The Silk Road and the Political Economy of the Mongol Empire

The growing importance of Central and Inner Asia and the Silk Road is much discussed at present. This book compares the nature of present day networks in these regions with the patterns of similar connections which existed at the time of the Mongol Empire in the thirteenth century and its successor states. It considers settlement patterns, technology and technology transfer, trade, political arrangements, the role of religion and the impact of the powerful states which border the region. Overall, the book demonstrates that the Mongol Empire anticipated many of the networks and connections which exist in the region at present.

Prajakti Kalra is a Research Fellow at the Central Asia Forum, Jesus College, University of Cambridge.

Routledge Studies on the Chinese Economy

Series Editor: Peter Nolan

Director, Centre of Development Studies; Chong Hua Professor in Chinese Development; and Director of the Chinese Executive Leadership Programme (CELP), University of Cambridge

Founding Series Editors

Peter Nolan

University of Cambridge and Dong Fureng, Beijing University

The aim of this series is to publish original, high-quality, research-level work by both new and established scholars in the West and the East, on all aspects of the Chinese economy, including studies of business and economic history.

60 Understanding China
The Silk Road and the Communist Manifesto
Peter Nolan

61 Being Middle Class in China
Identity, Attitudes and Behaviour
Ying Miao

62 Governing the Commons in China
Yan Zhang

63 The Economic Cycle and the Growth of the Chinese Economy
Li Jianwei

64 China's Rural Areas
Building a Moderately Prosperous Society
China Development Research Foundation

65 The Political Economy of Banking Governance in China
Xuming Yang

66 Reforming China's Healthcare System
China Development Research Foundation

67 Chinese Private Manufacturing Firms
The Challenges of Global Competition
Xiao Chen

68 The Silk Road and the Political Economy of the Mongol Empire
Prajakti Kalra

The Silk Road and the Political Economy of the Mongol Empire

Prajakti Kalra

Routledge
Taylor & Francis Group
LONDON AND NEW YORK

First published 2018
by Routledge
2 Park Square, Milton Park, Abingdon, Oxon OX14 4RN

and by Routledge
605 Third Avenue, New York, NY 10017

First issued in paperback 2021

Routledge is an imprint of the Taylor & Francis Group, an informa business

Publisher's Note
The publisher has gone to great lengths to ensure the quality of this reprint but points out that some imperfections in the original copies may be apparent.

British Library Cataloguing-in-Publication Data
A catalogue record for this book is available from the British Library

Library of Congress Cataloging-in-Publication Data
Names: Kalra, Prajakti, author.
Title: The Silk Road and the political economy of the Mongol empire / Prajakti Kalra.
Description: Abingdon, Oxon; New York, NY: Routledge, 2018. |
Series: Routledge studies on the Chinese economy; 68 | Includes index.
Identifiers: LCCN 2017056819 | ISBN 9780415786997 (hardback) |
ISBN 9781315226453 (ebook)
Subjects: LCSH: Silk Road. | Mongolia–Economic conditions. |
Mongolia–Commerce–History. | Mongolia–Foreign relations. |
Mongolia–History.
Classification: LCC HC430.25.K35 2018 | DDC 330.95/02–dc23
LC record available at https://lccn.loc.gov/2017056819

Typeset in Times New Roman
by Wearset Ltd, Boldon, Tyne and Wear

ISBN 13: 978-0-415-78699-7 (hbk)
ISBN 13: 978-0-367-43870-8 (pbk)

Book DOI: 10.4324/9781315226453

Dedicated to my father, Manu Kalra, with love and gratitude

Contents

Preface

The Eurasian region and the Silk Road today occupy much of the discourse on globalisation, international and regional cooperation and world trade. The usage and descriptions of both terms are manifold and reflect the pluralistic make-up of the region. The modern day understanding of Eurasia is informed by the particularities of the actors involved, which invokes a romantic notion of the past on the one hand but, also raises the spectre of suspicion and threat on the other. The politics of today which engages with the past continues to be coloured by misunderstandings and misrepresentations driven by modern frameworks and principles that do not necessarily reflect either the region or the individual actors. This book attempts to mitigate these distortions and takes a historical approach to inform present-day discourses on Eurasia as a consequence of Mongol governance.

In order to fully capture the essence of the region, then and now, one must consider the first moment in history which allowed for it to be connected under one polity. This is the story of that particular moment and covers the time period of Mongol control over the Silk Road in the thirteenth century and its legacy in order to shed light on how the mechanisms of trade and production along with innovations in technology helped make Eurasia the epicentre of the world. This book narrates the story through the prism of the political economy of the Silk Road as created and executed by Chinggisid Mongols. It traces the historical underpinnings of a *Mongol worldview* steeped in nomadic precedents which drove governance and policy in this period. The common thread which made for a Mongol Eurasia with its inherent flexibility and adaptability made political unification possible and in doing so created the conditions necessary for unprecedented economic and technological progress.

This book challenges the commonly held notions of the Mongols merely as destroyers and war mongers and instead presents evidence of an interconnected Eurasia. The sea of changes brought about by the Mongols is testimony to its impact in all the regions of Eurasia (China, Russia, Iran, Central Asia and beyond). The growth of cities (Muscovy, Beijing and port cities), the creation of new kinds of arts and crafts (miniature paintings), unprecedented trade flows, the availability of travel permits (*gerege*) which allowed travellers and caravans to travel across the territory, access to *caravansarais* with fresh horses, safe places to spend the night and a far reaching postal and communication system (*jam*) were the cornerstone of the Mongol political system. These same facilities are still necessary for travel today, whether by sea or land; the necessity for physical security for people, goods and now pipelines is as essential today as it was in the thirteenth century. The different aspects of trade and the processes through which the Eurasian space represented the Silk Road has to be juxtaposed with the modern understanding of state, economy and economic union in the same geographical space in the twenty-first century.

It is well known that the historic Silk Road under the Mongols connected Eurasia in ways that allowed goods and technologies to be transferred and traded all the way back and forth from China, Central Asia, Russia, Iran, India and Europe. The exchange of commodities can be compared with the varieties of people and ideas that traversed this space and led to interactions among societies which hitherto had not been closely connected. The Mongol attitude to religion also helped create conditions for these kinds of exchanges. The Mongol period is famous for bringing together cultural contact between different religions (Buddhism, Islam and Christianity) and protection of smaller sects within more established religions (Nestorian Christians, Manichaeans). Mongol courts served as meeting points for religious leaders who were often asked to have discussions and debates in the court (especially Qubilai Khan's court in China). This open attitude toward religion helped and guided trade as much as it created conditions for coexistence. These aspects of Eurasia have continued to be expressed in varying degrees since the Mongols and form the bulk of historical experiences of the region.

The historical evidence for the interconnectedness in Eurasia, geographically, economically, socially and culturally, echoes what was most definitively and coherently organised by the Mongol polity in the thirteenth century. The economic prosperity witnessed under the Mongols was a combination of the Mongol political system, the military and cultural habits which represented inclusiveness at their core. This book provides a snapshot of the historical place of the Mongol Empire in the building and sustaining of commercial activities across this swathe of territory which is being revived by different actors on the global scene today.

A look at Eurasian history from this perspective informs a regional understanding different from one accorded by European colonialism and creates space for Eurasian ideas with Eurasian precedents. This book showcases the importance of nomadic polities and the significance of the steppe environment (physical and conceptual) in the making of Eurasia. In the era of the Eurasian Economic Union and the One Belt One Road project, this approach provides the historical underpinnings for renewed regional cooperation. A reinterpretation of history based on the Silk Road in the Mongol period is timely and essential to the future imagination of the Eurasian region.

Acknowledgements

My interest in Chinggis Khan and the Mongols in the thirteenth century goes back to my undergraduate studies at Indiana University, Bloomington where I studied under Professor C. Atwood, Professor W. Fierman and Professor B. Eklof, who helped fill out the picture of Eurasia which has stayed with me till today. Professor J. Woods from the University of Chicago, where I completed my MA in International Relations, also deserves special mention, not only for teaching me but also for inspiring me with his annual expeditions to locate Chinggis Khan's grave in Mongolia. Subsequently, my time at Cambridge University and my interaction with Central Asia (the region and peoples) helped me refine my ideas and arguments to be able to write this book. I would like to particularly thank Professor Peter Nolan, Chong Hua Chair of Chinese Development and this series' editor, for recognising that my research should be published and for giving me the opportunity to write this book. I am indebted to Peter Sowden, editor of *Asia, Russia and Eastern Europe* at Routledge, Taylor and Francis Group for making it happen.

Time spent with scholars in Kazakhstan and Uzbekistan, conversations with Professor Meruert Abbusseitova (Head of the Oriental Studies Institute, Kazakhstan) and colleagues in the United Kingdom, United States and India have all gone into this piece of work. My research on regional organisations in Eurasia has furthered my belief in the historical significance of the Mongol period for this region. My association with various colleagues and students in the Cambridge Central Asia Forum and the Centre of Development Studies, University of Cambridge, Jesus College, Cambridge, along the way have allowed my ideas to grow and germinate to bring this project to completion.

The University of Cambridge Main Library has been a resource, office and home through the writing of this book and I am grateful for the helpful staff that saw me through the process. This book would not have been written without the work put in by my husband, Siddharth 'Montu' Saxena and my brother, Hargobinder Kalra, who read and re-read the chapters of this book for both content and language. Neira Kapo has drawn all the maps specifically for this book and she neatly captures the significance of the interconnectedness of the Silk Road across Mongol Eurasia. My friends and colleagues, Chokan Laumulin and Diana Kudaibergenova who pushed me to give the talk which showcased the idea of the significance of the Mongol Empire for Eurasia and globalisation deserve special mention. My discussions with Temur Yunusov, Ben Pingault and Boram Shin, with their questions, insightful comments and their unwavering encouragement helped me put pen to paper. My journey in Cambridge would not have been complete without my friends: Bruno, Marta, Yoni, Manar and Alessandra whose friendship has stood the test of time and geography. This book would never have been completed had it not been for the people who helped with taking care of my son: Emma, Pearl, Amy, Rebekah, Helen, Beth and Susanne. I would also like to thank my oldest friend, Aashita, who was there to share the moment I signed the contract for the book.

Finally, I would like to thank my family: my father to whom this book is dedicated has steadfastly supported my ideas and life choices without judgement or reserve; my mother remains my biggest supporter and my guiding light; and my husband who has been my partner in all things in life since the moment we met. My in-laws, brothers (Zorawar, Ajit and Vir), sister (Sehar) and sisters-in-law (Dillu, Sukhu and Mala), and my aunt (Chicki) who took an interest in this work and encouraged me deserve my sincerest acknowledgement. A special thank you to the next generation: Fateh, Amaara, Aaliyah and Ayaana. Last and most importantly, I want to thank my son, Shamsher, for giving me my purpose in life and who I hope will be inspired by this book.

Introduction

Eurasia is a particular place with a unique ecology encompassing varied polities: nomadic, sedentary and semi-sedentary. Of these, the nomads and particularly the Mongols were the most successful and the first to bring the natural connectedness of this region to the fore. The Silk Road once established in the second century has continued to evolve and shape the nature of interaction and exchange ever since. The near mythic stories of the opulence and prosperity of cities along the Silk Road, like Bukhara and Samarqand, along with Beijing, Tabriz and even Venice continue to evoke excitement and awe among readers. In connecting the vast expanse of the Silk Road from China to Europe the Mongols created a hybrid state which connected a large swathe of the world population and brought the most advanced societies of the time in closer contact with each other. They encouraged the free flow of ideas, peoples and goods while other parts of the world divided along religious lines restricted, limited and even forbade these kinds of interactions. The political unification under the Mongols surpassed every other earlier attempt and led to an explosion of interactions under Mongol aegis in Eurasia. The unification of Eurasia was a project initiated by Chinggis Khan and carried on by his sons and grandsons successfully along the historic trade routes going east and west. The expansion of the Chinggissid imperial project brought with it diverse groups of people, political and economic ideologies, religions and cultures. Over the period of the Mongol century, called the '*first global event*,'[1] and a '*turning point*',[2] the Mongol Khanates experienced transformations and adapted to local conditions but managed to contrive a Mongol ideology which was expressed in the form of the dignity of the figure of Chinggis Khan and the distribution of appanages. Both of these formed the backbone of the Inner Asian steppe tradition which exercised power and influence across Eurasia on the Chinggissids and continued to resonate even among successive empires.[3] Through this system of governance what the Mongols revealed was in essence the facilitation of quick travel and in greater numbers of goods, people and ideas than ever before.[4] In other words, the Mongols converted micro-economies on the Silk Road into a coherent macro-economy which enabled a much larger population to access Eurasia from end to end. This was to produce a golden moment in the history of Eurasian trade based on unprecedented connectedness and should signify a tremendous feat of Mongol agency.

Achieved through a particularly *Mongol worldview* and understanding of the world which was based out of a federal, cooperative structure of nomadic beliefs and institutions, Eurasia blossomed as never before.

The Mongols evoke as many dichotomies as the very landscape of Eurasia. For every atrocity committed there exists a counter example of Mongol clemency. For example, the exemption of taxes and levies which was given to all religious institutions; or the protection of Nestorian Christians across Eurasia who had been expelled from Christian lands in the Middle East and beyond; and even the protection of Muslim groups across Eurasia. The Mongols are accused of destroying everything in their path but these reports are juxtaposed with accounts of flourishing cities and groups of people like merchants and artisans (see Chapters 4 and 5, respectively) who did exceedingly well in the Mongol state machinery. The picture that has persisted pertaining to Asia and especially the Mongols, is one focused on destruction, killing and violence which can be found in contemporary sources of note as well as subsequent historical works all the way through till today. The Mongols depicted as the 'Storm from the East'[5] has overwhelmingly described the Mongol century. While there has been a lot of work done, especially by David Morgan, Thomas Allsen, Thomas Barfield, Renee Grousset and others, the Mongols have been relegated to being considered a negative force in Eurasia. The Mongol war machine is the only Mongol institution to have gotten grudging respect. However, this only goes towards hardening the idea of the barbaric Mongol on horseback with very little value for life. All this is pitted against the evidence from the cities and regions of the Silk Road which not only prospered but experienced unprecedented levels of growth and exchange in the form of ideas, peoples, technologies and goods which cannot be ignored even by the most ardent cynic.

This view is not surprising since most of history has been written through a predominantly sedentary lens of empire and state. The history of the Mongols and wider Eurasian region with Central Asia at its heart is one which is oral in nature, passed on to us through material written by neighbours, competitors and/or colonisers. The scarcity of sources left from the Mongols themselves, other than the *Secret History of the Mongols*, continues to leave the history of the Mongol period in the hands of their subject peoples: Chinese, Persian, Russian, Korean and Armenian along with other sources who represented their enemies (Delhi Sultanate, Mamluks of Egypt and Syria). This has been further exacerbated by the problem of understanding a particularly nomadic state, different from sedentary states, with unique characteristics and motivations. For the purposes of this book, the nomadic state is of vital importance especially its attitude to and encouragement of trade as a major source of economic prosperity. The success of Mongol Eurasia lay in controlling the Silk Road and ensuring seamless and safe trade across this vast expanse. Contrary to popular belief then, the Mongols were as famous for supporting trade as they were for war and pillage in world history. The fact that the Mongol state and its ruler, the *Qaghan*, understood the intricacies of commercial networks on the Silk Road and built infrastructure to ensure long distance trade is indeed remarkable. The Mongols established the first postal system to connect the far ends of Eurasia and provided amenities necessary to make mercantile activity comfortable and convenient. They were responsible not only for providing fresh horses, fodder, water and a place for merchants to rest but also created the necessary financial infrastructure for such activity. A collated census, taxation system and ready capital all formed the basis for commercial activity along the Silk Road. The Mongols were the facilitators and the *centre of east-west exchange*[6] in the thirteenth and fourteenth centuries.

These multifarious policies and practices in Eurasia can be summarised as a *Mongol worldview* which builds on the idea of *Eurasia as a unit of world history*[7] which presupposes geography and ecology to express the singularity of Mongol Eurasia. It serves as an example of governance which evolved from steppe traditions which had its own unique style of leadership and preferences for economic activity. The unique history of the nomads of Inner Asia unfolds through the centuries to create a composite worldview with its own set of historical precedence. Particularly for the Mongols, the pattern of nomads raiding and looting and periodically coming into contact with sedentary populations was broken with the arrival of Chinggis Khan. The Chinggissid nomad was very different from his predecessors and consequently the Mongol state and the legacy of the Mongols were of a very different quality. The Chinggissid ideology while informed by the steppe organisation was also informed by the demands of a system adapted to local conditions in newly acquired sedentary lands. The fixed dichotomies between centralisation, decentralisation, power sharing or monopoly over power did not exist for the Mongols, and thus did not percolate further down. The division of the Chinggissid Mongols into four Khanates (Yuan China, Ilkhanate Persia, Central Asia and the Golden Horde) by 1260 created four distinct Khanates with their respective Khans, yet each continued to acknowledge the existence of a composite Mongol system. This meant that the Khans or princes within the Mongol imperial family could be at odds with each other and still accept and associate with the Chinggssid ideology and express a *Mongol worldview*. A belief in the *mandate of heaven* and the destiny of Mongol domination persisted long after Chinggis Khan's demise in 1227 and eventually expanded to accommodate all of Eurasia. Princes could challenge the authority of the *Qaghan* without challenging the system of nomadic enterprise which retained its place as '… one of the universalist phases in Asian and Inner Asian history'.[8]

One of the most important consequences of Mongol presence on the Silk Road was the economic consolidation of the Eurasian region. The ancient Silk Road was transformed into a busy network of commercial activity, the revenues of which accounted for a large portion of the state treasuries and the goods and products which came into circulation under the Mongols represented their tastes and demands. Mongol institutions and bureaucratic practices were all directed toward increasing revenues and encouraging trade and commercial activity which could serve as the backbone of a nomadic economy with access to all of Eurasia. Specifically, institutions like the *keshig* (the imperial bodyguard), the office of *darugachi* and the *biceci*, represented by the who's who of steppe intelligentsia, worked together with the local administrative system to create a *Mongol megastructure* that was able to bridge gaps between disparate political and social groups in Eurasia. The openness of the Mongol system, most evident in their religious policies, reveals a deep understanding of Eurasia and the world. Mongol institutions, policies and practices were all geared toward improving connectedness and interactions across the Mongol Khanates which encompassed all of Eurasia. The impact on the sheer quantity and quality of goods moving on the Silk Road along with the numbers of people travelling long distances is what distinguishes the Mongols from their predecessors and marks this era as a turning point for Eurasia. An understanding of the natural eco-system of the steppe, in combination with steppe traditions which the nomads had adapted to in order to deal with the harsh environmental conditions can help explain the success that the Mongols experienced in their dealings in Eurasia. The Mongol presence on the Silk Road offers us so much more than what is commonly proffered. It laid the foundation for economic relations through attending to connectivity on the Silk Road which addressed the main aspects of communication and free movement across Eurasia.

The Mongols were able to consolidate societies, cultures and a wide variety of economic systems and this unique perspective on Eurasia allows us to use a non-binary lens in viewing interactions across systems: political, social, economic and cultural. It challenges the accepted Western notion of a zero-sum game in the context of political systems (communism and/or capitalism; majority rule versus guided forms of governance), religious affiliations and even cosmopolitanism. The historical basis for multilateral cooperation which existed among the Mongol Khans who jointly ruled Eurasia signifies a successful example of Eurasian cooperation informed by nomadic traditions, eastern philosophies and (Eur)Asian particularities. The shared idea of ownership carried with it the implicit reality of limited power which was guaranteed by requiring consensus among the Mongol Khans and princes. Viewed from an entirely nomadic perspective, Chinggis Khan managed to institute a system which required his descendants to work together and by delineating wealth and power he managed to create political unification based on shared goals and Chinggissid symbolism rather than centralisation which requires one superior authority. Mongol Khans could still lay allegiance to Chinggissid principles and yet question the election of the Qaghan, as in the case of Qubilai Khan in 1260. Akin to the sovereign nations of today, the Khans bickered, shared, cooperated, fought and competed for resources (material and otherwise) available in Eurasia. The *yasaq*[9] along with the very person of Chinggis Khan over time came to represent the source of the legitimacy to be able to rule Eurasia.[10] Subsequent rulers like Amir Timur (Tamerlane), and the Kazakh and Uzbek Khanates, continued to derive legitimacy from the *yasaq* and their Chinggissid lineage to rule over Central Asia and parts of Eurasia. The syncretic nature of Mongol ideologies which were visible in their institutions, practices, scientific and cultural endeavours and economic preferences contributed toward a functional, pluralistic system which was able to create an integrated system. It is important to note that an important aspect of Mongol Eurasia was that while the Mongols provided unification, the system of administration was symmetrical, not uniform.[11]

A closer look at the Silk Road, Eurasia and the Mongols in the thirteenth century challenges accepted ideas of Asia which continue to be understood and explained in binaries: control rather than cohesion, centralisation as opposed to coordination and styles of governance which necessarily highlight the incompatibility of democracy with other styles of governance. The Mongol Khanates were united by tradition and steppe practices but in adapting to the local conditions of the disparate regions they inhabited, they exhibited different governing styles. The by-word of the Mongol state machinery was flexibility in their relationships within the Khanates and with their subject populations.[12] In other words, while the administration of Mongol Eurasia could not be uniform because of its inherent adaptability, it nonetheless responded to the centre, i.e. to Mongol traditions which were shared by all the Khanates. The nomadic principles of ruling by consensus continued to influence the actions of the imperial family. The symbolism and sentiment so closely associated with Chinggis Khan's person and the system he initiated proved far more stable and alluring than anything else that the Mongols came in contact with, and that

> … historic continuity of the dynasty, which had remained Mongol in sentiment, tradition, language and customs, even beneath exotic appearances, in Persia and in China, and was therefore universally bound to its founders' policy in the fraternal government of the empire and plans for world conquest.[13]

This was further demonstrated by the fact that the efficacy of the Mongol system relied on access to resources in Eurasia even when they were not directly under the control of a particular prince. For example, Hulegu's army on its way to Iran and Iraq was amassed by peoples from China and Central Asia following censuses taken in these regions under Mongke and Qubilai. This signified a shared system which allowed the Khans and the princes to use the resources available to them throughout Eurasia whether they were their direct patrimony or not.[14] Even when the rivalries between the Khanates created alliances, i.e. between the Yuan and the Ilkhans on one side and the Golden Horde and Central Asian Mongols on the other, they all continued to pay allegiance to the Chinggissid ideology. The causes for rivalries between the Central Asian Mongols and Yuan China and the Golden Horde and the Ilkhans are discussed in Chapter 5, but suffice it to say a challenge to the authority of the Qaghan did not imply challenging the Mongol system. Far from it, the accusations against Mongol Khans were often expressed in terms of flouting Chinggis Khan's *yasaq* and abandoning the nomadic lifestyle.

The Mongol success in Eurasia described above requires one last point to be made. The Khanates ruling over more sedentary populations, namely China and Persia, have attracted the most attention and have consequently been accorded the most success. The sinicisation of Qubilai Khan in Yuan China and the Islamisation of the Ilkhans in Persia continue to dictate the achievements of these great civilisations. This of course has been pitted against the Golden Horde and the Central Asian Mongols who remained *more nomadic* and thus are deemed less successful and/or civilised as a result. For some time now the unquestioned cultural superiority of the sedentary populations has left no room for any possibility of arguing against the success of China and Persia as far surpassing the other regions of Eurasia, even under the Mongols. However, inconveniently the Mongol Khanates of the Golden Horde and Central Asia remained in power far longer than their cousins in China and Persia. Furthermore, the Golden Horde enjoyed economic prosperity and political control, at least parallel to the other Khanates, if not more than that enjoyed by the Yuan and the Ilkhanate. We have lesser evidence for Central Asia but its successes under the Timurids, immediately following the Mongol Khans, raises questions about the state of its economy in the thirteenth and fourteenth centuries. Embedded in this is the idea that in order to be civilised, the nomad has to be taken out or subdued. This is yet another binary which is challenged by the success of the Mongols. As we shall see in the following pages, none of the Mongol Khanates were overwhelmed by their sedentary populations, they continued to express and practise nomadic traditions, often in conjunction with newly acquired local practices but not to the point of abandoning the former. Even in Yuan China and Ilkhanate Persia the Mongols continued to live a life influenced by Mongol traditions and steppe practices. The Mongols overwhelmingly practiced their s*hamanistic* faith well into the thirteenth and even into the fourteenth centuries even while supporting, protecting and even practising other faiths.

The success of the Mongol Khanates was at its peak when Mongol Eurasia acted under the umbrella of shared proclivities. This is best showcased through the attention paid to trade and related activities which originated from the demands of a steppe economy and the open policies towards groups, peoples and religions which overcame divisions and adapted policies and practices accordingly. Finally, Eurasia offered resources ready to be marshalled and this was achieved primarily under Mongol unification of the region in the thirteenth century. The institutional framework of the Mongols set within its unique historical context then offers an example for nations today who often struggle with the idea of being overtaken and overwhelmed even to the extent of losing their sovereignty when operating in a regional context. The fear of China and Russia has paralysed efforts toward regional integration and is in large part driven by notions of power alien to the region itself. It is within the Asian and nomadic history that Eurasia needs to locate itself, not in the European history of colonialism and subsequent globalisation. This is essentially a move toward highlighting one of the most successful attempts at globalisation and a '…culminating point in pre-modern world systems'.[15]

The focus of the following pages is to provide a snapshot of a world of steppe traditions which with its specific institutions, leadership styles and traditions was able to give coherence to the diversity in Eurasia and created prosperity across the board as a result of a very *Mongol worldview*. I begin with Chapter 1 on the rise of Chinggis Khan which lays the foundation for both the steppe polity he came out of and the establishment of a Mongol state which would go on to engulf all of Eurasia. Chapter 2 covers the main institutions which the Mongols established across Eurasia and which had roots in the steppe polity and form the basis of a coherent Mongol policy across Eurasia. Chapter 3 adds another foundational step towards the *Mongol worldview* which was driven largely by the relationship the Mongols had with religion and religious institutions which furthered their ability to foster unfettered trade. Chapter 4 in offering a revisionists' view on the destruction of cities under the Mongols, proffers examples of how the Mongols achieved prosperity through the reconstruction and revival of cities on the Silk Road. Chapter 5 gives a description of trade relations, commodities and the trade routes which included old established routes and new routes which came up because of the Mongols. Chapter 6 summarises the way in which the historical narrative of the Mongols can be mapped onto the multilateral approaches that are visible in the region today. It focuses on the resurgence of the idea of a connected Eurasia through comprehensive development programmes both necessary and beneficial for countries across Eurasia. In doing so it strikes at the very heart of the possibility of building links and connections in modern times which echo the Mongol era. Organisations like the Eurasian Economic Union and the One Belt One Road (OBOR) initiative have been focusing on building infrastructure like roads, bridges, ports, storage facilities, financial institutions and creating a legal framework which reflects today's global interconnectedness in Eurasia. The 2008 financial crisis and the subsequent economic difficulties which spread like wildfire across the globe, and the more recent Anglo-American shifts away from globalisation have left a turbulent feeling in the world order. Countries like Russia, China and Central Asian republics realise the importance of regional interaction and are approaching economic unions with trepidation and hope. Earlier attempts at regional cooperation have often been half-hearted and continue to attract scepticism, especially by outside voices which feel threatened by the emergence of a strong regional entity. While both the Eurasian Economic Union and the OBOR have steered away from a political discourse, the former has maintained a steady approach toward integrating economies and the latter is focused on the building of much needed infrastructure and development projects in the Eurasian region. Much like the demonisation of the Mongols has persisted even when faced with an alternative narrative of prosperity and development, Eurasia continues to be viewed as a mystical continent which evokes both awe and fear. In these pages, I have attempted to unravel some of the mysteries by underpinning the success of the Mongols to their institutions, a uniform worldview and a continent which was just waiting to be brought together in meaningful and real ways. In this way, I have attempted to consolidate and contribute to the field of Mongol Eurasia and connect it to the historical legacy of Eurasia. The attempts to provide an amalgamated structure of economic and social development on the territory of this historic landmass are a continuation of centuries old interactions.

Notes

1 Adshead 1993, p. 53
2 Abu-Lughog 1989, p. 12
3 Jackson 2017, p. 97
4 Di Cosmo 2005, p. 392
5 Marshall 1994, title of the book
6 Allsen 2001, p. 4
7 Christian 1994, p. 175
8 Togan 1998, p. 151
9 Chinggis Khan's legal code
10 Togan 1998, p. 150
11 Allsen 1987, p. 222
12 Allsen 1987, p. 222
13 Olschki 1960, p. 317
14 Allsen 1987, p. 224
15 Di Cosmo *et al.* 2009, p. 4

1 Rise of Chinggis Khan

> By unifying all the Turko-Mongol nations
> into a single empire, by imposing iron discipline
> from China to the Caspian, Jenghiz Khan suppressed
> the endless intertibal wars and afforded the caravans
> a security they had never known.[1]

The rise of Chinggis Khan (1206–1227) and his empire in the thirteenth century had its roots in the historical, political and social structure of nomadic peoples of Inner Asia. He exemplified adaptation to the changing pattern of steppe society. His policies were a reaction to the anarchy that had descended on the steppe in the eleventh to twelfth centuries as a result of shifting alliances and weak allegiances. His innovative strategies and charismatic personality put him in a position to attract followers and revitalise the region. His polices and reorganisation of the steppe led to its transformation into a place of functional order and stability which was used as a springboard for uniting the rest of Eurasia. The creation of a supratribal identity associated with the person of Chinggis Khan was passed down to his descendants who expanded the Mongol ideology and applied it beyond the steppe. The politics and society in the steppe at the time of Chinggis' rise presented him with an environment of chaos and dysfunction which was crucial in determining his policies and their appeal to a majority of the tribes. Members of tribes that willingly chose to ally with him initially were dissatisfied individuals who found themselves on the periphery of existent tribes.[2] Chinggis Khan himself was an example of a dissatisfied member of a tribe that had left him and his family in their hour of need. His personal life experiences served as a backdrop for the principles which were to guide him in the governance of his empire. The paramount position of stable allegiances and loyalty remained at the centre of the institutions he created and remained the core of the Mongol state even under his descendants. Chinggis Khan's legal code (*yasaq*) and the establishment of the imperial bodyguard (*keshig*) served as the backbone of a Mongol system which valued elements that maintained functional order on the steppe and beyond. He attracted followers as a result of his military successes and his sense of fair play when it came to the distribution of rewards. He exemplified steppe traditions of generosity and reciprocity[3] by promising a share in the spoils of war for his army of conquest, returning favours to all the people who helped him in his struggle against his rivals (for example, he offered support to the Khitan brothers in their fight against the Jurchid for their help against his rival Jamugha) and opening trade routes for merchants.[4] The reorganisation of the steppe through the process of detribalisation created a system which bypassed fleeting tribal loyalties and provided stability in the form of the person of Chinggis Khan and his consistent policies. The order was guaranteed by rights which were formalised in the legal code and provided functionality on the steppe. His policies changed the content rather than the form of the insitutions and in doing so he was able to fashion something new without alienating tribes on the steppe. This principle was followed in Mongol Eurasia which encompassed diverse societies with historical traditions dating back centuries.

A brief overview of the history of steppe leadership and tribes is essential at this point. Inner Asia had seen numerous strong empires over the centuries: Xiong-nu, Kok-Turks, Uyghurs, the Kyrghyz, etc. They all showed evidence of a set of common features and styles of leadership which broadly reflected the make-up of tribal society. Nomadic empires embodied three major principles – '*qut*' ('mandate of heaven', 'divine right to rule'), '*anda*' (blood brother) and '*noker*' (companion, entourage)[5] which formed the backbone of the steppe imperial tradition. Steppe society until the thirteenth century had seen at least three distinctive styles of leadership. First, hierarchical leadership; second, leadership that changed hands due to civil wars, coups and weak emperors being replaced by stronger ones; and lastly, leaders that were elected by consensus.[6] Tribal groups at the time of Chinggis Khan's rise were roughly divided between two types of confederations: decentralised tribes (for example, the Mangut, Qongirrad) and tribes with hereditary leaders or centralised tribes (for example, the Kerait, Naiman).[7] Chinggis Khan adapted these traditions to formulate a Mongol system which was based on stability, loyalty and valued allegiance. There is no doubt that ideas and characteristics of the steppe imperial tradition of ancient Turks filtered down from the Uyghurs through to the Mongols.[8] To illustrate further, the full title of the *Qaghan* of the Xiong-nu was '*Tengri kudu Jenuye*' (*tengri* translates as Heaven) which continued to remain the divine blessing associated with the Chinggissids. Chinggis Khan's biography is riddled with references to the mandate given to him to rule by Tengri.[9] This can also be seen when Chinggis Khan was elected ruler of all the peoples in an official '*quriltai*' (election, decision-making body) in 1206[10] in accordance with old steppe traditions.[11]

Nomads had their own political culture which included characteristic features of charisma, dual kingship and models of rule, imperial titles and symbolisms (for example, *qan*, *Qaghan*, *yagabu*, etc.), specific succession patterns (for example, lateral), notions of collective and joint sovereignty and patrimonial modes of governance.[12] Not only did steppe tradition foreshadow the political nature of Chinggis Khan's empire, there was also a continuation of other steppe traditions that characterised the social strata (for example, the custom of marrying the widowed wife of a brother lost in battle, son-in-laws who lived with their in-laws for the initial one or two years before taking their bride with them, the importance of consort-clans where the majority of the wives came from, not shedding the blood of members of the imperial family) and illustrate the continuation of steppe tradition before, during and after Chinggis Khan's reign.[13] Furthermore, he continued to employ his predecessors, like the Uyghurs, who represented a successful steppe empire that had relied heavily on trade and control over neighbouring tribes.[14] The Uyghur were replaced by another tribe, the Kyrghyz, who are referred to as forest-dwellers who foreshadowed the Mongol Empire. As mentioned above their rule on the steppe is best described as disjointed and chaotic which was a result of shifting alliances and a breakdown of steppe order.[15] As a direct consequence, Chinggis Khan's power on the steppe stemmed from his ability to create institutions which could produce stability. The fashioning of an empire based on institutions, fairness and loyalty was an outcome of Chinggis Khan's military genius and administrative acumen. The conditions thus created which offered stability for economic, social and political development are not only noteworthy but deserve a special place in history, especially in light of the transformation of Eurasia under Chinggissid Mongols. The next section considers Chinggis Khan's establishment of the early Mongol state.

The state

In his struggle to become the *Qaghan*, Chinggis Khan was in no way guaranteed victory in the steppe. His accession to power was not smooth and uncontested. He came very close to losing to Jamugha, his *anda*, and Ong Khan (leader of the Kerait), his father's *anda*. Both, Jamugha and Chinggis Khan were young and ambitious men who wanted control of the tribes and neither would have accepted a subservient position willingly, leading to an inevitable rift.[16] This conflict was described by Togan as a fight to maintain tribalisation of the steppe tribes under Jamugha and detribalisation of the steppe represented by Chinggis Khan. Other historians have described this as a conflict between the old steppe hierarchical order clashing with the new democratic style of leadership of Chinggis Khan. According to the former argument, Chinggis Khan wanted to create a more stable and secure society free of shifting alliances.[17] He instituted a central structure of civil and military government and reorganised society into tightly bound units with the *Qaghan* at the apex. The organisation of the military in *tumen* based on the decimal system was already in use on the steppe and was transformed into a cohesive unit.[18] One of the main tenets of Chinggis Khan's *yasaq* refers to the punishment of death if soldiers abandoned their units. The reshuffling and reorganisation of *tumen* remained one of the easiest ways for regularising society as late as the fourteenth century. For example, Qaidu and Kebek in Central Asia organised society into *tumen* in the 1260s and then again in the 1320s. In the conflict between Chinggis and Jamugha, the former won and spurred the creation of the Mongol Empire which was to rule over one-fifth of the world. Tribal loyalty underwent a sea change as a consequence of the policy of detribalisation and moved away from to traditional kin-based loyalty and came to represent voluntary association to a leader based on his individual charisma.[19] This was best exemplified by the institution of *noker* which was to influence the creation of the *keshig* that formed the ranks of the core administrators and officials of the Mongol state. Steppe leaders had always had followers but now a *multitribal* or *supratribal* elite had been secured which was loyal to Chinggis Khan's person and his *yasaq*.[20] This new supratribal military unit superseded other loyalties and produced stability and security in society.[21] He also tried to streamline the succession process in order to avoid problems of lateral succession endemic to steppe society until then. According to Togan, the society thus created differed from older steppe societies and shared common aims and goals proposed by Chinggis Khan.[22] The *Mongol worldview* arose out of these elements which shaped a thinking informed by principles of loyalty, stability and openness. The creation of an army of conquest with an emphasis on securing trade routes gave added security to Chinggis Khan's empire and made him a popular leader to the members of the tribes.

While it is important to note that Chinggis Khan did institute new and long-lasting changes, he did so very much set in the framework of an existing steppe imperial tradition. In order to follow the course of their development, the personal journey and life of Chinggis and his family must be kept in mind. After the death of his father, his tribe (the Tayichi'ud) abandoned his mother and family, leaving them to fend for themselves in a highly unsecure environment. The insecurity that Chinggis Khan and his mother were subjected to in his youth and the kidnapping of his wife (Borte) and later himself by the Merkid, left an indelible mark on Chinggis Khan and heralded his decisions. They formed the driving force behind the administrative and social rules he later established. Chinggis Khan's insistence on carving out personal loyalty superimposed over kinship networks was a reaction to the way his family was treated by his father's tribe after his death. This betrayal left a strong impression on Chinggis Khan's psyche and resulted in a consultative approach of leadership. The special place of his military, made up of people who had joined his service voluntarily, was valued by Chinggis Khan. The security that he wanted to provide on the steppe included the provision of an environment that excluded the necessity of kidnappings of which he and his family had been a victim on more than one occasion. He learned and actively used older steppe traditions which had proved successful in the past in all spheres of the military, politics and society. For instance, the Liao dynasty had instituted a dual administration of collecting taxes from the conquered sedentary populations whilst retaining their inherent native nomadic traditions.[23] He introduced checks and balances on the steppe which translated into similar policies in other regions of Eurasia, integrating nomadic and sedentary practices and officials. The nature of Mongol institutions allowed for tribes and local dynasties to continue exercising flexibility and control within a larger structure. The offices of *darugachi* and *basqaq* were supervisory in many instances and were in place to ensure the demands of the *Qaghan* were met by local officials who were familiar with local customs.

Another aspect of steppe tradition which Chinggis Khan was insistent on changing was the transitory nature of alliances in society. His rise to power was plagued with experiences of friends and allies changing alliances as well as military setbacks. In 1184, Jamugha, Ong Khan and Chinggis Khan were allied together against the Merkid.[24] Some years later the rift between Jamugha and Chinggis Khan reached the point of a battle – Dalan Baljus (1187–1188) – where Jamugha even managed to defeat Chinggis Khan. Having suffered a setback, he persisted and regrouped with the support of Ong Khan in 1198–1199. In 1201 Jamugha was elected *Gurkhan*[25] by some of the tribes, however, soon after this Chinggis Khan triumphed. Later, in the same vein of shifting alliances, Jamugha convinced Ong Khan to abandon Chinggis Khan in a battle against the powerful Naiman. This plot backfired and Ong Khan did another turn-around and asked for Chinggis Khan's help against the attacking Naiman. In 1203 Ong Khan, leader of the Kerait, was killed by the Naiman.[26] In 1204, Chinggis Khan defeated and subjugated the Naimans.[27] This pattern of shifting alliances was weeded out by Chinggis Khan's later policies. His solution was the creation of an army of conquest to foster the feeling of loyalty towards the military unit they were assigned to or voluntarily joined. This policy helped dislodge the traditional steppe linkages and consequent multiple avenues of potential allegiances.[28] Furthermore, the *yasaq* stipulated that '...people were forbidden to leave their units'.[29] Chinggis Khan's army of conquest was formed on the following lines: hierarchy, clan structure, seniority, merit, valour and loyalty.[30] Principles of consensus, volition and redistribution of wealth were foremost in the army which was made up of representatives of all tribes. Under the Mongol Khanates the army was made up of troops who represented a cross section of Mongol princes and signalled the joint nature of Mongol Eurasia. Chinggis Khan's policies were directed toward the creation of stakeholders whether for the Chinggissids, soldiers, merchants and others, based on traditional principles of generosity and reciprocity. The importance of the *quriltai*, which was a consultative body which encouraged consensus, was retained throughout the Mongol period. The imperial family continued to use consent and elections in order to rule which was instituted by Chinggis Khan at the beginning of his career. The principle of generosity and distribution of wealth went beyond the imperial family. For instance, the soldiers of the army of conquest had a right to a share of the proceeds of war which signified personal gain. Merchants enjoyed the same generosity with access to investment, gainful employment and state infrastructure. This came through in the employment and use of local dynasties and rulers in newly acquired regions and served the dual purpose of minimising disruption in administration and secured loyalty for the Mongol state through the granting of privileges.

None of this would have been possible without the army of conquest and to this we must now turn briefly. While the bulk of the discussion so far has been about the changes thus instituted in the steppe which spread across Eurasia over the first half of the thirteenth century, a note on the Mongol army of conquest is essential. Chinggis Khan's charisma came as much from good governance and guarantees of economic prosperity as to his skill as a military leader. Based on traditional nomadic tactics, the Mongols under Chinggis Khan were a '... highly mobile cavalry, [and in this way] the nomads achieved an effect of surprise and ubiquity, which before any action began, disconcerted their adversary'.[31] In addition, the relationship between nomads and their horses is well documented.[32] Suffice to say the agility, skill and sharpness thus achieved, along with tactics like the *feigned retreat*, led to win after win for the Mongols. Based on tactics of hunters, the Mongols continued to forge ahead and quickly overcame most of Eurasia. Military tactics included propaganda and spreading information and rumours about the Mongol army's skill and ruthlessness. This last aspect led to towns and peoples submitting voluntarily and was an important part of Mongol strategy. As new populations were conquered, the Mongols would take prisoners on subsequent expeditions. In doing so, they would increase the numbers of their army and were able to spread information of previous conquests, often in devastating terms, to induce peaceful submission. For example, Chinggis took prisoners from Bukhara to conquer Samarqand, and Tolui took the rural population of Khurasan on to Merv to facilitate his military campaign.[33] Thus the conscription of Turks from Central Asia very early on into the Mongol army created a hybrid Turko-Mongol army.[34] The expertise of the Mongol army remained unmatched in Eurasia and the only instances in which it struggled was when they came against similar steppe Turkic groups in Mamluk Egypt and Syria in the west, and the troops of the Delhi Sultanate in the east. Faced with similar fighting styles and military tactics, the edge the Mongols armies had over their enemies decreased. In the conquest of Eurasia, the Mongols were helped first and foremost by Turks from Central Asia who joined the ranks of the Mongol army from as early as 1216. Following which the Mongols had access to resources – men, money and materials[35] – enabling them to forge a path into other regions of the Middle East, Southern China and further west towards Europe. The final word on the Mongol army of conquest remains the precedence of nomadic tactics, skilfully organised by Chinggis Khan and his descendants which achieved domination over all of Eurasia, and included everything from the Caspian Sea to the shores of Korea and everything in between, from the oldest civilisations of China and Persia to Muslim empires of Central Asia and Kiev, the centre of the Slavic world. The appanage system which underlined the idea of joint stakeholders in Mongol Eurasia created and supplied the possibility of recruits and resources from across Eurasia to come to the aid of expansion, turning the whole endeavour into a self-sustaining enterprise. As we shall see, the unification thus achieved made the sum of the parts work for the entire system and maintained the solidarity of Chinggis Khan's system.

The military under Chinggis Khan was also an administrative unit. Military ranks were given to important officials throughout the Mongol Empire: Mongols and non-Mongols. Chinggis Khan relied on his *noker* and *anda* who formed his retinue and were instituted into the body of the *keshig*.[36] The *keshig* in turn supplied personnel for nearly all the important offices in the Mongol state: *darugachi, basqaq* and *baurchi*. Another old steppe tradition which originated in the military was garrison troops, *tamamci*, who were left in border areas and served as administrators and kept unruly regions in check. Instances of establishing garrison cities and military colonies as late as the end of the thirteenth century in the border areas between Yuan China and Central Asia show the importance of these institutions for the Mongols.[37] Chinggis Khan's insistence on loyalty was a consequence of the impact of shifting alliances on military campaigns which was directly tied to steppe government. The organisation of the Mongol state was built on military enlistment which demanded extensive record keeping. It served as the paramount reason for having detailed records of the nomadic population, and became even more important after the inclusion of larger populations of sedentary peoples. Censuses were conducted under nearly all the early *Qaghans* and under Mongke an empire-wide census under central supervision was conducted for military reasons as well as reasons of resource allocation. All these aspects of Chinggis Khan's empire paint a description of Chinggis as an able administrator with the intelligence and skills for good governance. He surrounded himself with learned men in nearly all fields across ethnic and religious lines; he famously had Uyghurs, Muslim and Chinese advisers.[38] As much as he valued loyalty, he also emphasised meritocracy. The old steppe tradition of a preference for individuals with specialised skills dominated Mongol ideology from the start.[39] The inclusion of people with skills across tribal and ethnic lines included scribes, physicians, scientists, administrators, religious leaders and others, and was representative of the plurality intrinsic to the steppe. These remained the core features in the Mongol Khanates in the late thirteenth and fourteenth centuries. The structures and institutions established by Chinggis Khan included the appointment of his close friend and ally, Siqi Qutuqu to the post of chief judge to document all activities and rulings. This was to set legal precedent and record the peoples and lands assigned to family and military commanders.[40] These came to be Chinggis Khan's *yasaq* which served as a powerful tool in the governance of this vast empire for centuries to come. The use of people the Mongols trusted continued to play a role in the way the state was governed. The offices that exercised influence in Mongol Eurasia often had people who filled numerous roles in their service to the Khans. For example: Yeh lu Chu Tsai was initially a scribe and then became a *darugachi*; many officials started out as *baurchi* and went on to become governors and military commanders, like Ked Buqa and Bolad who held the position of *baurchi* and later filled other positions (Ked Buqa was military commander in the campaign against the Ismailis and Abbassids under Hulegu).[41] Chinggis Khan had managed to locate and utilise this *steppe intelligentsia* which in conjunction with the policy of transplanting people across different regions achieved the transmission of Mongol ideals. This policy continued under his descendants as well and reinforced the *Mongol worldview*. Chinggis Khan was much more than the military genius as he is most often described. He was descended from a long line of nomads who had evolved strategies for good governance through the centuries and he used and built on these to achieve unprecedented success. Chinggis Khan's main genius was the ability to merge disparate aspects of the steppe and create institutions which could be used beyond the borders of the steppe. Chinggis Khan initiated new roads to civilisations, accelerated the evolution of amalgamated practices across the steppe and brought a Mongol world system to bear; and it was his immediate successors, (his sons and grandsons) who proved that the system he created could be expanded to include all of Eurasia. They became purveyors of Mongol traditions. The result of this was the birth of interlocking networks and *a basic information circuit*[42] which spanned Eurasian societies and provided a *unified conceptualisation of the world.*[43]

Chinggis Khan in his time had already divided his empire into four *ulus*[44] between his sons. This division gave rise to centrifugal forces which eventually led to the independent nature of rule in the Khanates.[45] However, the Mongol system was able to overcome the political and economic divergence of these regions through a shared ideology which can be found in the very inception of the empire. The Mongol Khanates did not have to be run identically, and as a matter of fact, they could not be run along the same lines. However, they shared important aspects: steppe traditions, ancestral continuity from Chinggis Khan and the *yasaq.* As we shall see in the next chapter on institutions, the Khanates in adapting Mongol institutions to local conditions had already deviated from how these institutions were applied to a steppe polity. The deviance in itself was not a flouting of tradition but was part of the way the system could continue to operate in different regions. The culture of the Mongol Empire was one '...which freely combined political institutions, practices and personnel from all parts of the Mongolian world, integrated by an overall structure that was Mongolian'.[46] The distribution of appanages in addition to the division of the territories between his sons included joint ownership among the vast majority of Mongol princes, princesses and loyalists and gave them a personal share in the prosperity of the Mongol enterprise. In other words, a common feature among nomadic polities was the idea of generosity and reciprocity which fostered loyalty in the family, close allies, the army and society in general and was at work here as well. *Corporate sovereignty*[47] based on the appanage system laid the foundation for joint ownership of the resources of Mongol Eurasia. The institutions that showcase the interdependence of the Mongol system were: the *jam* (postal system), a composite army of conquest and shared rights to revenues from agriculture, manufacturing and trade.

Chinggis Khan was succeeded by Ogedei (1229–1241), his third son. Ogedei's reign signalled the entrenchment of the ideals of Chinggis' world and the conquest of the rest of Eurasia was begun in earnest. Ogedei's reign was a period of stability and prosperity and marked the establishment of the *jam* which connected the cities of Eurasia in essential ways. The death of Ogedei ignited a power struggle which was quickly overcome with Guyuk's (1246–1248) election. He died within two years and political manoeuvres on the steppe brought the Toluids (Chinggis' youngest son Tolui's family) into power. Mongke, Tolui's eldest son, became *Qaghan* with the help of his mother, Sorqoqtani Beki, and support from his cousin, Batu (Golden Horde). Mongke (1251–1259) initiated the conquest of the Middle East and consolidation of China by sending his brothers, Hulegu and Qubilai, to these regions respectively.[48] Hulegu was sent to Iran and Iraq to remove the authority of the Caliph in Baghdad and extend authority over the infamous *hashashins*[49] operating in Northeastern Iran.[50] Whether it was part of the mandate or not, Hulegu's successful campaigns culminated in the establishment of the Ilkhanate in Persia in 1258. At the end of Mongke's reign a civil war erupted between Tolui's sons Qubilai and Arigh Boke who vied for the throne. They were supported by the other princes of the Mongol *uluses*[51] and this led to the establishment of four powerful households, the Yuan in China, the Ilkhans[52] in Persia, the Golden Horde in Russia and the house of Chaghatai and Ogedei in Central Asia. With the accession of the Toluid branch of the family, the Ogedeids were deprived of most of their inheritance until the rise of Qaidu, Ogedei's grandson, in the late 1260s. Qubilai's election was severely contested but the Mongol system continued to bear influence and Qubilai and his immediate descendants continued to be the *Qaghans*. While the reign of Qubilai was fraught with challenges and assertions of authority by the Khanates, the overarching Mongolian world was still very much alive and well. Institutions and principles set by Chinggis Khan continued to form the basis of governance in all four regions. The conglomeration of Mongol traditions and local practices still operated on the lines of a *collective possession*.[53]

Despite the period of strife between the Mongol Khanates, inter-regional trade actually increased with the cessation of large scale conquest.[54] Mongke's government had instituted key changes: he systematised and regularised the administration and finances of the empire, reduced the power of the princes and their appanages, instituted a unified system of taxation, restricted the use of the postal system (*jams*) to official travellers, repealed seals and *paizas*,[55] and reigned in Muslim and Uyghur merchant companies operating in Mongol Eurasia.[56] These policies were designed to streamline practices in dominions which had expanded beyond the steppe to give rise to a Mongol Eurasia. Steeped in nomadic traditions, the Mongol princes and rulers across Eurasia continued to follow nomadic practices, lived in mobile capitals, moved between summer and winter pasturelands, organised hunts for practising military manoeuvres and followed *shamanistic* beliefs. Other shared aspects in the Khanates included the administrative organisation, the imperial bodyguard, make-up of the Mongol courts and distribution of appanages mentioned above.[57] Steppe traditions and laws which applied to a small nomadic population divided along tribes, clans and other groupings meant that power was shared with important personnel who served the Mongols and this continued to resonate in the Mongol Khanates. It existed even in the hereditary succession in offices which continued throughout the Khanates through the thirteenth and fourteenth centuries. Important and renowned *darugachis*[58] like Yeh lu Chu Tsai and Mahmud Yalavac passed down their positions to their sons who continued to retain their positions under successive Khans.[59] The joint ownership of the empire also meant that Mongol princes sent their own representatives to other Khanates and the imperial family shared the riches of all regions of Eurasia. The *Qaghan's* officials had to work with officials in the Khanates and with local officials who served as checks and balances at the intra- and inter-regional level and illustrated the extent of interdependence in the Mongol system.

The system which was thus created in Eurasia reflected Mongol traditions which were adapted to and intermingled with local conditions to tailor optimum policies. A supratribal identity with Chinggis Khan at the centre came into being and existed in conjunction with smaller groups or tribes in the shape of *tumens*.[60] In this way Chinggis Khan had managed to establish a new system of loyalty without abandoning more local, and thus, familiar customs among steppe nomads. Leadership could be flexible and the system was both centralised and federal simultaneously. This kind of centralisation was able to '…foster the development of a much more powerful confederation'.[61] The *Qaghan's* power was not limitless and was guaranteed by generosity and reciprocity which maintained allegiances essential for keeping control. The *Qaghan* depended on allies and friends who could support him in his election, conquest and administration. They in turn enjoyed equally high levels of prestige and power among their followers and this same principle percolated down, all the way to local officials. In this way, the very idea of centralisation of power was qualitatively different and not absolute and buttressed by the symbolic power expressed in a *Mongol worldview*. The relationship between the Mongol Khanates was one of a symbolic preservation of customs and traditions, rather than the centre dictating the actions of the four *ulus*.[62] The *Mongol worldview* based on these lines emerged and solidified in this period which stabilised Mongol rule within the regions and spurred government action, trade, cultural interaction and movement of peoples. As with any other world system, the Mongols brought with them new habits and interests which were to have a lasting impact on the societies of Eurasia and beyond. Steppe institutions and policies were further transformed as the Mongols came into contact with other societies. This raised the status of certain groups and led to the benefit of specific groups, peoples and cultures across Eurasia. The plurality of the Mongol system became a cornerstone of Mongol Eurasia and contributed to a hybrid culture. Among these groups and peoples, the ones worth mentioning include merchants, artisans, scientists and astronomers, along with people who could navigate and transmit the *Mongol worldview* further. The Mongol court became an engine for cosmopolitanism across Eurasia and a new (Mongol) Eurasian elite was created in the process, much like the global elite of modern day. These Eurasian elite were comfortable across cultures, were desirous of goods from all parts of the world and were in a position to enjoy everything an integrated system like that of Mongol Eurasia could offer. Finally, one of the most important consequences of this form of political unification was in the area of trade which blossomed in nearly every direction and accrued higher profits than from maritime trade.[63] Flexibility in the political system and nomadic mobility spurred exchange across Eurasia. Goods, ideas, peoples and technologies flowed on the Silk Road and served to reinforce Mongol traditions. In other words, Mongol centralisation and exercise of power was informed by their experiences on the steppe and the consequent strategies that were chosen to administer it. This led to processes of integration which naturally worked to unleash the power of Eurasia.

Mongol Eurasia was able to bridge seemingly divergent, if not contradictory, belief systems, concepts and peoples in far closer proximity than before and revealed a Eurasia which was more cohesive and comprehensive than before. Mongol flexibility was able to bring nomadic and sedentary aspects of Eurasia into much closer contact, as it did with established civilisations of China and Persia, and it brought the West (Europe) closer to the East (Central Asia and China). As prime movers of peoples, goods, ideas and habits, the Mongols were unsurpassed in logistics and this was visible in all aspects of governance.[64] The Mongols in form and content continued to provide security and investment for mercantile activity within and without their domains. The interdependence of the Mongols was visible from the very beginning, highlighted by joint appanages and the use of officials, personnel, artisans and military conscripts from one part of Eurasia in others. Mahmud Yalavac, a Central Asian administrator, was installed in Northern China; Yeh lu Chu Tsai, a Khitan was made *darugachi* in Bukhara; along with other instances even at the end of the thirteenth century when Qubilai Khan sent Bolad, a Mongol, to the Ilkhanate court and so on. Similarly, the armies of conquest were composed of troops from all the branches of the Mongol princes and allies, Hulegu's army sent to Iran and Iraq included contingents from the Golden Horde, Central Asia and China. The *Mongol worldview* was even able to circumvent immediate rivalries within the Mongol Khanates by creating alternative routes and/or by absorbing the risks as a result of wars and conflicts. The opening up of alternative trade routes which were to have a lasting impact on Eurasian commercial networks for the future was established by the Mongols. For example, Qubilai Khan who was at odds with the Central Asian Mongols, especially Qaidu, managed to open maritime routes in Southeast China and traded more with Ilkhanate Persia to compensate for loss in Central Asian trade. In a similar vein, the Golden Horde Khans brought the Black Sea trade emporia into the already multifarious network which represented the Silk Road in Eurasia. In Central Asia too, trade flourished throughout this period under the able and just administration of Qaidu and Masud Beg who focused on reviving and fortifying trade between cities and by closely tapping into the Golden Horde trade with Yuan China The multiplicity of networks which were inherent to the Silk Road were in this way further expanded, as we shall see in Chapter 5 on trade relations, and guaranteed by the Mongols who had an open door policy towards people across ethnic and religious lines. Mongol unity, far from being extinguished, simply changed and adapted to accommodate new conditions of an expanded Eurasia.[65] To reiterate, the Mongol Khanates continued to have a coherent policy with regards to economic relations and were deeply entrenched in their preservation of a common worldview which was driven by nomadic cultural norms passed down from antiquity.[66]

Summary

In summary, the rise of Chinggis Khan and his polity based in nomadic principles, reformed those practices and gave rise to a system which was based on loyalty and *choice* within the steppe hierarchy. The institutions of *noker* and *keshig* were voluntary retinue organisations of people. The inclusive nature of Chinggis Khan's policies also included the element of *choice*.[67] Sentiment and loyalty continued to be passed down with every detribalisation and reorganisation,[68] and eventually was visible in the Mongol Khanates of Eurasia who were able to formulate a shared heritage out of Chinggis Khan's *yasaq* and used it to build Mongol Eurasia. This explains why even when the Mongol Khanates were flexing their muscles against each other, they continued to nominally recognise the *Qaghan*'s authority and expressed a shared *Mongol worldview* driven by Chinggis Khan's transformation of the steppe as described above. What survived and even flourished in the steppe after Chinggis Khan's reorganisation and consolidation of the tribes was the *symbolism* it came to represent and the aforementioned sentiment which was associated with a common heritage and ancestry. These aspects of the Mongol Empire dictated particular attitudes toward government, trade, religion, science and culture which lasted far longer than the Chinggissids themselves.[69] While there were changes in the ways in which the Mongol Khanates interacted over time, they continued to express belief in the common enterprise of Mongol Eurasia. This was expressed through the respect for the authority of the *Qaghan*, family likeness in institutions and joint ownership of Eurasia which made the Chinggissids stakeholders in the overarching Mongol system. To elucidate, new Khans continued to be elected and installed with the blessing of the *Qaghan*, embassies were sent to Beijing to show respect, a peace embassy sent by Du'a in 1304/1305 to Temur Oljeitu Khan in Yuan China was an attempt to renew the bonds that had suffered due to war and conflict, officials were sent from Beijing to Persia and the Golden Horde and armies had troops from across Eurasia (Alans, Russians and Bulgars served in the Yuan armies well into the fourteenth century).[70] This exchange was the crux of Mongol success. The Mongols could harness skills from anywhere and apply them in places where they were needed. For instance: members of the Berkin tribe in Mongolia were used for their mountaineering skills in Iran in the late 1250s and they are mentioned again in Georgia under Timur (Tamerlane) a century later. In other places, Alan metal workers were used to produce chainmail, Chinese siege experts were used in Iran and food was brought from Armenia and Georgia to sustain troops in Hulegu's army when it campaigned against the Caliphate in Baghdad.[71]

The legacy of the Chinggisids did not end with the family of Chinggis Khan but continued to have resonance and formed the basis of legitimacy for centuries after. The Timurid Empire of the fifteenth century and the Khanates that succeeded the Golden Horde were indebted to their connection to the imperial family of Chinggis Khan and his *yasaq* to exercise power. The next chapter goes in-depth in describing Mongol institutions which formed the backbone of

Mongol Eurasia and created the conditions necessary for unprecedented levels of contact between the Khanates and across Eurasia. The Mongol Khans were the prime movers and instigators of exchanges and created innumerable opportunities across Eurasia for groups of people to be able to take advantage of the system which privileged innovation, activity and transmission.[72] At no point did the Mongols impose their own culture on subject populations, nor did they impose other cultures or religions on societies that came under their sway. The main purpose of relocations, transplanting officials and movement which came to be characteristic of Mongol Eurasia was a continuation of steppe traditions and helped exploit resources in the most efficient manner. Chinggis Khan's transformation of the steppe into a unified entity was successful and when applied to Eurasia only served to expand those same policies in a larger area. Khanates continued to represent a *superstructure* which was overlaid on local organisation and which created historical continuation and deep interconnectedness irrespective of separate policies and even immediate goals.[73] Much like the reshuffling of affiliations did not dissolve traditional groupings of people on the steppe, sedentary societies in Eurasia would remain unique even as part of a far more connected system. The Uzbek Khanate of the sixteenth century showed how Central Asian society continued to be governed by the two joint principles of Chinggissid legitimacy and its Islamic identity, even at the eve of Russian expansion in the eighteenth century. Mongol Eurasia came to represent '...the principal cultural clearing house for the Old World for well over a century'.[74] Central Asian and steppe identities even today continue to lie within similar forms of tribal groupings as they did in the thirteenth century and China and Persia persist in their cultural cache despite the impact of the Mongols in the thirteenth century which brought all these societies in far closer contact than ever before. The very notion of an *Eastern* cosmopolitanism which celebrates, rather than mitigates differences began with the Mongols who passed nomadic styles of coexistence on to sedentary cultures. This in turn created new and exciting opportunities for exchange and communication which has persisted through the centuries and come to occupy such an important component of today's societies. Eurasia continues to retain its position in the world as resource rich: human and material, and needs to be understood in terms of local conditions and preferences which capture its unique history.

The following chapters will highlight Mongol Eurasia's most salient features: multi-lingual elites, skilled professionals (artisans and merchants), technology, innovation and science, trade, flexible political and religious cultures, cosmopolitanism and generosity and reciprocity. All of which placed Mongol Eurasia as the precursor to modern globalisation which is based on similar principles. Nearly all the characteristics used to describe globalisation today can be applied to the Mongol world system. They include unparalleled profits from an interconnected world, freedom of movement, labour and brain-drain (and/or exchange), an urban elite who feels at home in global cities and institutions and organisations which guarantee modern globalisation. However, an important qualification lies herein; the Mongols saw themselves as the inheritors of Eurasia as ordained by Chinggis Khan and heaven which meant that Eurasia was one unit and implied that resources, people and material, continued to serve the *whole*, not merely the parts. The labour and brain-drain from Central Asia or China as artisans and officials moved to other regions in Eurasia continued to contribute to the development of the entire region, thus refuting the zero-sum interpretation commonly espoused today. The Mongol Khanates were parts of a whole and the Khans and princes understood that in order to maximise power, influence and success in the fields of politics and finance, they needed to act together. The Mongol philosophy passed down from the steppe was the foundation of Eurasia and had at its heart flexibility and the ability to adapt to disparate practices. The next chapter looks at the institutions as the building blocks of Mongol Eurasia which amplified the natural connectedness of Eurasia while maintaining unique aspects of the societies within it. Modern Eurasia requires a similar mindset and the history of Mongol Eurasia could help inform this discourse.

Notes

1 Grousset 1970, p. 252
2 Togan 1998, p. 131
3 Allsen 2001, p. 199
4 Ratchnevsky 1991, p. 72
5 Barfield 1989, p. 188
6 Barfield 1989, p. 188
7 Togan 1998, p. 11
8 Golden 1992, pp. 286–287
9 Parker 1924, p. 12
10 Ratchnevsky 1991, p. 89
11 For detail on the history of the steppe and Chinggis Khan, see Grousset 1970; Spuler 1971; Ratchnevsky 1991; Golden 1992; Bosworth and Asimov 2000.
12 Khazanov and Wink 2001, pp. 4–5
13 Golden 1992, p. 291
14 Barfield 1989, p. 157
15 Barfield 1989, p. 165
16 Ratchnevsky 1991, pp. 38–39
17 Togan 1998, pp. 137–138; Di Cosmo 1999, p. 19
18 Di Cosmo 1999, p. 21
19 Togan 1998, p. 133
20 Barfield 1989, p. 197
21 Togan 1998, p. 136
22 Togan 1998, p. 178
23 Mott 2015, p. 20
24 Ratchnevsky 1991, p. 37
25 Like *Qaghan*
26 Golden 1992, p. 286
27 Ratchnevsky 1991, p. 86
28 Togan 1998, p. 139
29 Togan 1998, p. 139
30 Togan 1998, p. 137
31 Grousset 1970, p. 224
32 For more information see Grousset 1967; Ratchnevsky 1991; May 2007
33 Grousset 1970, p. 243

34 Adshead 1993, p. 53
35 Adshead 1993, p. 63
36 Togan 1998, p. 144
37 Biran 1997, pp. 42–44
38 Grousset 1970, p. 250
39 Allsen 2001, p. 188
40 Grousset 1967, p. 167
41 Allsen 2001, p. 127
42 Adshead 1993, p. 53
43 Di Cosmo *et al.* 2009, p. 4; see also Adshead 1993, p. 70
44 Regions
45 Ratchnevsky 1991, p. 207
46 Buell 1999, p. 204
47 Jackson 2017, p. 103
48 Rashid al-Din 1960, pp. 974–975
49 Assassins/Ismailis
50 Rashid al-Din 1960, p. 974
51 Regions
52 Ilkhan translates as 'Subordinate (Il) Khan to the Grand *Qaghan*'
53 Golden 1992, p. 288
54 Biran 2013, p. 262
55 Official authorisation tablets from the *Qaghan*
56 Allsen 1986, pp. 499–500
57 Ratchnevksy 1991, p. 208
58 Governors
59 Allsen 1987, p. 223
60 Military organised along the decimal system/military units
61 Rossabi 1994, p. 31
62 Ratchnevsky 1991, p. 207
63 Allsen 2009, p. 103
64 Allsen 2009, p. 144
65 Adshead 1993, p. 88; Ratchnevsky 1991, p. 213
66 Allsen 2001, p. 202
67 Togan 1998, pp. 132–133
68 Togan 1998, p. 136
69 Togan 1998, pp. 137–138
70 Adshead 1993, pp. 87–88
71 Allsen 1987, pp. 211, 215
72 Allsen 2001, pp. 192–193
73 Manz 1994, pp. 10–11
74 Allsen 2001, p. 21

2 Institutional framework of Mongol Eurasia

> … the era of the unitary empire was the first (and the last) time in which a single pastoralist state dominated the entire length of the Silk Roads; and at no time did any sedentary state succeed in doing so.[1]

Chinggis Khan's rise sparked the creation of Mongol Eurasia which stretched from the shores of the Caspian Sea to the tip of the Korean peninsula. It came to include all of China, Central Asia, Persia and Kievan Rus. The establishment of this enterprise was based on steppe traditions which were adapted by Chinggis Khan, first to unify the steppe, and then were applied in wider Eurasia by his immediate descendants. At the time of Chinggis Khan's demise in 1227, Central Asia (the steppe and Transoxiana) and Northern China were under Mongol control, while the rest of Eurasia was yet to be conquered. According to the *Secret History of the Mongols*, Chinggis Khan divided his domains (conquered and the ones yet to be conquered) between his four sons which also included tribes, *yurt*, and territorial appanages. Jochi's *ulus* was farthest west and included the western steppe (Semiplatansk, Akmolinsk, Turgai, Khwarezm and everything west of the Volga), Chaghatai inherited Transoxiana, Ogedei was given the old Naiman territory (Imil and Tarbagatai) and Tolui received the patrimony of his father i.e. Mongolia (upper Onon valley).[2] Between 1227 and 1258 the Mongols had successfully laid claim to all of Eurasia. After 1260, Mongol Eurasia was run along four sub-divisions: Yuan China, Ilkhanate Persia, the Golden Horde and the Chaghatais and Ogedeis in Central Asia.[3] The governance of Mongol Eurasia while not centralised, shared certain Mongol characteristics which came from a uniquely Mongol perspective. Based out of nomadic traditions and a flexible style of leadership, the Mongols modelled the four Khanates on Chinggissid principles which formed the backbone of a unified Eurasia. The institutions and practices of the Mongols created a supranational administrative structure[4] which was able to combine distinct political structures in the societies of Eurasia.

As per steppe tradition, the *Qaghan* was elected in a *quriltai*[5] who had to secure a majority vote, and he ruled from an *ordo*, a collection of *yurts.*[6]

For Chinggis Khan and his immediate descendants this was Qara Qorum; under Qubilai Khan it shifted to Beijing in 1271. The principles that Mongol Eurasia was based on stemmed from steppe traditions and that included the idea of *corporate sovereignty.* Mongol Eurasia while being divided among Chinggis Khan's sons was considered the joint patrimony of the Mongol imperial family, '[I]n time honoured steppe fashion, the conquests were regarded as the property of the entire dynasty, and although presided over by a *Qaghan,* the empire was in effect run as a family firm'.[7] The appanage system which governed this nomadic custom shaped Mongol Eurasia and marked it as a shared resource, and signified a unitary system with centrifugal tendencies. This aspect of a Mongol run Eurasia informs the basis of an interconnected space which required, encouraged and spurred exchanges of peoples, ideas, goods and technologies, across this space. As a result of a conjoined political system, which nonetheless left room for manoeuvre by the Khanates and local dynasties, flexibility was allowed even in the economic sphere and led to phenomenal successes. The distribution of appanages remained a striking feature of Mongol Eurasia and continued to serve as a means to maintain support and loyalty throughout the thirteenth and fourteenth centuries.

The administrative structure set up under Chinggis Khan had its basis in nomadic traditions which were adapted to local conditions in China, Persia, Russia and Central Asia as they came under the sway of the Mongols. Other than a brief period of centralisation, under Mongke (1250–1259), Mongol Eurasia was administered in semi-independent ways. The Khanates as they came to be called shared certain features: Mongols (and steppe intelligentsia) in key positions, shared institutions, elevated position of merchants and open religious policies to name a few. The *Qaghan* at the apex of Mongol Eurasia enjoyed allegiance and loyalty along with tribute and a promise of troops in times of conquest. As mentioned in the previous chapter, Chinggis Khan unified different peoples on the steppe which included pastoralists, herders and semi-sedentary peoples and created a Turko-Mongol state which was represented by a mix of Mongols and Turks. Some of the early advisers of Chinggis Khan who came from the steppe's more semi-sedentary tribes continued to occupy places of influence and posts in the administration of Mongol Eurasia well into the reigns of Chinggis Khan and his successors. The principle of consultative governance which was evident in the election of the *Qaghan* was also reflected in military conquests. The army of conquest was made up of battalions from across the imperial family and guaranteed the interests of a cross section of Mongol Khanates. The various branches of the imperial family were engaged with the wider processes of governance and control across the territory of Eurasia. The consultative nature of the Mongol ruling style inherited from the steppe was visible even in the case of determining punishments. For example, in the instance of Arigh Boke's rebellion against his brother, Qubilai, the latter sent messages to confer with all the ruling Khans: Hulegu (Ilkhan), Berke (Golden Horde) and Alghu (Central Asia).[8] This point is particularly poignant because Arigh Boke was supported by Alghu in his struggle against Qubilai. This perspective is essential in analysing Eurasia under the Mongols. The Khanates were able to exercise a fair degree of independence and still remain a part of a composite Mongol state. This was most keenly seen in the unfolding of economic prosperity which was a direct result of burgeoning connectedness and openness on the Silk Road.

Chinggis Khan's distribution of appanages followed the principle of shared ownership and created a complex and co-dependent relationship between his descendants. For example, Batu (a Jochid prince) and Chaghatai had property and taxation rights in Northern China; Mongke had similar rights in the Golden Horde territory and so forth. This not only favoured cordial relationships between the Khanates but also spoke to the unification of Eurasia under Mongol overlordship. The ruling houses represented one philosophy and the government of all the regions in Eurasia shared features and officials. This organisation of the administrative structures gave Eurasia its *Mongol* 'flavour' and marks this period as a particularly special epoch. Mongol rule coincided with a period of unprecedented prosperity and commercial activity across the Silk Road and this needs to be understood in terms of the institutional frameworks put in place by the Mongols.

As has been mentioned in the previous chapter, the early Mongol institutional framework divided and organised society according to militaristic principles in a decimal system (tumen) with units of tens, hundreds, thousands, tens of thousands and so on.[9] All of society was represented in this way and the military administration and ranks were given to people who oversaw the civil administration as well. The system thus created was governed by a small aristocratic elite with the imperial family at the very top with their most trusted allies (military commanders and allies called *nokers*). This led to 'a more cohesive and powerful aristocracy' under the *Qaghan*.[10] Steppe societies by default are small due to the limited resources they have and thus the Mongols organised themselves in a similar fashion to their predecessors on the steppe. Far from the common perception of nomads and Mongols being unorganised and barbaric or lacking institutional frameworks before the inclusion of sedentary lands, the character of organisations on the steppe were precise and highly stylised to best adapt to the harsh ecological and geographical conditions. Put more precisely, the '… steppe was not an amalgam of heteroclitic and anarchic tribes, but a highly structured society […] the steppe nomad had a distinct historical tradition'.[11] One of the key institutions used by the Mongols for keeping checks was the *tamamci* which refers to garrison troops posted in border areas and newly acquired lands of Mongol Eurasia and dated back to pre-Mongol times. They were used for supporting Mongol *darugachis*,[12] spying and also functioned as vanguards for the newly established Mongol administration. They were used to ensure safety and stability across Mongol Eurasia and were vital for trade and revenue collection. These garrison troops served as private armies and auxiliary troops in times of war and conquest in Yuan China and were eventually used by the Ming to challenge Yuan authority well into the fourteenth century, testifying to their continued use.[13]

When the Mongols came into prolonged contact with the sedentary peoples of China and some parts of Central Asia, the nomadic principles of organising society were adapted to local conditions. Censuses were conducted from Chinggis Khans' times down to Eurasia-wide regularised censuses under Mongke. The period between 1251 and 1259 was one of centralisation and regularisation under Mongke and spurred taxation reforms directed by Mahmud Yalavac who managed to amalgamate Mongol and non-Mongol practices to best suit the populations of Central Asia and Northern China. Mongke also redistributed appanages which caused tension between the Khanates and deprived Ogedeids of their Chinggissid inheritance which had significant consequences for the unity of Mongol Eurasia.[14] However, even with rivalries and conflicts breaking out between the Mongol Khanates, the basic structure and governance of Mongol led regions remained fairly similar. Qaidu (Ogedei's descendant) and Qubilai were in charge of quite different populations – semi-nomadic as in the case of Central Asia under Qaidu and sedentary in China under Qubilai – but the court was made up of similar elements, openness in religious and commercial activities and overarching interests in skilled craftsmen and artisans among others. The main structure was almost identical, however, there were offices and officials which represented local conditions in all four regions.

The common features shared between all the Khanates can be summed up as the following: decentralisation, a consultative style of governance, staffing of courts with physicians, astronomers and religious clerics and the co-opting of local customs and cultural habits. It is important to clarify that while Mongol or nomadic unification implied certain similarities in administration, governance and other practices, the Mongols remained inimical to centralisation policies, as was evident from the aftermath of Mongke's centralisation drive in the 1250s.

Figure 2.1 Mongol Eurasia: The Khanates.

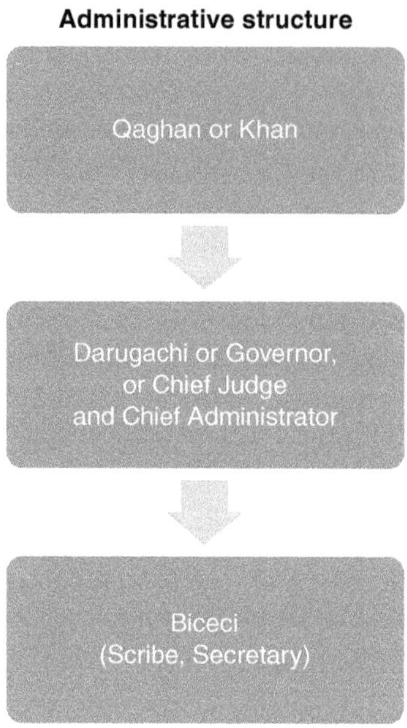

Figure 2.2 Government hierarchy.

The subsequent succession struggles which culminated in the election of Qubilai Khan clearly demonstrated that the Mongol Khanates were political entities in their own right. This did not preclude their allegiance to either the laws of Chinggis Khan or Chinggissid Eurasia. As stated earlier, the *Qaghan* continued to attract supporters and the fact that the princes of the imperial family jostled for power through supporting rival candidates depicts the system which was related through family ties and a shared political heritage. Similarly, the protracted conflict that erupted between the house of Ogedei and Yuan China in the 1270s was an outcome of a combination of factors that included circumstances which had diminished the position and prestige of the descendants of Ogedei. Qaidu's bid to reassert his authority on the regions which were assigned to his direct ancestors led to a conflict which impacted Central Asian cities, especially those bordering China. While it created alliances and anti-parties within the Chinggissid princes, it also served as an example for the importance of regional independence. Furthermore, it spurred the innovative strategies characteristic of the Mongol princes to carry on trading across the Silk Road by finding new routes, encouraging and streamlining trade within their regions and eventually, after the death of Qaidu in 1301/1302, to call for a peace that would resume earlier interactions. The peace embassy of 1304/1305 was initiated by Du'a (Chaghatai prince) and brought representatives from the Golden Horde and the house of Ogedei to Temur, Qubilai's successor in China. The peace embassy was clearly an important event because it recalled the *corporate sovereignty* of the Mongol Khanates, the importance of Chinggissid principles and proffered the resumption of large scale and unrestricted trade across all the Khanates.[15] The importance of this embassy is further corroborated by a letter sent by the then reigning Ilkhan, Oljeitu, to the King of France, alerting him to political unity among the Mongol princes. This letter further indicated that the Mongols were ready to form an alliance against the Mamluks of Egypt and Syria who had continued to resist the Mongols and Europeans.[16] The importance of a united front which echoed the ambitions of Chinggissid Mongols, and overcame the weaknesses caused by warring Khanates, was essential not only for expansion of territories but also for the continuation of trade. The correlation between trade and the ebbs and flow of Mongol power is reiterated in these interactions which refer to Mongol unification. It is clear that the Mongols used a variety of strategies to achieve these aims based on historical traditions and a common ancestry.

The administration of the four Khanates shared Mongol features and accommodated local conditions in order to achieve the best possible fit. To reiterate, the features that remained Mongol included the military which remained organised along *tumens* and served as the main administrative arm of the Mongol administration; ethnic Mongols (and steppe peoples) filled influential positions across the Khanates; traders and merchants were given special privileges; as were artisans and skilled professionals; and the Khans continued to travel between summer and winter pastures well into the fourteenth century. The main pillars of steppe society from Chinggis Khan's times were visible in all the Khanates with a level of alteration to reflect local conditions. The adaptive nature of Chinggissid practices as seen on the steppe was visible in all other parts of Eurasia. As a result, Mongol administration in China, Persia and Russia has sometimes been referred to as a *suprastructure* which was placed above existing structures. The act of combining was visible in spheres of administration, for example, the legal code in Yuan China under Qubilai was a conglomeration of Chinese and Mongol elements and included Mongol practices such as imposing monetary compensation for crimes committed in lieu of punishment.[17] The Mongols were also able to integrate the existing Secretariat Branches in China with the Mongolian socio-political system which is best described as a hybrid system of governance. Another aspect reflective of Mongol practices was the assigning of military ranks to all personnel (Mongol and Chinese) in the Yuan secretariat.[18] Mongol laws were incorporated within a larger administrative structure in some areas, while in other cases local customs were accommodated within Mongol laws. For example, in the Ilkhanate, local dynasties maintained control by paying allegiance to the Mongols in Tabriz. The presence of key Mongol and steppe figures in the government across the regions guaranteed a particularly Mongol imprint on governance and left enough room for local administrators to continue more familiar practices for the subject populations. This goes to show the ways in which the Mongols were able to foster cosmopolitanism fashioned out of what already existed as opposed to imposing an entirely new system alien to both the ruler and the subject. While there is no doubt that the Mongols impacted the regions they incorporated by directly transforming society, their policies of moving groups of people from one end of Eurasia to another also led to exchanges and transfers which continue to resonate today. Pockets of Central Asian artisans in China and conversely Chinese artisans in Iran still exist and have influenced the culture and habits of these places in innumerable ways.

The next section looks at the main offices which were set up in all Mongol Khanates following conquest. The main Mongol offices included: *darugachi, basqaq* and *biceci.* In addition to these, the four Khanates had offices which were reminiscent of older political systems: *sadrs* in Bukhara, Khojent and Ferghana;[19] Muscovite princes who were responsible for collecting taxation in Rus;[20] and local dynasties (Saljuqs, Qutlughkahnid dynasty in Kirman and Kurtids in Herat) who continued to rule in Iran as client rulers to the Mongols.[21] In some cases *darugachis* and *basqaqs* were positioned permanently, while in other places they were periodically sent in supervisory capacities to ensure that tribute due to the Mongols was being collected and sent as per the terms of surrender. As in the case of Bukhara, local rulers continued to mint coins in their own name (as opposed to in the name of Qaidu) and *darugachis* were sent rather than stationed there.[22] The system of joint patrimony and allegiance to the *Qaghan* also dictated the presence of representatives of other princes and the *Qaghan* in the Khanates across Eurasia. Appanages of the sons of Chinggis Khan were spread across regions and attest to the evocative place of integration in Mongol thinking. It speaks volumes toward the making of a Mongol Eurasia where successes and prosperity in one region signalled personal wealth and/or loss for the princes across Eurasia. Similarly, losses and defeats also echoed throughout the Mongol Khanates. Chaghatai and Hulegu's interest in a prosperous China came as much from their Khanates' ability to trade with it, as from taxation from certain regions which went directly to them. This practice remains relevant as much today as it did then, in light of an increasingly globalised world, and is particularly pertinent for Eurasia which is so deeply connected.

In the following sections, a closer look at institutions and administrative structures provides a snapshot of the ways through which the Mongols were able to create the phenomenon that was *Mongol Eurasia*. The institutions of: *yasaq, keshig, darugachi, basqaq, biceci,* and *tumen* are described in detail. Along with these offices, merchants and their unique place in state administration are discussed at length. These features of the Mongol Khanates are juxtaposed with the ways in which they were practised in and influenced local conditions across Eurasia. The purpose of this is to show both continuity and adaptability intrinsic to Mongol governance. The discourse shaped in this way helps in seeing the continuities within the overarching system and establishes the *Mongol worldview* so important for political and economic unification in Eurasia.

Chinggis Khan's *yasaq* (legal code) formed the basis of Mongol laws on the steppe and was used across Eurasia. It first appears in 1206 and was likely written by Chinggis Khan's close companion, Siqi Qutuqu. These conditions and laws included the distribution of appanages, treatment of *khatuns* (Mongol princesses), strict discipline in military ranks, involvement in economic activities and distribution of taxes including trade and pasturelands, and these continued throughout and across Mongol Eurasia in the thirteenth and fourteenth centuries. The *yasaq* gave ruling elites legitimacy and pointed to the importance of nomadic traditions and continued to have resonance for the Mongols even when they no longer lived on the steppe. The *yasaq* can be divided into regulations or laws pertaining to the civil, military, criminal code, private laws and the customs of the steppe. It was given to Chinggis Khan's second son, Chaghatai, to protect and impose. The penalties for not following the legal code were as severe as death in some instances. It also included a stipulation for religious tolerance which was invoked by later Khans in their treatment of religions across Eurasia.[23] It provided, whether written or oral, the justification and the means for unifying the steppe according to joint principles and even later as the Mongols went on to conquer most of Eurasia, it serves as a basis for unity in action and ambition among the Mongol princes and Khans. These laws were written down in 'blue registers' by Siqi Qutuqu. While the full text has not survived, fragments of it have been passed down in Persian, Arabic, Chinese and Russian sources of the Mongol period and in the following centuries. The *yasaq* along with the person of Chinggis Khan went on to form the very basis of Mongol ideology and legitimacy through the ages and was referred to as late as the end of the fourteenth century by Amir Timur to legitimise his rule in Central Asia. The Khanates of Crimea, Astrakhan, Kazan and later Uzbek and Kazakh Khanates continued to mention the importance of the *yasaq*, attesting to its long-lasting impact in the region.

A detailed look at Mongol institutions and administrative frameworks indicate that Mongol Eurasia was organised in a way that would encourage linkages and networks not only at the level between Mongol courts for purposes of political administration, but also for the purposes of engineering economic prosperity. The economies of the four regions were interlinked through a variety of institutions. One such key institution was the '*jam*' or '*yam*', a postal relay station, which connected the entire region and provided effective and efficient communication along with information flows. The *jam* was introduced by Ogedei throughout Mongol domains and continued to be expanded throughout the thirteenth and fourteenth centuries.[24] These were in essence facilities or checkpoints connecting different parts of Eurasia, provisioned with fresh horses, fodder, accommodation and other such requirements which would allow for quick movement of couriers, officials and traders. They formed the necessary infrastructure for imperial convoys to pass through territories, even during times of conflict. According to Marco Polo, for instance, '... each imperial envoy was protected by the so-called "tablets" or "piasters"[25] of gold and silver, which by imperial command rendered his person inviolable, under pain of death and terrible reprisals against any who should disregard them'.[26] These tablets functioned as visas which enabled safe passage throughout Mongol Eurasia. The *jam* was among the first to be set up in every region and province that came under Mongol sway and were a priority for all the princes and Khans across Eurasia. The upkeep of these stations was the responsibility of the local population which was supposed to maintain the stations through taxes. In China, Qubilai set up more than 1400 postal stations with numerous horses and other animals for merchants and envoys to use.[27] Along with providing seamless movement, they also ensured safety for travellers and traders who were often carrying expensive goods. They served as early warning systems for the military and were the fastest courier service. The officials running the service were granted military ranks which further indicated the special place *jams* were accorded.[28] In times of war and conquest, they served as patrol stations. For example, Qubilai built new postal stations connecting the provinces in the extreme west of China (Ajiqi and Chubei) to provinces in the extreme east (Muqali) in the late thirteenth century to keep Central Asian Mongols under Qaidu in check. This is further corroborated by Chinese sources which point to the building of 30 postal stations in this area which connected all the way to the region of the Uyghurs (Besh Baligh) in Central Asia.[29] Time and again the postal stations appear in the sources as part of the key infrastructural developments in Eurasia under the Mongols. In this way, the Mongol courts across the realm were connected and could get information in a speedy manner. *Jam* was therefore in many ways the backbone of Mongol governance which was used for key purposes of communication and information, fostered trade, encouraged economic activity and provided safety and facilitated travel.

The next important Mongol institution was the office of *darugachi* which can be traced back to Chinggis Khan's times. Along with the *darugachi* appears the office of *basqaq* which was appointed in each subdivision to supervise and keep local officials in check. These two offices at times are conflated and their responsibilities overlapped. For this reason, they are discussed jointly in this section. One can distinguish between the *darugachi*, the governor overseeing the administration of a region and the *basqaq* (sometimes more than one)[30] as a Mongol representative, especially in regions where local rulers were retained as vassals. Spuler further notes variation in the responsibilities of the *basqaq* based on the region. For example, in the Golden Horde they were commandants; in Persia, their role was more supervisory; and in Transoxiana (Central Asia) they oversaw civil and financial administration. On other occasions, the sources conflate the offices of *darugachi* and *basqaq*, and in some cases the hierarchy is determined by the person in the office.[31] In the *Secret History of the Mongols*, the term *darugachi* refers to 'chief local administrator, controller, local resident commissioner, governor, overseer and even someone who exercised control' and his functions were tax collection and recruiting people for military service and labour, derived from the Mongol word *daru*.[32,33] *Basqaqs*, on the other hand, ensured that the demands of the central *ordo*[34] were fulfilled and the office has been associated with being military commanders and protectors of the *darugachi* as well.[35] The responsibilities of the *basqaq* included monitoring activities of local vassals and overseeing the census along with ensuring tribute was paid according to the terms of submission.[36] A description of the responsibilities clearly indicates the importance of aspects of administration which were important to the Mongols: census and taxation. The economic significance of these two administrative offices is proof enough that the Mongols were aware of the need for economic integration. There was an unequivocal attempt at monitoring, regularising and sharing of information which essentially shaped Mongol Eurasia. The fact that these offices were filled by Mongols or the steppe intelligentsia[37] and by Central Asian and Khitans who were aware of the Mongol system and its nomadic nature speaks to the prevalence of an overarching philosophy. These offices were filled by the most trusted advisers and closest allies of the Khans. It is essential to point out that the people who filled these offices are as important as the office and highlights the Mongol attention to administration. They ensured that the Mongols had final say and control over the populations across Eurasia. Among the people who filled these positions was Sigi Qutuqu, who served as the first *darugachi*. He clearly enjoyed great authority; his rulings especially in granting and resolving disputes related to appanages formed the basis for all future judgements as late as the middle of the fourteenth century.[38] Under Ogedei, Cinqai was *darugachi* and his duties included serving as the '… supervisor of princely representatives and head of joint imperial administration'.[39] The appointment of officials, especially the post of *darugachi*, requires further clarification. An important Mongol addition to the administrative structure of Eurasia was their policy of employing people of different ethnicities. This policy was first introduced by Chinggis Khan to bypass tribal loyalties to local leaders and foster allegiance to the Chinggissids. Even when the Mongols moved into lands beyond the steppe, this policy was enforced to great satisfaction. In principle, the appointment of *darugachis* was done by senior Chinggissid princes and they were representatives of the entire royal family (reflecting the appanage system and joint ownership of the regions). For example: Yeh lu Chu Tsai from Northern China and an ethnic Khitan was made governor in Central Asia, while Mahmud Yalavac, a Muslim Central Asian financial administrator from Central Asia was installed as governor in Northern China. Yeh lu Ahai (another ethnic Khitan) was *darugachi* of Bukhara and his son inherited the position after he died. Under Ogedei, Korguz (a Uyghur) was the *darugachi* of Khurasan and Mazandaran. According to the Yuan Shih, Kitai (Qongirrad Mongol) was made governor of Rus and his appointment coincided with organising Rus along Mongol lines and the taking of censuses and imposition of taxes.[40] Similarly in Ilkhanate Persia high ranking officials were from Central Asia (Khwarezm and Khurasan).[41] This aspect of joint ownership was evident even in the offices of *darugachi* and *basqaq* with Mahmud Yalavac and Arghun Aqa who were responsible for multiple Khans, Mongke and Qubilai in the case of the former and Mongke and Hulegu for the latter.[42] Through this strategy of using ethnically different officials the Mongols were able to avoid rebellions and managed to encourage transfer of technologies from one region to another. This was especially true in Mongke's time when the system was regularised across Eurasia in such a way that resources could be utilised across the expanse of the territories. For example: Chinese technologies were used in Persia and Central Asian colonies in China exercised influence in the culture of cities like Hangchow. Along with officials representing the Mongols, there were local officials whose work was supervised by the Mongol *darugachis*. The local officials represented the language, customs and conditions of the region and provided the necessary knowledge and skills to administer newly conquered regions. In these instances, *darugachis* provided checks and balances between princes and the local population. In summary, the office of *darugachi* encompassed all matters related to a functioning appanage system, collecting taxes, taking censuses,[43] supervising local officials in the subdivisions and reflecting Mongol traditions across Eurasia. The duties of the *darugachis* also included: time keeper of the *Qaghan's* seal, military commander, adviser, chancellor and governor. In the late 1240s Cinqai even received emissaries, embassies like that of Carpini, drafted letters to the Pope and had subordinate *darugachi* and *biceci,* Qadaq and Bala respectively.[44] Closely associated with these two offices was the office of *biceci.* The office of *biceci*, which has been translated as scribe or secretaries, was filled by Yeh lu Chu Tsai under Chinggis Khan. He was '... in charge of official documents in Chinese with that of court astrologer-astronomer'.[45] He travelled with Chinggis Khan to Central Asia, and under Ogedei was made *darugachi* in China. The importance of writing and paperwork is worth mentioning here. While nomads in general are considered to have an oral culture, the Mongols were interested in writing and even devised a writing system based on the Uyghur alphabet early on in the establishment of Chinggis Khan's Eurasia. The inclusion of Uyghurs, Khitans, Chinese, Central Asians and Persians within their domains spurred writing and maintaining documents. The main responsibilities of the Chinese secretariat (*chung-shu cheng*) under Yeh lu Chu Tsai was to draft decrees, official documents and keep records in multiple languages.[46] This is further attested to by the fact that the Central Asians who were multi-lingual did exceedingly well in the employment of the Khans. The language of the court remained Mongolian in all regions which led to the employment of translators in huge numbers and the subsequent rise in prestige of the career is noteworthy. The language of Mongol courts remained Mongolian well into the fourteenth century whether in Yuan China, the Ilkhanate, Central Asia or in the Golden Horde. In Central Asia, documents from Turfan have been found in Mongolian as late as 1369.[47] Persian officials had to learn Mongolian in the Ilkhanate to further their careers, and Mongolian was used in the Yuan court as well. Mongol Eurasia gave rise to many multi-language dictionaries and grammars which included Eurasian regions and also adjacent regions of India and Egypt.[48]According to Juwayni, *biceci* were employed in all languages (Persian, Uyghur, Chinese, Tibetan and Tangut).[49] From very early on the main edicts and charters issued by the Mongols were written down by *biceci*, mostly Uyghurs in Chinggis Khan's time. These officials held the imperial seal (sometimes held by *darugachi* as mentioned above) which had to be used to verify every document.[50] Thus the scribes exercised great authority and opportunity to influence the Mongol Khans. In time, there was an attempt at balancing local officials with Mongol officials to ensure checks and balances. The division of responsibilities between these offices was blurred and often determined by the person who filled the office. However, these offices and descriptions of responsibilities point to Mongol involvement in day-to-day functioning more than is usually accepted, especially in sedentary regions.[51] This section has provided examples of the ways in which the Mongols (Khans and officials) impacted governance in Eurasia.

A further look into the early officers of Mongol Eurasia helps us determine the importance of the steppe intelligentsia in early Mongol statehood. The foundations of Mongol Eurasia, along with the key practices and responsibilities were derived from steppe traditions. There is little doubt that nomadic practices lay at the heart of the administration of Central Asia and the Golden Horde. However, even in Yuan China and Persia these Mongol offices and officials exercised influence and impacted governance. In other words, '[F]rom the beginning the nucleus of Mongol administration had lain in the imperial household guard and it had remained there since …'[52] irrespective of the overwhelmingly sedentary populations in some regions of Eurasia. The integrated system, political and economic, which this produced, was guaranteed by Mongol officials who understood the intricate workings of Mongol Eurasia based on nomadic principles in close contact with sedentary populations. The officials not only had to mediate between two different populations but also had to guarantee the smooth functioning within the Chinggissid imperial family which oversaw Mongol Eurasia as a joint patrimony which often led to disputes over revenue.[53] As mentioned above, this practice was visible in military services as well, i.e. Mongol princes sent troops to make up any army of conquest. For example, Guyuk, Mongke and others went as military commanders on the expedition to the west, even though it was expressly under the control of Batu of the Golden Horde. Hulegu's army on its way to the Middle East had troops from the Golden Horde in 1258.[54]

This brings us to the institution of *keshig* (the royal bodyguard) which has been described as the *most impressive innovation* of Chinggis Khan. Originally, *darugachis* were chosen from Chinggis Khan's *keshig* or royal bodyguard.[55] The imperial guard or *keshig (kesigten)* was the main administrative institution of steppe polity. After the inclusion of sedentary populations, the *keshig* served as the central government and had the responsibilities of collecting taxes, taking censuses, recruiting for military purposes, keeping records and distributing spoils of war.[56] The members of the guard were rotated on a regular basis, returning to the court after a period of service in far flung places to renew their ties with the *Qaghan*.[57] The guard existed in all the Khanates. The *Qaghan* and the princes all had their own personal guard which looked after their private household. This institution was built along old ties which '… bound retainers to a prince or *Qaghan* [and] were forged by the military discipline of the guard and further reinforced by daily social interaction with their patron'.[58] In exchange for this personal loyalty, the patron had substantial responsibilities, the most important of which was to keep the guard satisfied and to apportion fair reimbursement for their services. The *keshig*, exclusively Mongol commanders, enjoyed privileges and special positions in Yuan China and the Ilkhanate throughout the thirteenth century and up to the middle of the fourteenth century.[59] The role of the people that made up the *keshig* included the office of *baurchi* (loosely translated as the cook), always selected from the royal bodyguard and represented closeness to the person of the Khan and the imperial household. Examples of people who held this position include Bolad and Ked Buqa, both of whom played an important role in Yuan China and Iran. They were *baurchis* but also commanded military campaigns in Iran and Northern China.[60] The *keshig* occupied important positions in government, and very often oversaw local officials in order to accommodate conditions peculiar to where they were.

Mongol institutions with the khan on top, followed by *darugachis* (senior and junior) and then *biceci* were found in nearly all the Khanates. Siqi Qutuqu, Cinqai, Yeh lu Chu Tsai, Yeh lu Ahai, Mahmud Yalavac and later Arghun Aqa to name a few, represented the Khan in numerous roles and very often became the eyes and ears of the *Qaghan* in distant lands. While, the *Qaghan* did not have the direct right to dictate policies for all the Khanates, the Mongol system based on integration through shared officials, common offices, taxation, appanages, *jam* and *corporate sovereignty* connected Eurasia in deep and meaningful ways. The Mongol Empire was not a Westphalian state but exhibited a shared historical and ancestral continuity which legitimised its rule over Eurasia. The subsequent economic success is testament to the veracity of this particular Mongol strategy especially in the environment Eurasia. The key players in making this situation tenable, other than the Khans, were the ministers, advisers and governors in the form of *darugachis* and *biceci*. They fulfilled numerous roles, their stock went up and down but they served as the pillars of the Mongol state and continued to pass on Mongol traditions as set out by Chinggis Khan and his descendants across the region. As per Allsen, in the Mongol state, '[E]ach individual appointed to a specific office could have taken over duties of any other office without major difficulty'.[61] This was visible in Mongol Eurasia throughout their existence and in this way, the Mongols and their allies continued to control this vast geographical space.

Before a discussion on the role of merchants in Eurasia, a note on taxation is essential. Taxation was a combination of Mongol and non-Mongol elements. In general, it was carried out according to local conditions with additional Mongol

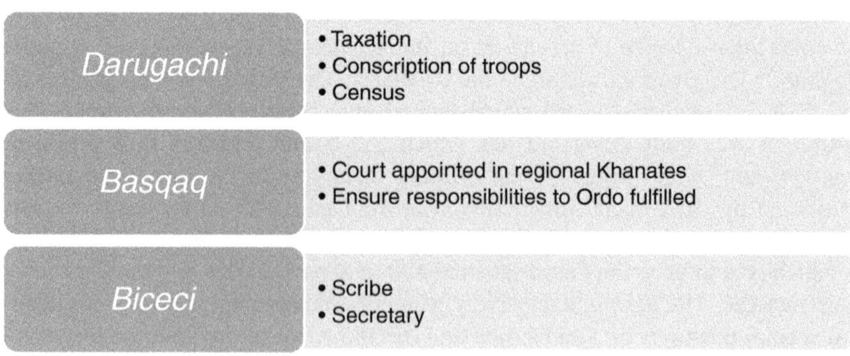

Figure 2.3 Mongol offices (institutions) and their responsibilities.

taxes. The taxation system included Mongol-inspired tribute payments and traditional taxes (agricultural and trade related). The basic categories of taxation were: *tamgha* and *qubichir*. *Tamgha* referred to commercial and manufacturing taxes, and the sedentary population also had to pay *alba* which refers to the tribute that the local princes collected and sent to the *Qaghan* to convey continued allegiance. In addition, *qubichir* was charged sporadically and referred to special taxes, such as those levied in times of war or for the upkeep of the postal relay station.[62] Taxes for military operations made up the largest portion of special taxes imposed on sedentary populations throughout the Mongol period.[63] Taxation was received both in cash (coins, paper) and kind (especially fabrics).[64] Most taxes were collected locally per local conditions, other than under Mongke, when tax collection was done under the supervision of a court appointed *darugachi* sent from Qara Qorum. On average, the Mongols retained traditional revenue streams and added nomadic taxes into the mix. Mongol Khans spent a considerable amount of time and effort regularising taxation in their realms. For example, in 1229, Yeh lu Chu Tsai as head of the regional administration in Northern China proposed reforms to regularise the tax base according to three categories: household, land and commercial which led to increased revenues in 1234 under Ogedei. Mongke is attributed with regularising the taxation system for Mongol Eurasia; Mahmud Yalavac was the administrator who executed the changes. Over the years, the Khans of the four Khanates reorganised and regularised taxation at various intervals expressly to increase revenue and weed out corrupt practices. There are instances of financial reorganisation under Qaidu in the 1260s, and again under Kebek in the 1320s in Transoxiana. In Persia Ghazan Khan and his financial adviser, Rashid al-Din, undertook major reforms to rectify hardships and corruption on highways and at entry points into markets. The Golden Horde Khans also undertook reforms and renewed treaties with Genoese and Venetian merchants in response to conditions in the markets. In most instances, the reforms led to prosperity and cleaned the system of corruption and complacency as documented in Chinese and Persian sources. This naturally brings the discussion to the class of merchants who served as the most prominent group under the Mongols.

Merchants not only served and benefitted as an economic class but were key players in the state apparatus of the Mongols. They served as administrators, governors and financial officers after the conquest of large parts of Central Asia, Northern China and the Middle East in considerable numbers. According to Allsen, merchants were specifically well placed to be in positions which were often far away from their households, since they had experience of doing just that as part of their profession. Merchants proved effective to the Mongols in both their transferable skills and their loyalty. In one instance, in Shabankarah in Iran, merchants and *ortoys* were handed the administration when the Mongols were left with no local heirs to administer the region.[65] Merchants were able to buy their freedom if they were abducted in military operations and continued to become influential and wealthy under the Mongols.[66] According to Rashid al-Din, Chinggis Khan saw the profession of merchants as a hereditary vocation, akin to the soldiers teaching their sons to shoot bows and arrows.[67] In many cases sources refer to them as ambassadors rather than merchants. The relationship between the Mongols and merchants has been described as, '[In] the expanding Mongolian state the traders had found a powerful ally that actively promoted commerce by providing patronage, capital, and protection'.[68] Under Ogedei, merchants continued to exercise influence on imperial policy and were given special privileges. This is attested to by Chinese and Persian sources in their descriptions of the court.[69]

The relationship between merchants and the Mongols through the inquiry of the office of *darugachi* is important not only for the purposes of looking into commercial activity in the Mongol state but also to gain insight into the workings of the Mongol realm. The term *ortoys*, a Turkic term meaning 'partner' was applied to merchants in the Mongol era. It came '... to denote a merchant operating with capital supplied by a Činggisid prince or court official'.[70] The earliest partners of Chinggis Khan were Uyghurs, and after the conquest of Khwarezmshah's domains, Central Asians, both of whom were traders and involved in long distance trade for centuries. Within the context of the steppe, the Uyghurs had long been central to and controlled trade with China. It is not surprising then that the relationship between merchants and Chinggissids was so close and intimate. Merchants joined Chinggis Khan's retinue from very early on; the first of them might be Hasan at least, as reported by Juvayni. In other words, merchants were part of the government in some form or the other from the very inception of the Mongol state.[71] 'In 1215, when Peking [Beijing] fell to Mongolian arms, [Hasan] became the first imperial agent (*daruyači*) appointed in the conquered territory'.[72] Merchants not only benefitted from the largesse of the state and princes and through the patronage of the Mongol rulers but also because they were often the moneylenders in regions like Northern China. In times of need, *ortoy* also provided loans to the Mongol princes and princesses.[73] The partnership in essence meant that the investor (in this case, the state and Mongol princes) financed a commercial venture undertaken by a merchant, who returned the investment along with a profit after a specified period of time. While the merchants had a share in the profit, the investor bore all losses.[74] In all this, Central Asians, especially merchants, benefitted most by lending money to sedentary populations in order for them to meet the tax burdens.[75] Most of the merchants were Muslim or Uyghur which gave Central Asia and the Chaghatais a special place in Mongol Eurasia and a significant presence on the Silk Road. Their networks were old and widespread, further encouraged by the appearance of a connected Mongol Eurasia. Qaidu and Du'a built Andijan for mercantile activity of the Ferghana region to flourish and later in the 1320s to 1330s there were regular tribute missions to Yuan China which became important trade routes for Muslim and European traders. Among the traders there were Iraqis, Indians and Syrians as well.[76] According to the Yuan shih, Qubilai Khan provided not only capital but also transport, especially ships. Merchants also received simple loan agreements and their goods were often insured by sovereigns so they would incur fewer losses if anything went wrong. In the Golden Horde, merchants were even given tax exemptions, for example, the merchants of the Hanseatic League were allowed to enter Russia without paying taxes in order to trade with Novogorod.[77] The Yuan shih mentions that merchants were checked when entering cities to ensure they had the right licences, correct stamps and paperwork in order to be able to do business there. These posts were like toll booths to collect octroi taxes today and kept checks on the merchants and people entering territories.[78] In summary, merchants had knowledge, access to trusted long-distance networks, information, luxury goods and linked Eurasia. These were all essential ingredients for the Mongol enterprise in Eurasia and were accessible to them through their close partnership with merchants.

While the sources point to an exaction and pressure for revenues from the sedentary populations, the very opposite is true for merchants who were charged very low duties in order to encourage trade in Mongol Eurasia. The Mongols were able to encourage overland trade which was more expensive than sea trade and made the Silk Road one of the most productive and commercially viable routes in the world. The sea trade in the thirteenth century was controlled by Byzantine and Muslim rulers from Syria and Egypt (Mamluks) who charged excessive taxes and restricted access to trade from non-denominational merchants. For example, the Genoese were not allowed to enter Muslim lands and conversely Muslim traders were kept out of Byzantine lands. The Mongols had no such reservations and encouraged traders and travellers from across religions and charged smaller duties which translated into bigger profits. As a result, overland trade flourished and scores of Muslims and Christian travellers, traders, merchants and missionaries traversed across Mongol Eurasia. There are various instances of Mongol Khans giving free transit to merchants and guaranteeing their safety. For example, in a letter to Grand Prince Iaroslavic (Muscovite Prince) as late as 1370, the Khan of the Golden Horde promised freedom and safety to all merchants in his territory.[79] The cities across Eurasia flourished and became commercial hubs in the thirteenth and fourteenth centuries and continue to remain important even in modern times. The Genoese, Venetians, Muscovites, Bulghars, Central Asians, Chinese and Persians traders were all present and enjoyed unprecedented profits from trade on the Silk Road.

The integrative nature of the Mongol state in Eurasia assured that the continuities and connectedness on the Silk Road worked to the benefit of a much larger swathe of the population than before. The *Mongol worldview* with its specific institutions, cadres (merchants and artisans along with other skilled professionals), religious tolerance and economic practices to bolster trade all led to the creation of a limitless Eurasia. After the main thrust of the Mongol conquest was successfully executed, the running of Mongol Eurasia and the desire for economic sustenance drove the activities of the four Khanates. Much is made out about the Yuan and Ilkhans evolving into sedentary entities, while the Chaghatais and the Golden Horde remained nomadic and thus 'truer' to their Chinggissid roots, but a deeper analysis of the Yuan and Ilkhanate also points to a singularity of Mongol traditions especially in the upper echelons of court and society. The Silk Road as the connector of Eurasia under the Mongols took on a life of its own which hitherto had not been seen or permissible under more sedentary styles of governance. The veracity of the sources on the Mongols which have been mostly written by sedentary people who themselves belonged to the people who were subjected by the Mongols has to be questioned and furthermore critically appraised when it comes to their judgement of Mongol traditions and laws. These misrepresentations have been exacerbated by infighting and accusations within the Mongol subdivisions of being less 'Chinggissid' or nomadic in a bid to strip away legitimacy from each other, but the evidence overwhelmingly supports an adherence to nomadic principles in the Yuan and the Ilkhanate as much as in the Golden Horde and Central Asia. As mentioned above, Qubilai Khan and Hulegu travelled, and moved capitals for access to summer and winter pastures in nomadic tradition. Mongol administrative structures were added to the already existing bureaucratic apparatus and there was a parallel nomadic and sedentary administration for most of the thirteenth century in all the regions of Mongol Eurasia. Furthermore, people identifying themselves as Mongols retained high positions in the military ranks of each region and continued to enjoy privileges and special status. The multi-cultural environment favoured by Mongols could be seen across Eurasia, and was represented by the bureaucracy and administration and at court.[80] Yuan China eventually reflected a kind of supranational government with the inclusion of Mongols, Persians, Central Asians, Europeans and Chinese within its ranks. This reflected the make-up of the early Chinggissid state which was made up of a steppe intelligentsia of various tribes and confederations.[81] To explain this point further, according to Ratchnevsy, '...if the Mongol empire, as a total system, seems to be politically heterogeneous in many respects, that feature can be taken as expression of the hybrid character proper to the steppe intelligentsia itself'.[82] While at the same time it is also true that Mongol Eurasia was under different rulers, it is a fact that despite infighting there was uniformity across the expanse of Eurasia, something which was touched upon earlier in the description of the key institutions introduced by the Mongols in Eurasia. According to Jackson, despite differences, there were key elements which pointed toward a cohesiveness of Mongol Eurasia: joint patrimony, Turko-Mongol aristocracy (especially the royal bodyguard, *keshig*), *jam*, loyalty to Chinggis Khan and the system embodied in the *yasaq* and his desire for unity.[83] At no time in history previous to the Mongol epoch was Eurasia connected so intimately, and the Mongols also brought Europe into the orbit of China which had hitherto been impossible. This connection between the East and West was facilitated by structures, institutions and practices which encompassed an eagerness to promote economic functions across the Mongol realm.

Having said this, it is also important to point out the extent of local autonomy which was maintained in the regions of China and how imperial rule in many ways was exercised in less direct ways. Mongols and se-mu (Western and Central Asians) occupied positions of *darugachis* and expressed the demands of the Mongols to the local populations through local intermediaries. In steppe tradition, imperial governors supervised local tribal leaders and this continued throughout Mongol Eurasia. Trade and the conditions for merchants became a focal point of policies in state, especially in China, where international trade had long been seen as a drain of wealth as opposed to the Mongol perspective of merchant activity as a means to create wealth.[84] In Yuan China, 'a hybrid fiscal regime that drew on both the nomadic tradition of tribute and the administrative tradition of agricultural taxation'[85] was implemented, much like in other sedentary regions of Eurasia. The Yuan bureaucracy kept the old bureaucrats in office but changed some of the key features of the way China was governed.[86] Under Qubilai Khan the system of examinations was abolished, there was a segregation of classes based on ethnicity in the court and there was fiscal decentralisation. Under both Qubilai and Toghan Temur, taxes were increased and pressure on the populace was cited as reasons for discontent among the Chinese population and many attempts were made to ease the pressure: regularisation and the reform of taxes, founding new avenues of regional trade and encouraging agricultural production. Steppe traditions continued to serve as the backbone of governance in China under Qubilai along with necessary adjustments to the policies to reflect local conditions. The establishment of certain offices like the one for horses or for textiles was a particularly Mongol response to the objects and goods that they considered essential. In addition to the above-mentioned institutions for spurring trade across the Silk Road in Eurasia, the Mongols also paid attention to efforts to curb smuggling, especially smuggling of horses in China. Qubilai Khan created an office for horse administration in order to guarantee enough horses for the Mongols and there were severe punishments for flouting state control of horses. Horses had always been in demand in China and previously the nomads from the steppe sold horses to the Chinese to meet their demands. This was a major cause for concern for Qubilai and he ensured a supply of horses and strict protections and guarantees for the availability of horses in postal stations across China.[87] By the end of his reign there were up to 55,000 horses available in over 167 postal stations in Yuan China.[88] There was also a Bureau for Imperial Household Production which was established specifically to deal with fruit trees that the Yuan court received as part of tributes from all over, the significance of which can be traced back to the importance and symbolism surrounding trees in Mongol tradition (with attributes of *tree of life, longevity and rebirth* associated with them).[89] In a similar vein, Qubilai set up many offices for textiles (silks, gold brocade, cotton, etc.) in order to exercise control over these essential commodities which not only brought wealth but also provided security and stability for the economy as a whole. Official monopolies also existed and were an important source of government income for the Mongols. In China, these official monopolies existed on salt, liquor, mining, smelting gold, silver and iron. Similarly, Central Asia and the Transcaucasus region also had salt monopolies which were in the hands of the Mongol princes.[90] It was at the behest of the Mongols, specifically Qubilai Khan, that merchants and trade took centre stage and Chinese cities became essential hubs of commodity exchange. China was a largely agrarian society and the Confucian principles on which it was organised did not place the merchant class in a high position. However, in Central Asia, merchants, especially Muslim merchants were commonplace and Uyghur and other merchants from the steppe had long-standing trade relations with China. After Qubilai Khan settled his capital in Beijing and it became the seat of the Mongol Qaghanate in 1260, not only was there a revival of agriculture which was essential for revenues for the state but with the implementation of the paper currency and improvement in roadways and internal waterways there was overall economic revival. Of course, the conquest of China had caused disruption to the economy and the Mongols were very keen on rectifying that situation both for political and economic reasons. Similarly, in Persia as well the Mongols had to institute policies to stabilise the economic situation. For example, Hulegu and his descendants not only used the administrators from pre-Mongol times but also revived old practices which included confirming old land titles, insisting on a limited period for land deeds, restructuring of procurement manufacturing of arms, banning tax-farmers, restoration of old gold and silver coins, helping standardise coinage in Mongol Eurasia in general, restricting access to postal relay systems to state-sponsored traders and merchants and limiting abuse by the political bureaucracy of old.[91]

In the time period under consideration certain policies in Yuan China require further attention. Trade and commercial activity of the kind seen under the Mongol tutelage had not been an essential component of China's policies. As Kwanten explains, '[T]his period was one of the few in which foreign trade was an important factor in the Chinese economy'.[92] Not only commercial activity, but the introduction of paper money (balishi) in 1260 in Yuan China which was pegged to silver and copper serves as one of the most exciting and innovative policies instituted under the Mongols. Paper money has since continued in China with very little disruption through the ages and enjoys a special place in the innovations of the Mongols in the thirteenth century, forming the basis of the modern economy, even in the West, at least until BrettonWoods when the US Dollar replaced metals as a standard. Not only did Qubilai Khan create a convertible paper currency, he also created offices and measures to avoid counterfeiting and restricted the number of places where the money could be converted. This measure was beneficial for commerce, introduced ease in trade and encouraged merchants to travel across Mongol Eurasia. As per documents and contracts left by Pegolotti, not only was currency convertible in Yuan China but traders could convert goods into metals when travelling to other parts of Mongol Eurasia where metal coins rather than paper was used. A merchant could travel through from the Mediterranean to Yuan China through Persia and on to the Indian Ocean with a convertible currency and under a uniform tax regime devised by the Mongols.[93]

Trade as a consequence of Mongol control also prospered on the Black Sea under the Golden Horde, and continued to thrive in Central Asia and Iran under the Chaghatais and Ilkhanate, respectively. By the 1260s and despite the subsequent challenge to Qubilai's election to *Qaghan*, Eurasia was already well on its way to an explosion of inter and intra-regional trade supported and encouraged by the Mongols.[94] The very core of the Mongol state was based on the ability to be able to guarantee loyalty, which in steppe tradition was guaranteed by the availability of goods and luxuries required to trade across Eurasia. The appearance of Mongol courts all along the Silk Road only increased the already existing networks which transformed into an *interlocking system*.[95] Chapter 5 on the relationship between the Mongols and the reconstruction of cities will elucidate how Mongol conquest after initially disrupting economic activity became the harbinger of commercial activity in cities across the Eurasian region. Far from the common belief that the Mongols only destroyed and decimated cities and populations, there are numerous counterfactual examples of Mongol cities which were created and thrived due to Mongol presence and economic policies. The close relationship between the Mongols and the merchant class described above showcased the importance of Mongol presence in Eurasia especially in relation to commercial and economic activity. The steppe economy even before the inclusion of much of Eurasia under the Mongols was heavily dependent on trade which was an important pillar of commercial activity. With the acquisition of the rest of Eurasia, the royal family, princes and even *khatuns* (princesses, wives and other important women in the Mongol court and family) became drivers of mercantile and commercial activity throughout the thirteenth and fourteenth centuries. They created new markets, production centres and trade routes in order to fully exploit the continent of Eurasia. The Mongols were able to direct military conquest and set up Mongol Khanates across Eurasia in ways which guaranteed exchanges and movement of peoples and goods for reasons of economic prosperity, not only for the Mongol elite, but for a larger section of society. While they displaced old traditional elites, they also gave rise to new classes and groups of people who found opportunities in the new system with new professions and roles which were an outcome of the Mongol state culture.

There are as many conflicting perspectives on Mongol Eurasia as there are the number of states and entities that trace their origins to the Mongols. Oft repeated, the Mongols gleaning talent and incorporating local experts rather than expelling them, is attributed as much to chance or a foregone conclusion as to an active policy of governance. As a matter of fact, the policy of collecting skilled men can be traced back to ancient steppe traditions which would have been passed down to the Mongols and survived them to pass into the hands of the Timurids as well.[96] Furthermore, the incorporated local officials became subaltern auxiliaries in the Mongol army which bolstered the number and technologies for subsequent conquests. Movement of peoples was another aspect of Mongol governance, troop movements and groups of skilled craftsmen between appanages depending on the needs and requirements of Mongol princes was commonplace and spurred contact, interaction and exchange of a very unique quality. The story of Mongol Eurasia which began with Chinggis Khan was one in which nomads and their institutions ruled a large swathe of territory to produce political unification and economic prosperity across Eurasia. Trade, as the pulse of Mongol Eurasia, began with the nomads' desire for goods (essential and luxury) for personal use and to ensure loyalty. This was guaranteed by the ways in which they exercised power and resulted in inter-regional trade at unprecedented levels. Commercial revenues continued to be the main source of financial stability for the Jochids even after Russian principalities paid massive tributes to the Golden Horde. While in China and Persia the Mongols controlled centres of production and collected large sums in agricultural revenue which, in combination with trade revenues, represented a vast bounty for the Mongol courts which was in turn was used to build and maintain infrastructure and fund mercantile activity.

It is not difficult to see the imprint of Mongol institutions on the structures and society of the regions which represented Mongol Eurasia. Mongol Eurasia as a geographical, political and economic entity was a product of the policies of the Mongol Khans in the region. The Silk Road already existed much before the Mongols appeared on the scene in Eurasia, however, the political ramifications of becoming part of one global system which was connected via the Mongol royal family and subsequent institutions were an altogether new experience. The arrival of the Mongols in Eurasia created fresh demands on the populations of Eurasia, sedentary and nomadic, and the Mongol state went about formulating ways and means through which these demands could be met. This chapter has described the essence of the core Mongol state and how the four Khanates faced with local realities responded to those demands. The steppe traditions and nomadic state apparatus interacted with the institutions and bureaucracies of local peoples and a hybrid system modelled on Chinggis Khan's initial unification of the steppe tribes and confederations into the Mongol state was created in Eurasia. The fact that Mongol polity beyond the steppe could adapt its own system to the ones it found among its subject populations, and still not be overrun by them, is testament to the ability of the Mongols. The Mongol elite remained in important positions across Eurasia and continued to choose, select and transfer exchanges which best supported the *Mongol worldview*. In other words, the Mongols were able to appreciate the value of free movement and exchange, economic and cultural, and acted on it with alacrity and skill to bring out the innate features of Eurasia and fashioned a reality out of a geography which until then had been highly differentiated.

The main consequence of Mongol control over Eurasia was the creation of greater opportunities for contact across Eurasia, of goods, peoples, ideas, culture and technologies which '... produced the outlines of an interlocking set of institutions ... or world networks'.[97] It created an overlapping system with particular demands which gave rise to increased exchange and influence across Eurasia because of a 'dramatic infusion of new knowledge'.[98] People like Rashid al-Din, Yeh lu Chu Tsai and even Marco Polo exploited these opportunities to the maximum and became part of a Eurasian elite which developed in the Mongol trans-Eurasian state.[99] The thirteenth century creation of Mongol Eurasia is by all means the first historical moment in which the empirical evidence of a Eurasian powerhouse can be located. Steppe empires like the Kok-Turks in the fifth and sixth centuries had limited success in connecting trade routes across Eurasia. However, '[t]he emergence of steppe empires coincided with the first appearance of a flourishing trade route across Inner Eurasia'.[100] This took on incredible proportions under the Mongols and has left an indelible mark on the societies of this region. The Silk Road and overland trade saw volumes and profit of unprecedented quantities and was achieved due to the presence of a *Mongol Union* across Eurasia. Mongols '...provided such effective protection for the major trade routes across Eurasia that it created a single economic, cultural, and epidemiological world system'.[101] Much like a customs union of today there was a uniformity and continuation of policies essential for commercial activity to take place unfettered. Not only was there geographical unity under the Mongol umbrella for a substantial portion of the thirteenth and fourtheenth centuries, which created abundance of goods and commodities and accrued huge profits for the Mongol court and the merchant classes, but the successor states to Mongol Eurasia were in many ways products of policies and interactions with Mongols. Amir Timur in Central Asia went on to build another version of Mongol Eurasia in the late fourteenth century; Muscovite Russia arose in large part thanks to the interactions with the Mongol Khans of the Golden Horde; Italian merchant states of Genoa and the Venetians attained their golden age in the time of Mongol Eurasia and benefitted from their role as partners to the Mongols. The successive Chinese dynasties after the Yuan continued to use the legacy of the Mongols, Mongol institutions and paper money in their economy to great success.

One of the key aspects of Mongol courts was their cosmopolitan nature which was in large part guaranteed by the open policy toward religion which was a cornerstone of Mongol policy in Eurasia. The next chapter will look at the religious affiliations of the Mongols throughout their presence on the Silk Road. Mongol religious policy is of paramount importance since it forms part of the *Mongol worldview* which is inclusive and adaptive as opposed to a delineating force between groups. The Mongol approach to religion echoed what had always been the case on the Silk Road. Commercial networks on the Silk Road had encouraged interaction between different religious and ethnic groups and thus had made the Silk Road a home for multiple religions and faiths. The Mongols in turn expressed an interest in all religions while at the same time keeping their faith; this policy was exemplified in their encouragement of religious groups and communities irrespective of the denomination to move around freely across Eurasia. The combination of Mongol preference for trade and an open religious policy gave Eurasia an edge over other empires of the time which were closed off to each other, namely Christian and Muslim empires which were engaged in the Crusades at the time.

Notes

1 Jackson 2017, p. 211
2 Grousset 2002, pp. 254–255
3 Referred to as Central Asian Mongols henceforth
4 Kwanten 1979, p. 197
5 Election
6 Tents

7 Jackson 2009, p. 37
8 Boyle 1971, p. 264
9 *Tumens*/military units
10 Di Cosmo *et al.* 2009, p. 2
11 Kwanten 1979, p. 288
12 Governors
13 Rachewiltz 2004, pp. 1002–1003
14 Ratchnevsky 1991, p. 105
15 Ch'i-ch'ing, 1994/1998, pp. 503–504; Biran 1997, pp. 71–74
16 Biran 1997, p. 71; see also Mostaert and Cleaves 1962, pp. 55–85
17 Rossabi 1988, p. 130
18 Allsen 1994/1998, p. 361
19 Biran 1997, p. 100
20 Halperin 1985, p. 31
21 Jackson 2017, p. 242
22 Biran 1997, p. 100
23 Saunders 1977, p. 43
24 Jackson 2009, p. 35
25 *Paizas*
26 Olschki 1960, pp. 87–88
27 Rossabi 1988, p. 124
28 Ratchnevsky 1991, p. 185
29 Boyle 1971, p. 326; Allsen 2001, p. 105
30 Jackson 2017, p. 251
31 Jackson 2017, p. 108
32 Rachewiltz translated *daru* as 'to press down'; Cleaves translated *daru* as 'oppressor'
33 Rachewiltz 2004, p. 961
34 Court
35 Ratchnevsky 1991, p. 178
36 Jackson 2017, p. 251
37 Coined by Paul Buell, Ratchnevsky 1991, p. xx
38 Ratchnevsky 1991, p. 75
39 Ratchnevsky 1991, p. 101
40 Allsen 1987, p. 104
41 Jackson 2017, p. 273
42 Allsen 1987, p. 104
43 Vasary 2007, p. 188
44 Ratchnevsky 1991, p. 102
45 Ratchnevsky 1991, p. 141
46 Ratchnevsky 1991, p. 151
47 Jackson 2009, p. 63
48 Di Cosmo *et al.* 2009, p. 4
49 Jackson 2017, p. 110
50 Ratchnevsky 1991, p. 185
51 Morgan 1986, pp. 108–111
52 Jackson 2017, p. 284
53 Allsen 1987, p. 105
54 Spuler 1971, p. 23
55 Barfield 1989, p. 196; Jackson 2017, p. 110
56 Allsen 2002, p. 52
57 Allsen 2002, p. 53
58 Allsen 2002, p. 53
59 Rossabi 1988, p. 128

60 Allsen 2001, p. 127
61 Allsen 2001, p. 198
62 Allsen 1987, p. 144
63 Allsen 1989, p. 100
64 See Allsen 1997
65 Allsen 1989, p. 124
66 Allsen 1989, p. 114
67 Allsen 1989, p. 125
68 Allsen 1989, p. 94
69 Allsen 1989, p. 95
70 Allsen 1989, p. 85
71 Allsen 1989, p. 87
72 Ibid
73 Rossabi 1988, p. 123
74 Allsen 1989, p. 117
75 Allsen 1989, p. 101
76 Biran 2009, p. 62
77 Halperin 1985, pp. 80–81
78 Allsen 1987, p. 162
79 Di Cosmo 2005, p. 392
80 Di Cosmo *et al.* 2009, p. 3
81 Kwanten 1979, p. 238
82 Ratchnevsky 1991, p. 96
83 Jackson 2017, p. 123
84 Barfield 1989, p. 220
85 Brook 2010, p. 260
86 Martinez 2009, p. 92
87 Rossabi 1988, pp. 128–129
88 Rossabi 1988, p. 124
89 Allsen 2001, p. 121
90 Allsen 1987, pp. 162–163
91 Martinez 2009, pp. 90–91
92 Kwanten 1979, p. 211
93 Ciociltan 2012, pp. 106–109
94 Martinez 2009, p. 89
95 Di Cosmo *et al.* 2009, p. 3
96 Allsen 2001, p. 202
97 Di Cosmo *et al.* 2009, p. 3
98 Allsen 2001, p. 105
99 Allsen 2001, p. 80
100 Christian 1994, p. 182
101 Christian 1994, p. 183

3 The place of religion in Mongol Eurasia

Empires in the medieval ages were motivated by religious ideologies and the spread of religion and proselytising was amongst the main motivating factors for conquest. Mongol Eurasia was an anomaly to this rule and one can argue that the absence of religion as a guiding force allowed the Mongols to encompass such a large geographical space and helped create unprecedented commercial interactions across Eurasia. Overland trade which served as a quintessential revenue source for the Mongols, and served as a means to acquire luxury and other products, brought with it many benefits which were very much part of a larger *Mongol worldview* and came out of the economic necessities of the steppe and of a nomadic economic system. One of the key policies of the Mongols to bolster trade was the movement of traders of multiple denominations across Mongol lands without prejudice and persecution. Mongol religious policy was yet another foundation stone which assisted the creation of a unified Eurasia and echoed Mongol institutions in their ability to be able to adapt steppe traditions to local conditions. Mongol courts, mobile and otherwise, continued to attract religious leaders and figures throughout the thirteenth and fourteenth centuries and led to a burgeoning of cultural and economic activity as a result of Mongol policies. This chapter looks at religion in the framework of an institutional, functional practice which enabled the Mongols to construct an inclusive worldview and its examination allows a window into Mongol practices in Eurasia. While there will be some discussion about the theological aspects, the main thrust here, like the previous chapter, is to showcase the ways in which steppe traditions had an impact on creating a world which encouraged contact, exchange and interaction across Eurasia under the Mongols. The idea of the legitimacy of the Chinggissids' right to rule originated and lay in Chinggis Khan's person and his *yasaq* which is qualitatively different from the *divine right of kings* as seen in other parts of the world. The next section describes the role and place of *tengri*[1] in the Mongol belief system. While Chinggis Khan's right to rule was in part buttressed by the '*mandate of heaven*' (*tengri*), his continued legitimacy came from each new success in military conquest. Furthermore, his descendants could rely on their success but equally their Chinggissid ancestry. The legacy of Chinggis Khan was to last far longer than the Chinggissid imperial family and maintained a firm hold in Central and Inner Asian political systems as late as the eighteenth and nineteenth centuries. The Timurids, Kazakh and Uzbek Khanates and even the Mughal emperors of Hindustan derived legitimacy from their association with Chinggis Khan

Mongol Eurasia was home to many religions and the Silk Road had historically been the route through which religious ideas had travelled from the east to the west, for example, Buddhism, and from the west to the east as in the case of Nestorian Christians. The steppe itself was populated by different sects of Christians (Nestorian, Manichaean and Franciscans) and Muslims, the nomads themselves, especially the Mongols, were *shamans.* The religious policies of the Mongols coming from this mileu were as per steppe tradition open and tolerant. They were used to acting in an environment which was multifaceted and thus were used to adapting and navigating their beliefs in relation to multiple belief systems extant on the steppe. Not only were they open to religions but as has been articulated earlier were innovative in nearly all aspects of cultural and political thinking. Their skill lay in being able to adapt their own beliefs to the systems they came across, without abandoning their own traditions. In the time period under consideration, this was indeed at odds with the way the Christian and Muslim empires in the Middle East and Europe acted. The following sections are a brief summary of the policies and practices of the Mongols across Eurasia with regards to religious activity. The territories that the Mongols inhabited and unified were home to the biggest and most influential religions of the world and it is indeed noteworthy to consider that the Mongols were able to harness the skills and ideas of different religions to create opportunities for trade and exchange based on commerce and transfer of knowledge and ideas. As a place frequented by various merchants and travellers from pre-Mongol times, the heart of the Silk Road had long witnessed many religions and people traversing it, and had developed ways in which to be able to navigate between them successfully. The Mongols reflected this policy and echoed their belief in the Eternal Heaven while seeking out new and interesting ideas from religions they were exposed to on the steppe and the ones they came into contact with during their conquests.

The system of religious beliefs that the Mongols inherited were driven by the ecological and geographical conditions prevalent on the steppe. Shamanism is a combination of elements in which nature and the sky god are worshipped in the form of *tengri.* They were concerned primarily with earthly and practical matters; the worship of *tengri* was to influence their life on earth, not for rewards in an afterlife. These beliefs were commonly found among the numerous tribes on the steppe. The Mongols believed that there were spiritual forces in land, earth, water, mountains and rivers, and they were harnessed to imbue positive forces for human action. The use of signs and ancient spirits was common and was used in the founding of Qara Qorum, the Mongol capital under Ogedei which was built on the site of previous capitals used by Uyghurs. This was done in order to maximise the forces of successes of their predecessors passed down in folklore to the Mongols. Magic and omens were used extensively in deciding grand political ambitions, actions like establishing capitals, and even for mundane everyday actions to maximise the forces of ancestral successes.[2] As a consequence, the place of oracles and soothsayers in Mongol society was elevated, as was the place of medical practitioners and scientists (astronomers) who were seen as being part of a group of people who could tell the future. They were consulted before any conquest, battle or any other major activity which required divine interference. Famously, Hindustan was not overrun by Chinggis Khan because the oracle predicted failure by looking at ox bones. Even in the case of Arigh Boke's challenge to Qubilai for the title of *Qaghan*, a strong wind that destroyed Arigh Boke's camp in Almaliq was meant to have signalled his future defeat and was immediately followed by him being abandoned by his Mongol supporters.[3] In Chinggis Khan's *yasaq*, religious tolerance was stipulated along with showing no preference for any particular sect.[4] The Mongols continued to hold *shamanistic* religious beliefs; *shamans* were consulted and futures read but religious leaders were firmly subordinated under the Mongol Khans. Akin to their adoption of local traditions in fields of political, social and everyday habits where the Mongols took that which was compatible with their own beliefs, religious principles and certain professions became closely associated with the Mongol courts across Eurasia. The tradition of Mongol courts to look for and build cultural and social elements from subject populations using traditional Mongol and steppe elements which they were familiar with, led to the elevation of certain peoples with respect to religions as well and included doctors, astronomers, sorcerers, charmers and Chinese pulse specialists and others who resembled *shamans*.[5] Not only did the Mongols accord respect to other religions in their domains, Mongol openness to religion in general can even be classified in terms of a secular paradigm. They were not just tolerant of other religions but they went a step further and extended the policy of employing talented people even from minority faiths that did not leave an impression on them.[6] What followed from this policy can best be understood in terms of the Mongol preference for meritocracy. Accordingly, these policies have been variously understood as anti-religious by observers who saw the Mongols break the monopoly of Muslims and Confucian scholars in Persia and China respectively. However, set against the perspective of a *Mongol worldview* these policies exhibit a different picture.

Within the groups of people the Mongols came across, there was a special place and value for people able to tell the future, read fortunes and symbols, much like the occults and spiritual leaders in the steppe. Astronomers, scientists and physicians at that time were associated with religion in some form or other and thus along with traditional leaders of major religions, these people also enjoyed special privileges and had the ear of the Khan. Furthermore, these skilled and learned people allowed the Mongols access to the knowledge, wealth and resources of the subject peoples across Eurasia. Astronomers, especially, represented a group which was included among religious people who could help the Mongols access and understand the supernatural and their natural environment which closely resembled what the *shamans* did on the steppe.[7] Astronomers were 'time keepers' and were often consulted before starting out on any important military campaign, and occupied positions of influence and power in Mongol courts across the realm.[8] They were ascribed with religious and spiritual qualities which were important to the Mongols. Muslims and the Chinese had a highly developed knowledge of astronomy and consequently continued to fare well under the Mongols. The famous figure of Nasr al-Din Tusi, astronomer and scientist, who served Hulegu in many capacities (advisor, administrator), not only enjoyed special treatment in the Ilkhanate court but was also commissioned to build an observatory near Tabriz.

As mentioned above, medical practitioners had knowledge and healing powers which came to be admired by the Mongols who saw them as tapping into the magical-spiritual beliefs so highly regarded by the Mongol Khans. *Shamans* and medicine men along with other soothsayers were part of the imperial bodyguard (*keshig*), the most powerful body in all Mongol courts. An interest in medicine men and longevity was expressed as early as in Chinggis Khan's times. He invited the Taoist monk, Chang Chun to visit him to discuss matters of esoteric knowledge. The monk was famous for his magical-spiritual beliefs and was supposed to have been over 100 years old.[9] Chinggis Khan's special treatment and interest came from wanting access to Chang Chun's knowledge of the elixir of life and immortality. From the very beginning then, physicians travelled with armies of conquest and were part of the Khan's retinue. As the Mongols continued to add territories, their access to physicians from China, West Asia and eventually Iran was established. For example, in the conquest of West Turkistan, Chinese physicians accompanied Mongol armies and Hulegu's armies to Iran in 1258 also contained a large number of Chinese physicians. The Ilkhanate court maintained its fascination and interest in Chinese medicine throughout the thirteenth century. The movement of large retinues of physicians in Mongol courts gave certain communities, especially Nestorian Christians, the Chinese and Uyghurs a lot of importance. Nestorian Christians had long been transmitters of West Asian medical practices in China in pre-Mongol times and they continued this in Mongol times as well. Famous Nestorian physicians who were prominent in Yuan China and Central Asia included Simeon and Isa who were both born in Rum, travelled to Mongolia in the 1240s and ingratiated themselves with Ogedei and his successor, Guyuk. While Simeon returned to Iran and served in Hulegu's court as a physician and was able to support and protect Christian communities in Muslim dominated cities like Tabriz, Isa continued on in to Qubilai's service in Northern China and headed the Bureaus for medical practices until his death in 1308. Nestorian Christians remained closely associated with Western (modern Central Asian and Persian) medicine, also called Muslim medicine in China well into the fourteenth century.[10] There was even a Bureau to oversee diviners in Qubilai's court which included supervision of other religious faiths under it as well.

Over the years, the treatment of Mongol religious policies have experienced many ups and downs. The Mongols have been called religiously tolerant but they have also been accused of threatening the very existence of Islam and Christianity. According to Gumilev for instance, the Mongols had a well-developed religion already worked out with cosmology, mythology, a deity, the idea of ethics and demons which survived its rival faith, Nestorian Christianity, on the steppe. Similarly, when faced with Islam and Christianity, the Mongols' beliefs in *shamanism* continued to thrive and associated practices were not abandoned even after the conversion to other religions in some cases.[11] In the texts of early Muslim authors in the thirteenth century, especially in Mamluk Egypt and Hindustan (Delhi Sultanate) the Mongols were accused of being anti-Islamic since they destroyed the seat of the Caliphate. In a similar vein, the destruction of Kiev under the Mongols has been reported as a threat to Orthodox Christianity and Mongol conquests of Europe have been seen as directed against Catholicism and the Pope's authority. Similarly, the Mongol policy of openness broke the monopoly of Confucius scholars in government offices in Yuan China and has been described by some scholars as being part of an anti-religious policy. All this paints a rather bleak picture of Mongol respect for religion, however, along with being the seats of these noteworthy religions, Baghdad, Kiev and Rome were political empires which dominated huge swathes of lands and the Mongols as an upcoming political entity saw them as peoples to be subjected. In other words, evidence suggests that the Mongols went to war with Baghdad and Kiev not because they were Muslim or Christian but because they were political competitors. In the case of Confucians too, the Mongols broke the traditional system which was in place in order to establish their control. While they continued to use Confucians in the court, they no longer had the exclusive right to office. Furthermore, both Orthodox Christianity and Catholicism did exceedingly well under the Mongols. After the initial destruction of the Caliphate, the Muslims in Persia were not subjected to any particular hostilities, and in Central Asia Muslims made up the merchant class which was treated with great admiration and accorded special positions in administration and society. Medical practitioners and scientists were also largely made up of the Chinese and Muslims which furthered their influence in court.

If anything, after conquest, Mongol policies were designed to benefit religious institutions.[12] All religious institutions, Mongol and otherwise, were exempt from paying taxes throughout Eurasia. The clergy of most religious faiths were given letters of authority (*paizas*), were exempt from paying taxes along the way and were not subjected to the demands of conscript labour. The respect accorded to learned men across religions is said to have been recorded in the *yasaq* of Chinggis Khan. Edicts given to all religious clergy by the Khans followed a certain pattern. They recalled edicts of previous rulers and exempted the subject of their obligations (especially *alba* and *qubichir*[13]) in exchange for heavenly blessings bestowed on the ruler.[14] We have exemptions for Buddhist monasteries from either paying taxes or offering troops for the military as far back as Chinggis Khan's times, and then again in 1223 Chang Chun, a Daoist monk, was exempted from any taxation.[15] Under Ogedei, these were extended to Muslims (*imams*, *shaikhs*, etc.) and under Mongke it continued, except for rabbis (who were not numerous). Mongke even declared in 1255 that the five religions of Islam, Christianity, Buddhism, Taoists and Confucians were like the five fingers of his hand.[16] The correspondences with European religious leaders and kings always mention the Mongols' exemption of their religious institutions in matters of taxation, and a respect for their faith.[17] Ratchnevsky and some others have argued against[18] this but on the whole the Mongols practised a policy of exempting religious institutions of paying poll tax, though at times they were charged tax for commercial enterprises they were engaged with as well as a land tax.

The Mongol approach to religion was one of pragmatism and was directed towards building bridges via open dialogue and discussion which was seen throughout Mongol courts across Eurasia. A quick look at the religious affiliations of the *Qaghan* and the most important Khans of the four subdivisions of Mongol Eurasia can give us a clear picture of the place of religion under the Mongols. Among some of the most important Chinggissid princes, the sons of Tolui were all brought up as Christians, though none of them had been baptised. They continued to also be *shamans* and, as in the case of Qubilia showed a keen interest in Tibetan Buddhism, and Hulegu (Ilkhan) who also expressed an avid interest in Buddhism. However, this did not preclude Hulegu from being a protector of Christians in the Middle East either. The Khans of the Golden Horde, which had substantial populations of Muslims and Christians, did not favour one group over another, no matter their personal inclinations. If anything, the Mongols continued to keep religion in the background and followed political and economic policies without paying heed to religious differences. The Silk Road remained a place for religions to interact and with the Mongols in control that interaction got a further boost and religious sects even innovated in the new Mongol framework to remain or extend their influence on local populations. Christian and Muslim sects which had been driven out of their homelands found safe environments in Mongol regions and at least in the case of the Nestorian Christians and *Sufi* sects found space to operate and remained relevant far longer than they would have if the Mongols had not been in control.

Importantly, in economic terms the link between the support of religious institutions and trade needs to be highlighted here. Religious leaders of almost all denominations were involved with commercial activity and the capital and support of the Mongol court was at their disposal to carry out trade operations. By leaving capital in the hands of the churches and monasteries the Mongol courts benefitted through taxation on commercial enterprises and was able to garner goodwill from religious institutions. There is also evidence in the case of Simeon, the Nestorian medical practitioner, who was involved in trade with the Mongol court, supplying both support and capital to mercantile activities. Not only were the religious institutions part of the commercial networks on the Silk Road, but the policy of Mongols allowing people of all denominations to trade in their domains bolstered trade between Muslim and Christian mercantile communities which hitherto continued to be subject to penalties in other regions beyond Mongol control. In combination with these basic principles, the fair treatment of religions helped the Mongols create freedom of movement in unprecedented numbers across Eurasia. In addition, all the advantages that merchants enjoyed with the arrival of a connected Mongol Eurasia applied to religious travellers as well. Mongol policies towards religion sprung from a place of tolerance and inquisitiveness which was mixed up with their ideas of magic and spirituality inherited from steppe traditions as mentioned above. The Mongol religious policy was yet another building block of the impetus to trade which was seen in political and social institutions of importance in building Mongol Eurasia.

The safety and possibilities offered to people (merchants and others) and the increased transmission of cultures, knowledge, labour and technology, along with religious tolerance, changed the Eurasian landscape under the Mongols. According to Abu-Lughod, the variety of religions in Eurasia across the Silk Road including Christianity, Buddhism, Zoroastrianism, Islam and Confucianism along with various smaller sects and religious ideologies, all worked to encourage and facilitate trade rather than hamper it.[19] The character and nature of the Mongols and steppe culture proved to be the necessary combination of conditions required for global trade at a time when divisions along religious lines and ethnic differences were the norm. Additionally, the use of religious leaders in the submission of populations was another reason why the Mongols were benevolent toward religion.[20] By treating religious leaders and institutions with care, the Mongols accrued favour for themselves and managed to gain loyalty, whether by the Orthodox Christians or the Buddhists in China. Even the religions which felt most threatened by the Mongols (Islam in the Middle East and Confucianism in China) and were displaced with the arrival of the Mongols as the new political elite, were still employed by the Mongols in the administration. As has been mentioned previously, while the Confucians may not have been the sole cadre of Chinese officials in Yuan China they still retained important positions and even rose to high office as part of Qubilai's policies of appeasing the Chinese intellectual elite and the local population. Similarly, the Ilkhans of Persia and the Central Asians who administered large Muslim populations continued to hold positions in the Mongol apparatus, including non-Muslim Yuan China. While the Caliphate and *ulema* may have suffered, especially in the early years of the conquest, the Muslims, particularly in the merchant class, did exceedingly well and were even seen as the favourites of the Khans. The Christians also did remarkably well and communities like the Nestorians survived longest in Mongol Eurasia than in other parts of the world, to the bane of co-religionists like Catholics who sought favour from the Khans. Tolui's wife Sorqoqtani Beki and Hulegu's wife Dokuz Khatun were Christians who used their positions to evoke the protection of the Khans in Mongol Eurasia.[21] Qubilai Khan was openly pro-Christian, at least until he went to China where he was exposed to the doctrines of Buddhism which greatly impressed him. Nestorian Christians were also protected by Hulegu throughout the Middle East and enjoyed the favour of successive Khans as well. These policies sometimes fuelled rivalries within certain religions, for example, the protection of Nestorians caused jealousy among both Catholic groups and Franciscan monks who travelled through Mongol Eurasia in the middle of the thirteenth century. Hulegu is said to have given one of the palaces of the Caliph to a Nestorian patriarch in

Baghdad in the 1258.[22] Much like the treatment of Confucians in China could be taken as being anti-Confucian since they were no longer the sole occupiers of administrative positions, or the Muslim merchants who tended to be seen as occupying prominent roles in Mongol courts, the Nestorians were seen as overly prominent, especially in proportion to their population. Since they were physicians to the Mongol Khans, just like the office of *baurchi* (the Khan's cook), their presence near the person of the Khan gave rise to jealousy and rivalry which has been documented in contemporary sources. In Yuan China especially, Mongol practices and policies in employing medical practitioners from Central Asia led to a feeling of discontent among Confucians who felt threatened by the influx of foreigners so close to the Khans. However, in the long run, as part of the transformations brought by the Mongols, the Confucians began to become doctors and specialise in medical practices in order to be employed in the court.[23] Accusations of Mongol religious policies as favouring one or other religious groups are abound, except when looked at comprehensively, the Mongol Khans maintained an open-mindedness which was a product of their steppe traditions and their interest in promoting trade across their domains. To reiterate, especially in the context of the Crusades which were still being fought outside Mongol Eurasia, these policies did much to protect, promote and provide interaction between religions which was not possible in many other regions of the world at the time. The next sections provide a more detailed examination of religious policies in the four Khanates with special emphasis on the personal and the public.

The individual and the group

The complex relationship of the Mongol Khans and religion can be divided into two categories: the personal and the public. As individuals, Mongol Khans over a period of time supported, protected and even converted to different religions, however, religious persecution was not a feature of Mongol Eurasia, and widespread conversions were not common until well into the fourteenth century. Publicly, the Mongols were inheritors of wider Turkic beliefs of *shamanism*, *Tengri* and *the mandate of heaven* and demanded submission to the *Qaghan* by various rulers, irrespective of religious affiliations. Saunders has argued that the *yasaq* of Chinggis Khan and the person of Chinggis Khan came to represent a kind of religious zeal similar to the seventh century Arab nomads and Islam,[24] however, there was no attempt at converting sedentary people to these beliefs. If anything, the division between nomad and sedentary people was maintained. However, the steppe and nomads were not of one faith. From as early as the fifth and sixth centuries, nomadic tribes like the Kerait, Naiman and Onggud had converted to Nestorian Christianity. Semirechye, Almaliq, Samarqand, Uyghuria and the Tarim basin had a concentration of Nestorian communities. Additionally, Catholic communities were also present in Central Asia, probably from a mission to China.[25] The Uyghurs and other Turkic tribes had also converted to Islam and the steppe tribes in Northern China were Confucian scholars. Thus, from the very beginning Mongol courts were cosmopolitan in nature and were populated by members of a variety of religions and sects including Buddhism, Zoroastrianism, Nestorian Christianity, Islam, Confucians, etc. The Mongol princes spurred building of religious centres across Eurasia and as will be seen in the following sections, these formed part of any rebuilding efforts in the cities and regions the Mongols conquered. According to William of Rubruck, Qara Qorum had 'twelve idol temples, two mosques and a Christian church', because the city along with other Mongol cities had religious buildings as an integral part of their make-up.[26] Even in later years when Qubilai Khan's Buddhist sympathies were not hidden, and the Golden Horde had become Muslim, persecution based on religious beliefs were not common. Muslim Khans of the Golden Horde issued *yarlighs*[27] giving privileges to the Russian Metropolitan and received princes Ivan II and, Basil of Tver in Sarai.[28] In Yuan China, Qubilai allowed the three important belief systems to continue: Taoism, Confucianism and Buddhism. Buddhism enjoyed a special place, especially Tibetan Buddhism, but it did not lead to suppression of other faiths. In 1289 Qubilai even set up the Directorate of Christian Affairs in Beijing.[29] Churches were built in Almaliq during the reigns of Iljigedei and Chagshi in the mid-fourteenth centuries, though by then the Khans were adherents of Tibetan Buddhism.[30] Though Qaidu in Central Asia followed shamanism himself, he also encouraged the building of mosques in Central Asia. Even after Ghazan Khan's conversion in 1295 to Islam, his court continued to be a place where religious debate and discussions between leading figures was commonplace, as it was in the Yuan court, Golden Horde and in Central Asia. In general, Mongol policy toward religion and religious institutions was one of tolerance and even inquisitiveness, as is evidenced by their desire to have religious leaders discuss the merits of their respective religions.

On the individual level, things were often different. Often, along with practising traditional *shamanistic* or Turkic observances, the Mongol elite in Persia and Central Asia followed *Sufi shaikhs* or Buddhist and other monks; in Yuan China Buddhist and Taoist monks were equally popular. Berke, the Khan of the Golden Horde, was the first to officially convert to Islam. By the end of the thirteenth century, the official conversions of the Khan became a means to gain legitimacy in the population, for example, the famous instance of Ghazan's (Ilkhan) conversion to Islam in 1295 has been discussed at length by historians like DeWeese and Komaroff.[31] With his conversion, not only did the Muslims in Iran and Iraq benefit but there was a further impetus for the opening of trade relations with the Mamluks in Egypt and Syria, who had until then been the sworn enemies of the Ilkhanate because they were not Muslim. In addition, the sympathies and interest of Qubilai Khan in Chinese religions, especially Buddhism, and the consequent rise of Tibetan monks, is no secret. However, this did not translate into the persecution of other religious populations by the Mongols. On the contrary, '... in Mongol fashion...[they] avoid[ed] giving preferential treatment to any one faith'.[32] The following section provides further details on the Khans' policies in the Khanates and their relationships with diverse religious groups even when they openly accepted a particular faith.

The Khanates

Mongol courts for the most part remained hotbeds of religious activity, where different religious figures gathered to discuss the merits of their respective religions habitually at the behest and encouragement of the Khan. On the whole, even after a Khan's conversion, he did not stop practising his *shamanistic* customs and beliefs.[33] Conversion was often a means to garner legitimacy and support from the populace. The Golden Horde due to its make-up had the Christian principalities of Rus, as well as the Muslim populations of Khwarezm and Volga Bulgars. The Muslim population represented the commercial heart of the region. As a result, one can see that the Mongol Khans of the Golden Horde chose between Islam and Christianity throughout the thirteenth and fourteenth centuries. While, Berke (1257–1266) of the Golden Horde was the first Mongol Khan to convert to Islam, Sartaq (Batu's son) was a Christian and dealt with Russian affairs, while still continuing with *shamanistic* practices.[34] Berke had converted to Islam but went on to found an Orthodox Bishopric in Sarai and was also friends with the Mamluks at the same time, especially as the Mamluks were enemies of their rivals, the Ilkhans of Persia.[35] The Golden Horde did not convert to Islam until the middle of the fourteenth century under Ozbeg Khan (1313–1340), most likely for external reasons. Their cousins, the Ilkhans, had converted to Islam and fostered ties with the Mamluks, who had previously traded almost exclusively through Golden Horde territory. Thus, for the Golden Horde, converting to Islam was an economically beneficial decision.[36] With the Ilkhanate-Golden Horde rivalry, and the Golden Horde allying with the Mamluks, as well as the importance of trading communities like the Volga Bulgars and Khwaremians it is not surprising that Berke turned toward Islam.[37] Relations with the Christian Genoese and the Venetians also had an impact on the faith of the Khans, and intermittently one or the other Khan turned to Christianity. Like other religious institutions, the Russian Orthodox Church was given tax exemption officially in 1267 which was subsequently renewed by all the Khans. They were issued *yarlighs* or patents which gave them immunity from taxation.[38] Even though the Golden Horde increasingly became accepted as part of the Islamic world, the Catholic and Orthodox Churches remained undisturbed and enjoyed tax exemptions. Not only were they allowed to carry on their own religious practices but Franciscan Catholics even carried out proselytising activities among the Mongols.[39] Furthermore, the Orthodox Church was able to accumulate huge amounts of material wealth under the Mongols. Russian clerics were also free from recruitment to the army.[40] The subsequent centrality of the Orthodox Church over the following centuries, at least in part can be traced back to Mongol presence in the region and their accordance of a special status to religious institutions, including helping the Church to acquire its vast wealth and become a symbol of Russian identity.[41]

Central Asia or Transoxiana as the domain of Chaghatai was the most religiously diverse with the presence of Islamic, Nestorian Christian and Buddhist communities. The majority of the population was Muslim but there were large

Nestorian communities in Samarqand, Kashgar, Uyghuria (Eastern Turkistan) and Yarkand among others. A large portion of the Berkin tribe which was part of Qaidu's army was also Christian. Nonetheless reflective of the general population, building activities under the Khans, *khatuns* and commanders and governors was directed toward Muslim buildings. There were a number of mosques, *madrassas* and *Sufi khanqahs* built in Bukahara, Samarqand, Almaliq and in other important cities of Central Asia. As early as Chaghatai's times, one of his officials, Habash Amid built a *khanqah* in Almaliq which attracted a large Muslim scholarly community from around Central Asia.[42] Under one of the most famous female regents, Orghina Khatun (the wife of Qara-Hulegu who ruled from Besh Baligh), Muslims of Central Asia enjoyed special privileges and protections.[43] Her reign was peaceful and one of the best-known examples of a female ruler in a Mongol Khanate. Her son, Mubarakshah, is also said to have been Muslim and Central Asian Muslims enjoyed peace, prosperity and privileges in this period. According to Hookham, religious figures of the Muslim church were among the few groups along with merchants and the Mongol elite that did exceedingly well in Mongol Central Asia.[44]

There was no change in religious policies in Central Asia even after the division of Central Asia between the Chaghataid and Ogedeid princes. One of the most prominent Ogedeid princes, Qaidu (1271–1301/1303), remained a *shaman*. He has been described as a sun-worshipper and was buried according to Mongol custom, high in the mountains. Despite being steadfastly *shamanistic*, even in Qaidu's court in Central Asia, the *ulema* enjoyed special favour. His successors continued to be sympathetic to Muslims as well. Examples of religious activity under Qaidu include the construction of Masud Beg's *madrassa* and construction of mosques in Bukhara in 1299. Mongke's wife and Masud Beg built colleges in Bukhara and Transoxiana where *hadiths*[45] were written and other religious activities took place, as well as science, astronomy, poetry and medicine, etc. was taught. Masud Beg's teacher Baba Kamal Jandi[46] also enjoyed considerable authority over both nomads and sedentary people in the Jaxartes region. Bukhara continued to be a centre of *Sufi* activity and many *Sufi* sects continued to flourish in Bukhara, including Bakharzi's sect which held sway in the Golden Horde as well. Bakharzi had a *waqf*[47] in Bukhara which had been started by a grant from Mongke's wife.[48] The *waqf* continued to be important and prosperous throughout the fourteenth century. Bukharan Kurbawi *Sufis* originated in Bukhara and went to India, Kashmir, China, the Volga region and other parts of the Khanates and served as important cultural brokers in Mongol Eurasia.[49] In addition, Qaidu had religious leaders in positions of power in various towns across Central Asia. While Muslims and Islam definitely attracted the attention of the Mongol imperial family, William of Rubruck has furnished information on the prevalence of Buddhist temples in Central Asia along with the ease with which Christians were allowed to practise their faith under Qaidu.[50] The scholarly activities, religious and otherwise, continued under the Mongols and in the 1320s Delhi Sultanate rulers enticed scholars from Transoxiana to the court in Delhi for their religious knowledge and expertise.[51] Late in Tarmashirin's times when many of the Mongols in Central Asia had converted to Islam, there were many *khanqahs* built by Tarmashirin and his *amirs* (commanders).[52] The Central Asian Mongols on the whole practised an open policy toward Islam which was a mark of Mongol religious policy in general as opposed to springing from any particular political gain.

In the Ilkahnate, Hulegu and most of his early descendants, including Ghazan Khan who later converted to Islam, was Buddhist for most of his life and built *pagodas* and Buddhist temples in Khabushan and Maragha.[53] The early coins and their motifs point to an appropriation of Islamic customs within a *Mongol worldview*, and much like the use of local institutions and governors to understand and rule local populations, the Mongols used religious symbols for political and economic benefit. Among the Mongol *amirs* there seem to have been conversion to Islam and up to 30 per cent of Mongol names in the upper echelons reflected conversion. There are various examples of Mongol *tumen* in different parts of the Middle East and even India where the Mongols converted to Islam.[54] There is also some information available on the influence of *Sufi khanqahs* on the wives of Mongols Khans especially in the Ilkhanate. There are instances of endowments, land grants and protection documents given to *Sufi* dervishes. Qutlugh Malik is said to have been a follower of Shaykh Zahid Ibrahim, founder of the Safavi order which later became the Safavid Dynasty and ruled Iran.[55] Mongol interest in spiritual powers and worldly saints with magical powers go back to Chinggis Khan's time but this relationship was often between individuals and the question of conversion remains muddled and at odds depending on the sources. Even in the Ilkhanate, illustrations of rulers show them with a hawk perched on his wrist, recalling the very Mongol symbol in which birds of prey represent a link with the sky god *Tengri*.[56] These illustrations point to a syncretism of religious beliefs. Mongol traditional symbols appear side by side with motifs easily recognisable to the local population. In other words, these illustrations point to a move towards '… Mongol symbols of religious and temporal authority neatly synchronised with comparable traditions'.[57] Conversely in the case of Yuan China, Khans were retrospectively turned into Buddhist rulers to appease Buddhists and make the Mongols a more long-standing legitimate political entity in China.[58]

Qubilai Khan has been more heavily associated with Buddhism over other religions and compared with other Mongol Khans is considered to have been outwardly religious. At the beginning of his career, he was supposed to have been openly sympathetic to Christians and one argument offered for Mongke sending him to Northern China was to remove Qubilai from Christian influences. Over time his interest in Buddhism was much talked about and formed the basis of accusations of him being anti-Muslim, anti-Confucian and so forth. Obviously Qubilai expressed an avid interest in religion; this is clear from the number of religious debates that took place in his court as well as the number of religious buildings that he constructed. His later religious policies were directed to increasing his legitimacy in Yuan China. His election to *Qaghan* had been disputed from the offset and while Yuan China continued to have Mongol elements in government, Qubilai also wanted the support of the Chinese population. Much like the conversion of Berke and Ghazan to Islam signalled an attempt at becoming closer to their subject population; Qubilai and his successors felt the need to fortify religious support in China from Buddhists, Taoists and Confucians. In order to achieve this, Qubilai built temples in Beijing; the Great Temple was established to please Confucian elites and the temple housed shrines to Mongol ancestors of Qubilai Khan, including Chinggis Khan's parents, Chinggis and his four sons, along with Qubilai's predecessors (Guyuk and Mongke). He also built altars of Soil, Grain and other natural elements revered by the Chinese. He even built a temple for Confucians and had Confucian texts translated in Mondol. This kind of religious activity can be seen as a means through which Qubilai wanted to appease his Chinese subjects but all this was done in addition to his personal beliefs and interests in Buddhism and Shamanism which he continued to practise.[59] Qubilai's Buddhist adviser was Hai-yun and Qubilai had his successor (Temur Khan) tutored by two monks, Yao Shu and Tou Mo To, Confucian scholars and the Tibetan monk, Phags-pa.[60] Phags-pa was given the title of State Preceptor in 1260 and following that was also made an official in Tibet and mediated between with Buddhist monasteries there. In 1264 Qubilai exempted all Buddhist monasteries from taxation.[61] The lama remained close to Qubilai and eventually Phags-pa's brother married a Mongol princess and they enjoyed special offices in the governance of Tibet. Nepalese craftsmen built various Buddhist temples across China; A-ni-ko, the most famous of those craftsmen was given high offices and rewards throughout his service to the Khan.[62] One of Qubilai's two daughters mentioned in the Chinese sources, Miao-yen, became a Buddhist nun.[63] The Taoists also enjoyed Qubilai's attentions especially because of their purported magical powers and spiritual abilities. Qubilai funded Taoist temples, especially the Chang-Chun temple built for the Taoist monk favoured by Chinggis Khan.[64] Overall, Qubilai Khan's religious activities included all three major Chinese belief systems and in exchange all three sects provided Qubilai and the Yuan legitimacy and brought them closer to the Chinese population. Despite Qubilai's preference for Chinese sects, especially Buddhism, and a brief period of anti-Muslim policies in the 1280s including banning meat to be slaughtered in the Muslim way, there was no policy of keeping Muslim officials out of bureaucratic or important positions throughout Yuan China.[65]

Looking back, the period appears to be marked by a religious lens which limits analysis of the situation in Mongol Eurasia. Very often the Mongol policy of placing officials of different faiths in the regions they governed were interpreted as anti-Chinese and anti-Muslim but if we look at the policies from the perspective of steppe traditions and historical experience, these policies do not lend themselves to the same conclusion. Looking at Mongol Eurasia comprehensively it would be difficult to conclude that the Mongols in the thirteenth century were operating in favour of any particular religious denominations. The key officials from Central Asia were merchants and they were used extensively to govern the regions of Mongol Eurasia and even though they are described as Muslim, there is no evidence to show they were selected based on religious criteria. In the same way, the Khitans or Jurchen who are often referred to as Chinese were in a large part people of the steppe who had become Confucian and were installed in places like Bukhara and Samarqand not because of their religious affiliation but because of their talent and knowledge of sedentary populations and agricultural practices. An overwhelming number of sources have verified that Chinggis Khan and the early Mongol Khans could spot talent and used those people across Eurasia as it came under their control. The reporting of history in religious terms limits the reader's ability to be able to remove the bias of that religious lens, but in terms of Mongol policies this is an essential condition because most of the other information we have about the Mongols negates this point unequivocally. This in no way removes personal bias, the Mongol khans on occasion showed anti-religious sentiments, but the overarching driver of policy was based on economic consideration and the installation of peoples best suited to administer irrespective of their faiths. As mentioned previously, the Mongols were not on a religious mission, though of course every success was viewed as a *mandate of heaven* in tune with *shamanistic* principles. Over time many princes and princesses and groups of Mongols converted to different religions but at least until the mid-fourteenth century, nomadic traditions and rituals were practised in conjunction with other religious practices.

The relationship of the Mongols with Islam and Christianity deserves more comment. In a world which was divided between these two religions, the Mongols represented both an independent entity and were candidates for possible conversion. In the beginning, as has been described above, the Mongols while open to religious debate continued to follow their traditional religious beliefs either exclusively or sometimes in conjunction with newly acquired knowledge. One of the most important features of Mongol Eurasia remained its open-door policy to religions within their domains and those outside Eurasia. Intellectuals and learned men in general played an important role in the courts of the Mongol Khans and with each new conquest the number of these people increased. The cosmopolitan nature of Mongol courts gave rise to enmities and rivalries which were often written about and experienced in religious terms. When, for example, merchants were privileged, their ethnicity became important and often a bone of contention. Or, when the Khans chose Nestorian Christians as their physicians, other people reacted to their religious affiliation. The following section raises some of the religious issues that Mongol policies created and provides a framework to redirect the discussion back to Mongol customs and principles.

Islam

The overall relationship between the Mongols and Islam, like other religions, was dictated more by how the state functioned than anything specifically to do with religious preferences of the Mongols. In general Muslim merchants in Central Asia, Persia and in the Golden Horde did well, enjoyed prosperity and high office in government as *darugachis* and/or governors. They became partners to the Mongol Khans, but the merchant class across Eurasia also enjoyed these privileges. As described in Chapter 2, the merchants in Eurasia were an institution unto themselves and were important in Mongol administration from the beginning of the Mongol century. That many of the merchants were Muslim was not a matter of Mongol preference but rather the state of affairs as they found them. Merchants were not only an important commercial class but were also key advisers and repositories of knowledge and information required for the governance of such a large geographical space. They represented the connections and linkages across the region which was bolstered under the Mongols to reinvent and revive the Silk Road. In other words, it was because they were skilful, knowledgeable and ready partners that they were important in Mongol Eurasia not because they were Muslim. As a result, Muslims not only did well within Mongol Eurasia but Muslim elites who migrated to Mamluk Egypt or the Delhi Sultanate (India), which became havens for Muslims escaping the Mongols, saw a further spread of Islam and over the next few centuries saw a further burgeoning of the Muslim faith. Eventually the Muslim faith, with the conversion of Mongols and non-Mongols alike, also saw an increase in Muslim groups and sects.[66]

An equally compelling argument exists which asserts that the Mongols were anti-Muslim to begin with. In order to prove this, the examples cited are: the initial assault on Khwarezm which was ruled by a Muslim ruler, Hulegu's destruction of the Caliphate in Baghdad and even refusing audience with Muslim Khans. As mentioned above, Qubilai had issued an edict forbidding slaughter of animals according to Muslim ways in light of Muslim merchants refusing food from his table. This edict led to divisions in court and Christian factions taking advantage of the situation. Officials like Isa Tarsa Kelemechi, Ibn Ma'ali and Baidaq among others profited and plotted against their Muslim rivals. This edict was in effect for a limited time since it was negatively affecting Muslim merchants coming to the Yuan court.[67] Other Christian efforts at an anti-Muslim coalition with the Mongols included commentaries from Christian scholars and letters from the Pope directed to such ends. In general, the Mongols continued to employ talented people from across religious groups based on their skills and knowledge. Knowledge existed in as wide a range as the expanse of Eurasia offered: Uyghur script, the Mongol government system, local administrative practices along with alchemy, medicine, science, religion and so forth.[68]

The conflict between the Golden Horde and Ilkhanate Persia has also been variously described as having origins in Berke's conversion to Islam, the first of the Mongol princes to do so, and his opposition to Hulegu's destruction of the Caliphate in Iraq. However, while this may have played into the overall rivalry, there is evidence to show that the rivalry was primarily due to the politics in Qara Qorum and the usurpation of parts of the Golden Horde's territory by the Ilkhans, particularly the regions of Azerbaijan and Arran which were important for trade and also offered opportunities for grazing with lush pasturelands in high demand by the Mongols.[69] The Golden Horde and the Ilkhans remained at odds for most of their existence, though that did not always mean that trade was not allowed to pass through. However, one of the major reasons for the establishment of the Black Sea trade and the creation of a new route through Central Asia was the blockades and stoppages between the Golden Horde and Ilkhanate territories. While we cannot argue that Berke's religious bent did not influence his actions against the Ilkhans, there is ample evidence to prove that the complex relationship between Berke and Hulegu was not limited to or even driven by religion. The Golden Horde alliance with the Mamluks against the Ilkhans is also often expressed in religious affinity but again there is evidence to show that the slave trade with the Mamluks dictated the relationship with the Golden Horde, the alliance against the Ilkhans was an added bonus. In other words, while religion indeed may have been one of the contributing factors, we cannot say that it was the main motivating factor propelling Mongol action. However, by the 1340s the Golden Horde had become Islamic, following the reigns of Ozbek and Janibeg.[70] The conversion of the Golden Horde has been attributed to a number of factors which were beginning to become problems for the administration of their vast lands especially in the context of their (by then) Islamic rivals, the Ilkhans, becoming Muslim. By the time Ozbek Khan became ruler of the Golden Horde, Volga Bulgar merchants who were Muslim occupied high positions. There were a growing number of Muslims in the military and ties with Muslim Mamluks against the Ilkhans were becoming more important.[71] As is evident from the discussion so far, the Mongols retained their ability to adopt practices which best suited governance. They exhibited steppe flexibility in their relationship with Islam and as we shall in the next section, with Christianity. The *Mongol worldview* continued to find resonance and drive Mongol policies in Muslim and Christian lands of Eurasia.

Christianity

The Christians in Eurasia fared reasonably well under the Mongols. Along with different sects of Christianity, Orthodox Christians, Nestorian Christians and Catholics were all able to find a place in Mongol Eurasia. In opening up the Black Sea trade emporia, the Golden Horde opened the east to Western missionaries, merchants and other groups. There was construction of churches and religious institutions under the Mongols, sometimes by the Mongol princes and princesses, but also by religious leaders in the region. For example, in the 1230s, Nestorian churches were built and crosses erected by Simeon Rabban-ata in Azerbaijan.[72] Samarqand in Central Asia was a seat of both the Metropolitan See of the Nestorian Church and a Latin bishopric. In addition, the city was reported as the centre for Christian activity and a place where Christian sects dominated, as well as there being a grand temple.[73] Hulegu is said to have built large idol temples in Arran and Azerbaijan.[74] By the fourteenth century there was a Catholic mission in Khan Baligh. The latter half of the thirteenth century witnessed papal missions and Christian/European merchants frequenting Mongol Eurasia.[75] Despite Ghazan's conversion to Islam in 1295, his policies included a re-establishment of contact with Christian communities in Iran.

A note on the relationship of the Mongols with Christian kingdoms in the thirteenth and fourteenth centuries is necessary at this point, along with the position of the Mongols in the context of the Crusades. The Mongols benefitted from the religious conflict between the Mamluks and Byzantium. With the waning of power of the Byzantium Empire and an embargo on trade with Muslim kingdoms like the Mamluks, the Mongols of Eurasia received papal embassies and letters asking them to become part of the Crusades. However, as mentioned previously, the Mongols were open to relationships with kingdoms across religious faiths as long as they accepted Chinggissid supremacy. As it happened, this did not take place, but the Golden Horde and the Ilkhans forged relations and treaties with Genoa and Venice who were given permission by the Pope to trade in the Black Sea in the middle of the thirteenth century. The Genoese and the Venetians were major players in the Black Sea and Eastern Mediterranean trade. Beginning in 1261 with the permission of Michael VIII (Byzantine Emperor) the Genoese followed quickly by the Venetians became intermediaries in the Black Sea trade going to Europe. The Genoese and the Venetians signed treaties with Mongol Khans to allow them to set up colonies and quarters in the Black Sea region, through which they could easily access Central Asian markets. The cities of Tana, Caffa and even Trebizond around the Black Sea were populated by large numbers of Genoese and Venetians. Other cities further afield, especially Beijing, also had Christian quarters but the Black Sea trade was the main entry point for the Italian maritime empires of Genoa and Venice and they enjoyed special privileges and access to trade. The Black Sea region was the main supplier of grain and foodstuffs for Western Europe,[76] so much so that a trade embargo of 1340 by the Pope which forbade trading with the Mongols in the Golden Horde and the Ilkhans resulted in dire conditions in Crete which was besieged by a famine, inflation and general upheaval. This indicates quite clearly that Mongol policies in Eurasia were generally positive for merchants irrespective of their faiths. Even during the Crusades there were papal letters given for trade within the Black Sea region and this did not change until some of the Mongol Khans began to lose power. After 1335, the Mongol Ilkhans began to lose control, and new challenges to the Golden Horde brought about a resurgence of pre-Mongol religious policies directing trade behaviour, which meant that embargos and blockades came back into fashion. As a result only in the middle of the fourteenth century did the Genoese and the Venetians stop trading with the Mongols and that too for a brief period of five years (1343–1347).[77] In other words, the Mongols had good relationships with Christians in Eurasia, whether it was Nestorian Christians who had been ejected from other Christian lands, Orthodox Christians in Rus or for that matter Catholics who were not part of Mongol Eurasia but who had special relationships with the Mongols as a result of their mercantile interests. There was a resurgence of old religious rivalries once the non-Mongol elements in Eurasia found traction again.

Summary

The treatment of religion under the Mongols deserves to be understood in light of two important precepts of the Mongol state; (i) trade was of paramount importance and required freedom of movement unperturbed by religious or any other restrictions as was the case in Islamic and Christian lands at the time; and (ii) the 'Mongols, from the outset of their imperial enterprise, demonstrated a decided preference for individuals with specialised skills'[78] which blurred divisions based on religious affiliations and ethnicities.[79] Mongol religious policies were driven by their interest in, and fascination for new ideas which they incorporated into a complex network of magical-spiritual beliefs. This led to spaces and outlets for discussions among different religious figures who gathered in Mongol courts. An open religious policy also allowed the Mongols access to commercial networks and spiritual power both for their own use and to keep subject populations in check. Both by co-opting local officials and treating the clergy of all the religions they encountered with respect, the Mongols managed to harness their power and standing in society for their own benefit.[80] As a consequence, people and groups across Eurasia adopted Mongol customs, habits and redirected their skills to participate in careers and professions which were required in a Mongol dominated Eurasia. This included raising the status of professions like clerks, translators and physicians; groups that responded to these changes in Eurasian societies benefitted, like the Uyghurs and Nestorians, while groups like Confucian scholars who initially resisted Mongol pressures found themselves out of office. The same is true for the *ulema* and religious people in Central Asia and Persia who as a political class were dislocated by the Mongols and thus initially considered the Mongols anti-Muslim. Even Rashid al-Din who owed much to the Mongols expressed disapproval of the continuation of *shamanistic* activities under Ghazan Khan and in the *ordos*[81] of princes and princesses. Mongol laws that contradicted Muslim laws were indeed flouted and this caused much indignation.[82] However, Mongol Eurasia was a composite system which encompassed diverse peoples, cultures and societies and was necessarily informed by a combination of global and local factors.[83] Mongol religious policy was an outcome of decentralised and flexible governance and guaranteed stability in a diffuse region by focusing on talent and not religious or ethnic characteristics.

Mongol rule in Eurasia continued to spur religious activity in the region and the Silk Road remained a place with many religious groups in close quarters and ways and means had to be devised through which they could coexist and curry favour from the Mongols. What we do know is that the Mongols across Eurasia protected Christians, Muslims, Buddhists and a variety of sects within these faiths throughout the thirteenth and fourteenth centuries. The Mongols themselves paved the way for religious activity, debate and building in all major cities and did not participate in persecution of any particular religions. Eurasia remained a place where religious interaction continued to flourish. The Mongol approach to religion was one of flexibility and openness and if anything, religious sympathies were used to foster new lands, peoples, ideas and most importantly to keep the flow of trade going. The Mongols are credited with using the Silk Road for exchange and flow of goods, peoples, ideas and information; religious concepts and ideas key among them. The Silk Road is as much remembered for economic relations as it is for the transfer and exchange of religious ideas. Mongol Eurasia yet again stands out as a golden moment in time which, because of the intrinsic nature of nomadic steppe traditions and the Mongol approach to religion, allowed the religions of the book and the religions of the East to interact. Mongol Khans encouraged religious debates and discussions in their courts, princes and princesses often brought up in one faith practised *shamisnistic* and other religious faiths in tandem. Religious institutions across the board were protected thanks to Chinggis Khan's *yasaq*, a stipulation which was carried out throughout Eurasia under the Mongols and was applied to all religions the Mongols came into contact with. In Yuan China, Buddhism, Confucian scholars and Taoists all did reasonably well and enjoyed high office. Confucian officials were not the only ones allowed to enter the ranks of the bureaucracy and civil service which can be seen as breaking a monopoly and encouraging social mobility. Since there were numerous Confucians still in office, there is no evidence to suggest persecution; rather it represented an opening up of a closed or limited system. Similarly, in Ilkhanate Persia Muslims still enjoyed positions of high office, though the State was no longer imposing *sharia* law. The fall of the Caliphate was not so much an attack on a religious faith but the conquest of a powerful kingdom which happened to be the seat of Islam. The Golden Horde represented a mixed territory of Christians and Muslims and the individual preferences of the Khans showed how both the faiths had reasonably strong attractions and influences. Central Asia with its predominantly Muslim population and possibly home to the most nomadic societies in Mongol Eurasia remained a bastion of Chinggissid principles with a mix of Islamic elements which over the years crept into the administration. However, it also represented the territory where smaller sects in both Islam and Christianity survived the longest, Nestorian Christianity and Manichaeism or *Sufi* sects which survived through the centuries and even developed further after the thirteenth century. The prevalence of all major religions in Central Asia attests to the open and flexible environment for religious practices that existed throughout time in the heart of the Silk Road. Viewed especially in the context of the Crusades which were still going on in the thirteenth century, Mongol Eurasia offered itself up for a far more cosmopolitan and free geographical space than what either followed immediately after the Mongol century or even what is in place today.

In summary, economic relations and commercial interests could dictate Mongol policies without being muddled by religious limitations. Mongol Eurasia was traversed by the Chinese, Indians, Central Asians, Iranians, Iraqis, Venetians, Genoese and other Europeans (including French and German artisans) representing a variety of faiths and religions. What is even more interesting is that many states that replaced the Mongols, Muslim (Amir Timur's Central Asia, Safavids). Christian (Russia) and Chinese (Ming) all owe their rise to power and in some cases as in Timur even their legitimacy to Chinggis Khan and the presence of a Mongol Eurasia.[84] Whether the Mongols were religious or not, or whether they became more religious as time went by, their main contribution was to create opportunities and conditions for trade across the Silk Road and across Eurasia to include a huge number of people and unprecendented quantities of goods and products, spurring a whole new system for future centuries. According to scholars like Abu-Lughod[85] and Jack Goody,[86] Mongol Eurasia was a precursor to modern day economic relations especially in the context of globalisation. The next chapter looks at the growth of cities as commercial hubs as a result of the institutional framework and religious policies of the Mongols which accelerated the reconstruction, revival and growth of a variety of cities across Mongol Eurasia. It considers the variety of ways in which the Mongols interacted with cities which were sources of economic prosperity, human capital, symbols of legitimacy and prestige and economic and political centres.[87]

Notes

1 Sky god
2 Allsen 2001, p. 209
3 Boyle 1971, p. 260
4 Riasonovsky 1965, p. 34
5 Allsen 2001, p. 207
6 Jackson 2017, p. 313
7 Allsen 2001, p. 205
8 Allsen 2001, p. 175
9 Hookham 1962, p. 35
10 Allsen 2001, pp. 149–151
11 Gumilev 1987, p. 282
12 Golden 1992, p. 297
13 Mongol taxes
14 Schurmann 1956a, pp. 324–325
15 Jackson 2005b, p. 264
16 Gumilev 1987, p. 209
17 Jackson 2005b, p. 265
18 Ratchnevsky 1991, pp. 197–198
19 Abu-Lughod 1989, p. 354
20 Jackson 2005b, p. 263
21 Gumilev 1987, pp. 194–195
22 Grousset 1970, p. 357
23 Allsen 2001, p. 158
24 Saunders 1965, p. 84
25 Biran, 2009, p. 64
26 Cunliffe 2015, p. 443
27 Edicts/commands
28 Ischboldin 1973, p. 52
29 Gumilev 1987, p. 210
30 Biran 2013, p. 270
31 See Komaroff 2006 and DeWeese 2009
32 Jackson 2005b, p. 270
33 Jackson 2017, p. 329

34 Gumilev 1987, p. 310
35 Gumilev 1987, p. 201
36 Saunders 1977, p. 65
37 Golden 1992, pp. 297–298
38 Halperin 1985, p. 77
39 Vasary 2009, pp. 78–79
40 Ischboldin 1973, p. 45
41 Morgan 2006, p. 434
42 Biran 2013, p. 262
43 Thackston 2012b, p. 46
44 Hookham 1962, p. 38
45 Islamic teachings
46 *Sufi* shaikh/teacher
47 *Waqf* means Islamic charitable endowment
48 Biran 2009, p. 65
49 Biran 2009, pp. 65–66
50 Biran 1997, pp. 93–95
51 Biran 2009, p. 65
52 Biran 2013, p. 274
53 Pfeiffer 2006b, p. 371; Jackson 2017, p. 300
54 Pfeiffer 2006b, pp. 374–375
55 Pfeiffer 2006b, p. 378
56 Fitzherbert 2006, p. 393
57 Fitzherbert 2006, p. 395
58 Allsen 2001, p. 55
59 Rossabi 1988, pp. 133–134
60 Rossabi 1988, pp. 137–138
61 Rossabi 1988, p. 143
62 Rossabi 1988, p. 171
63 Rossabi 1988, p. 226
64 Rossabi 1988, p. 146
65 Rossabi 1988, p. 201
66 Jackson 2017, pp. 381–382
67 Boyle 1971, p. 294
68 Jackson 2017, p. 312
69 Ciociltan 2012, pp. 46–47
70 Hambly 1969, p. 119
71 Golden 1992, p. 298
72 Jackson 2005b, p. 262
73 Bretschneider 2000, (Vol. II) pp. 58–60
74 Thackston 2012b, p. 58
75 Abu-Lughod 1989, p. 144
76 Carr 2015, p. 129
77 Carr 2015, pp. 127–128
78 Allsen 2001, p. 158
79 Jackson 2017, p. 311
80 Allsen 2001, p. 200
81 Military encampment/headquarters
82 For more information see Jackson 2017, pp. 297–327
83 Mott 2015, p. xiv
84 Hambly 1969, p. 110
85 For more information see Abu-Lughod 1989
86 For more information see Goody 1997
87 Biran 2013, p. 257

4 Mongol cities of Eurasia

> But there is a great deal more to the Mongol impact on world history than havoc and massacre.[1]

Inhabiting a multiplicity of locations is intrinsic to the nomads and the Mongols were no exception to this rule, even after their conquest of traditionally sedentary societies. The blurring of the urban-rural spaces for a steppe nomad is inherent in his movement patterns; his location signifies the rural and the urban simultaneously and is driven by the availability of pasturelands. In this context, the Mongols created multiple capitals, summer and winter camps, which represented cities even when they existed beyond so called city limits. The Khan's court attracted merchants, artisans and religious figures and became the hub of commercial and other activity, often in combination with extant cultural and commercial hubs in the vicinity. In a continuation of nomadic custom, Qubilai Khan moved between his summer capital (Shangdu) and winter capital (Beijing) in Yuan China. Similarly, the Ilkhans moved between their favourite winter and summer pastures and carried the entire court with them. Sarai, the capital of the Golden Horde, has famously been described as a 'tent' city or a 'mobile' city. Qaidu constantly moved around in Central Asia all through his reign, as did his successors, Du'a and Kebek who also had summer and winter capitals. The 'moving' capitals represented the nuclei of court activity and were where important political meetings like *quriltais* – which elected Khans – took place as in the case of the Ilkhanate.[2] Along with the royal courts, these moving sites included spaces for hunting which was essentially military exercise as well as a typical steppe activity, and artisan and manufacturing quarters as in the case of Sultanniyeh in Iran. Central Asian Mongols (Chaghatais and Ogedeis), supposedly the most nomadic, also had an impact on urbanisation (though opinions are divided on whether the impact was positive or negative overall) in Central Asia which went hand in hand with the creation of markets and production centres in this region. Cities like Baghdad, Tabriz and Samarqand came to represent hubs of commercial activity as the backbone of a comprehensive Eurasian economy and included trade in all directions: north-south and east-west. The essence of Mongol Eurasia was one which spurred economic activity across borders and this necessitated safe passage to and from commercial centres. An examination of the complex relationship of the nomadic Mongols with cities is then imperative to this discussion.

Mongol Eurasia is as much a story of birth (as it is of destruction) with numerous examples of cities and regions which gained prominence in the thirteenth century and continue to retain their position even today. The speed and efficiency with which the Mongol military went through the process of conquest to connect Eurasia inevitably led to destruction and left upheaval in its wake. This has been highlighted by historians writing during the Mongol era and has informed understanding of the nature of Mongol conquest in subsequent centuries through to the present. The disruption in trade during conquest was inevitable but equally important is the Mongol attempts at stabilising conditions and resuming normal activities. The Mongols implemented policies of reconstruction almost immediately after they gained control in every region. After initial conquest, a further disruption took place when the infighting between different Khanates in 1260 began in earnest and caused roads and routes to be closed off, especially between Yuan China and Central Asia and the Golden Horde and the Ilkhans. Cities also suffered from policies of relocation of skilled men which temporarily impaired local economies. As mentioned previously, the policies of the Mongols need to be understood in global terms of world market economies and particularly the economy of Eurasia in order to gain perspective on the events of the thirteenth century. The unification of Eurasia under the Mongols brought with it both disadvantages and advantages which hampered and helped different regions and communities across the Eurasian space. New systems bring with them a disruption of the old to make room for the new and in this case the Mongols brought about one of the biggest upheavals in world history to an already prosperous region and still managed to increase productivity, commercial activity and exchanges of the cultural, social and religious variety. However, the 'complete' destruction of the previous world order would be a gross overestimation because as much as the Mongols caused disruptions, the Central Asian cities, for example, 'recover[ed] and thrive[ed] as the trade networks were re-stablished'.[3] If anything the Mongols tried to sustain the connections which had persisted over centuries. Their institutions and policies were designed to highlight the connections across Eurasia and they did this successfully by employing people and using them where they were most needed. The economic recovery of Eurasia was quick and was at the behest of Mongol Khans and princes. The integrated nature of the economic system was most visible in the movement of peoples which has been referred to as labour and brain-drain and is particularly applicable to the cities of Central Asia. Easily the closest population to the Mongols in terms of sharing a common heritage and worldview, the Central Asians were essential to the Mongol state and thus were mobilised in significant numbers. This is as common today in the modern market economy as it was during Mongol rule and has to be analysed with a global perspective in mind. The unprecedented infusion of ideas, peoples and goods following the period of conquest, overall reduction of customs duties and the building of *caravansarais*, courts and urban centres boosted the overall conditions in Eurasia.[4] As early as 1218 Bukhara was already undergoing a revival. An examination of the major cities which were destroyed during the first half of the thirteenth century requires an equal examination of the cities which saw the most rapid revival under the Mongols. Samarqand, Baghdad, Merv, Herat, Tabriz and Tus to name a few underwent rapid reconstruction and were functioning commercial centres soon after conquest. Equally important is to point out the fact that the Mongols spared cities which submitted voluntarily. The cities that did suffer destruction were supposed to serve as examples for others.[5] This is clearly important and goes against the popular images of the Mongols as blood-thirsty barbarians. As a small population from the steppe they were keen to gain access to resources without entering protracted battles which would impact their own numbers and would be detrimental to trade and economic activity.

The *Mongol worldview* percolated down to the creation and revival of cities under the Mongols. Mongol cities formed the basis for Mongol power and continued to symbolise wealth and prestige, showcasing both nomadic and sedentary characteristics. Mongol cities were intimately tied to nomadic traditions and Mongol institutions and policies, foremost among them being their religious policies discussed in the previous chapter. In traditional nomadic style, the Mongols had multiple capitals and they served different sets of purposes.[6] With this in mind this chapter divides the kinds of cities that sprang up under the Mongols into the following categories: commercial hubs (overland and coastal towns) on trade routes, for example: Bukhara, Samarqand, Tabriz, Almaliq and Sarai (Old and New); agricultural towns; capital cities (Qara Qorum, Beijing, Sarai); artisan towns and cities (Cinqai, Bolad); and mobile courts. Mobile courts had a huge impact on surrounding areas and impacted the growth of cities nearby even in regions where there was no obvious city associated with a Khan as in the case of Qaidu. Mongol cities were closely associated with religious buildings:[7] churches, *khanqahs*, mosques, *madrassas*, monasteries and temples, something which would have gone hand-in-hand with a near blanket exemption of taxes for religious institutions. The institutions of note for the growth of cities were the postal stations, merchants in key positions and the *keshig* which supplied key officials for the Mongol state. Seen individually, the establishment of postal stations in themselves serve to show how connecting cities (commercial, political and even mobile courts) was a top priority for the Mongols. *Jams* were established as much for free-flowing information for military and political purposes as for economic gain, especially in order for merchants and diplomats to be able to travel far and wide unencumbered and with ease. They often gave rise to or culminated in *bazars* and included buildings for storage of goods and commodities. The importance of merchants also naturally prioritises reviving commercial centres. Seen in the context of Mongol policies then, it is not surprising that the Mongols were drivers of new towns and cities and their efforts were directed as much to provisioning for mercantile activity as for preserving political and familial connections. In addition, the Mongol policy of moving artisans and other skilled craftsmen from one part of Eurasia to another led to the growth of artisanal and manufacturing centres along with scientific and scholarly communities in different parts of the region which left lasting imprints on the cultural psyche of certain cities like Almaliq and Cinqai among others. In addition, there were also garrison towns and military colonies which established towns and centres around them in border areas.

The administration and institutional structure to govern Eurasia has already been discussed in previous chapters. The relationship between the Mongols and cities is indeed noteworthy in light of the fact that nomads have complex relationships with urban centres and this can be seen through a look at the different kinds of cities which sprang up under the Mongols. The Mongols initiated, encouraged and developed all four Khanates in order to gain maximum benefits from Eurasia. As we have seen previously, merchants served as one of the key classes in Mongol administration and so the importance of trade and commercial activity was among the most important elements of Mongol Eurasia. There were at least three ways in which cities were recognised, cities like Bukhara and Herat had to be revived after a period of destruction; new cities were founded through the creation of capitals and Mongol courts; and the idea of mobile tent cities[8] or travelling capitals which were organised around the *ordo* or court of a Mongol khan and were a travelling contingent of thousands of tents, followed by *bazaars* (markets) and households, the best example of which was Sarai. In addition to these there was also a rise of new centres in regions which were ruled through vassals, for example Muscovy where Muscovite princes gained prominence through their service to the Khan, defeated Novogorod and other competitors and became the capital of Tsarist Russia and the modern Russian state.

Mongol policies geared toward the revival of the economies of their regions was not limited to trade, manufacturing workshops and infrastructure for building roads and waterways, but agriculture also attracted attention. It remained in the able hands of Chinese and Muslim administrators who had more direct experience with agriculture and sedentary societies. While the focus here is the Mongol interest and encouragement of trade, a note on Mongol policies to revive, improve and promote agriculture needs attention. Since the Mongols were pastoralists, and many of their newly acquired subjects engaged in agricultural activities, their impact on agriculture is studied very little and requires more research. As will be evident from the following sections, the revival of cities was not limited to building infrastructure for trade but concerted efforts were made throughout Eurasia to improve the conditions for agriculture. Grain and foodstuffs were also part of the commercial exchanges, for example, the Golden Horde was a key player in providing grain to the Genoese traders which was essential for Europe at the time.[9] Additionally, agricultural production was required for internal consumption as well, for example, Qubilai Khan invested in securing grain for Northern China through a system of canals and waterways which led to the growth of rural areas and cities sprang along the north-south route. Farmers had access to storage facilities and the securing of roads and waterways went a long way in boosting agricultural production and dissemination. The exchanges between the Yuan and the Ilkhanate included agricultural and food technologies in a large part and as a result, Chinese and Muslim irrigation technologies along with fruits and foods formed the bulk of exchanges in one region. The spread of cotton production in Yuan China is attributed to Qubilai Khan; and conversely Chinese communities in Khui impacted what was grown locally and introduced Chinese agricultural techniques in Iran.[10] The creation of a cosmopolitan Eurasian elite also led to the opportunities for using ingredients and foodstuffs from other regions to replicate the tastes and flavours that the elite wished to consume and furthered exchange in agricultural technologies. Central Asian Mongols under Qaidu and his adviser, Masud Beg, also created conditions to improve agricultural production in the oases societies of Bukhara and Samarqand. Kebek in the 1320s concentrated heavily on the revival of agriculture and instituted reforms to bolster production.[11]

This chapter focuses on cities as commercial hubs and production centres established under the Mongols. The revival of Tabriz and Baghdad under Hulegu in Ilkhanate Persia, the creation of Tana and Caffa as important port cities in the Golden Horde where Italian merchants along with merchants from across Eurasia came to make their fortunes and the establishment of artisan, military and agricultural colonies across the Eurasia space speak volumes to the agency of the Mongols. The creation of Andijan as an important commercial hub in the Ferghana region, true even today, was carried out under the Central Asian Mongols, as was the revival of important cities like Bukhara and Samarqand which were both prospering cities in accounts left by Chinese and European travellers in the 1230s. Or for that matter the cities of Hangchow and Quangzhou, which became bustling artisan cities, centres of porcelain and silk production for the court in Beijing and for markets in Iran and Iraq under the Ilkhans. The Golden Horde is also credited with the emergence of various towns and cities for artisans as production centres. In Mongol fashion one of the main elements of the creation of cities was the transfer of populations across Eurasia which gave rise to agricultural and artisanal colonies of the Northern Chinese in Iran and Muslims from Iran and Central Asia in Northern China. Khui in Azerbaijan and Hangchow in China are famous examples of two cities which were inhabited by the Chinese and Muslims respectively[12] but these are two examples among many more; Samarqandi artisans were relocated to China in 1218 and there were Chinese military-agricultural colonies in Merv and Tabriz as well. These populations continued to practise their own local habits and this gave rise to further opportunities for diffusion of Chinese and Muslim cultures and are testament to the transformative nature of Mongol Eurasia. The development of cities and trade relations is directly linked with the steppe intelligentsia in office. Mongol princes along with *darugachis* and local administrators are credited with the revival and reconstruction of old commercial and cultural hubs, the birth of new cities and the creation of infrastructure between regions which naturally led to urban growth and cities. Time and again the figures connected to prosperous cities are Mahmud Yalavac, Masud Beg, Yeh lu Chu Tsai, Cinqai, Bolad and Rashid al-Din who all served as governors or were important officials under the Khans. The other figures of note are all Mongol Khans and princes who oversaw, drove and created capital cities, mobile courts and revived coastal towns and bolstered agriculture which led to comprehensive development in Eurasia.

All these point to a far more complicated relationship between Mongols and the region of Eurasia, a far cry from an unlimited siege of destruction and death caused by Mongol conquest. As Jackson has said, the Mongols caused a lot of havoc and chaos but without a doubt left a far more interconnected Eurasia than before.[13] Not only were cities renowned for their place on the Silk Road revived but as a result of population transfers of artisans and in order to meet demands of the Mongol courts of the Khans, princes and princesses spread across Eurasia, even the remotest part of the steppe saw the founding of production centres. This made them attractive enough to be visited by merchants and allowed a connection between them and other parts of Eurasia. The Mongol policies of moving populations around meant that while cities like Samarqand lost up to 30,000 of its artisans, they were replaced by Chinese, Tangut and even German artisans and miners from other parts of Eurasia which would benefit or help in repairing the damage done to the local economy. The production centres nearer the sources of raw materials not only meant a larger network for mercantile activity but also created new links and interactions, furthering transfer of skills, technology and communication and bringing Eurasia and its different populations closer together. The birth of more cities along the Silk Road further led to the burgeoning of commercial activity because caravans could travel shorter distances between cities which helped in the overall security of goods and products traversing through the region. The variety of contacts, transfers and exchange led to an increase in the goods produced as well, for example the production of white and blue porcelain in Quangzhou, China for sale in cities of Ilkhanate Persia led to new expertise and new opportunities for artisans and traders. The availability of a larger variety of goods either because the merchants could travel the extent of the Silk Road or because centres of production were closer to markets was a direct consequence of changes instituted by the Mongols in Eurasia. Mongol presence highlighted the contiguous nature of the Eurasian continent. Interconnectedness especially in the thirteenth century without modern modes of communication was surmounted by the Mongol nomadic vision of Eurasia. The list of cities and regions developed and revived by the Mongols is not exhaustive by any means but a description of the main cities and regions within the Mongol Khanates sheds light on the extent of the impact of the Mongols on the Silk Road and Eurasia as we understand today. The next section delves into the cities of note in all four of the Khanates and briefly discusses the kinds of efforts made by the Mongol Khans to achieve resumption of urban centres in Eurasia.

Mongolia

The Mongols established cities in the steppe and the most famous of these was Qara Qorum, located in the Orkhon valley. Before 1218 the centre of authority had been somewhere between the Onon and the Kerulen rivers. Already in

Chinggis Khan's time the centre of authority had started moving toward the Orkhon valley and after 1218 Qara Qorum increasingly became important. Ogedei established it as his capital and turned it into a walled city with permanent imperial residences in 1235.[14] It remained the capital until Qubilai moved the capital to Beijing in 1265. Qara Qorum was built by Chinese architects and the palace was impressive and has been described by travellers, missionaries and scribes in contemporary sources as such. It attracted goods and products from across Eurasia and its markets were flooded with a wide variety of merchandise. It also held manufacturing centres populated by artisans and craftsmen from across Eurasia which produced a cross-section of Eurasian goods locally. The city could boast of Chinese, Central Asian and Persian bureaucrats, officials, elite, artisans and the like, and also had colonies of Europeans (missionaries, merchants and famously a French engineer who built a fountain of alcohol for Mongke).

Cinqai Balqasun, a city in West Central Mongolia was populated with artisans from China by Cinqai in 1212. Cinqai later served under Ogedei Khan in important positions such as that of *darugachi* and has been referred to as Prime Minister by Ratchnevsky.[15] The city was founded as an agricultural colony and was most likely set up as a base camp for military activities against the Khwarezmshah. The city became a centre for goldsmiths, and jewellers as artisans from here were relocated to China in the 1260s. The city prospered and offered a place for lively interactions between Muslim and Chinese artisans.

Central Asia

Out of all the Mongol Khanates, Central Asia has received the most devastating account of Mongol rule. The Central Asian Mongols were the most easily identifiable as nomadic throughout their rule. In addition, the Turkic population of Central Asia was not much differentiated from its Mongol rulers which worked against both the Central Asians and Mongols in any historical analysis. These aspects combined with the protracted war with Yuan China persisted in describing Central Asia as a devastated region. However, this image is at odds with the place of Central Asia and Central Asians at the crossroads of civilisations and the heart of overland trade. The region retained its importance and the rule of the Mongols even gave rise to important cities on the Silk Road which represented the very essence of the connections which made the Mongol era so productive. The Mongols were well aware of the riches of Central Asia, and it was much more than a battleground for the Mongols: it was the centre of Mongol Eurasia and effort was poured into keeping it peaceful in large part for overland trade.[16] Furthermore, the educated elite of Central Asia were partners to the Mongols in the creation of Mongol Eurasia; they formed the multi-lingual base necessary for Mongol administration across regions and had experience of nomadic polities which meant that they moved and emigrated in larger numbers out of Central Asia compared with any other ethnic group.[17] The similarities between the Mongols and Central Asians based on common steppe traditions and customs made them natural allies to the Mongols. Even when conflict between Yuan China and Central Asia was at its peak, i.e. under Qaidu (1271–1301/1303) there is evidence of prosperous cities (Bukhara, Kashgar, etc.), minting of a large number of coins across Central Asia, mention of weaving workshops which were important as sources of revenue and even building activity which all indicate that local trade was taking place even if regional trade with the Yuan and the Ilkhanate was impeded.[18] Central Asia under Qaidu was a matter of establishing Ogedeid control in the style of the other Khanates as opposed to a fight for the title of *Qaghan* of Mongol Eurasia. Most of the fighting was made up of border skirmishes and small battles between the Yuan and Central Asia which left the larger parts of Central Asia and Yuan China free from conflict. This combined with the economic reforms under Qaidu clearly indicate that the Central Asian Mongols were only fighting for their share of the Mongol Empire. They wanted access to their territorial possessions on which they depended for revenues.[19] The historical background for this conflict has been discussed previously, but to reiterate since the election of Mongke, the line of Ogedei had continued to lose territorial possessions due to the divisions and re-divisions under Chinggis and then under Mongke which finally gave control of the Mongol Empire to the Toluid line of the Chinggissids and sparked rivalries between the Mongol princes. Qaidu in Central Asia succeeded, at least briefly, to create a Ogedeid line with control over parts of Central Asia in joint partnership with the Chaghatais. Eventually, it was at the behest of Du'a (Chaghataid prince) who took full control after the death of Qaidu, that a peace treaty was initiated with Yuan China and the Ilkhanate which resumed overland transcontinental trade through all of Central Asia. The concerted effort to bring peace between the Khanates was to put an end to instability and the destruction of cities which had economic repercussions for all of Mongol Eurasia. The early part of the fourteenth century – 1304, 1310 and 1323 – saw more concrete moves toward stabilisation in order to allow for traders to move unfettered, and there are instances of traders from Egypt and Syria (rivals to the Ilkhans) travelling to Transoxiana in the 1330s according to al-Umari, signifying both that it was safe to travel and that Transoxiana had regained its position in commercial activities.[20] Pegolotti had previously noted how the route from Tana to Cathay was the safest in the thirteenth century. Diplomatic missions were often accompanied by *ortoy* with money from the Khan to trade for him personally and thus the Khans had a personal stake in embassies travelling safely through to their destinations and back.[21]

The revival and creation of cities in Central Asia followed a deliberate pattern of ancient cities on the caravan routes to Bukhara and Samarqand, namely Garganj and Khiva, and were among the first few to attract the attention of the Mongols, both for conquest and revival. The following is an extensive but not an exhaustive list of cities in Central Asia which received attention from the Mongols from very early on. Already under Chaghatai, cities like Almaliq and his mobile court which was near Almaliq, became centres of court activity and attracted travellers, traders, diplomatic embassies, etc.[22] After 1260, Central Asia suffered due to the infighting within the Mongol Khanates and their protracted war against Qubilai. Central Asian cities were harassed by both the Yuan from the east and the Ilkhans from the west. This situation led to the emigration of many Central Asians to Mongol courts in China where officials like Sayyad Ajall, Ahmad and ‘Abd al Rahman attained high office.[23] Central Asians continued to play an important role in Mongol Eurasia whether located in Central Asia or more likely in Yuan China. The Ogedeid prince Qaidu ruled Central Asia but since he officially jointly ruled with the Chaghatai princes, the conditions in Central Asia vis-à-vis other Khanates was more complex. Qaidu never built a capital, and moved constantly, living primarily along nomadic lines, whether for showcasing his closeness with Chinggissid ideals or for fear of upsetting the partnership with the Chaghatais is up for conjecture. However, his successors are more closely associated with cities, for example, Kebek Khan moved to Qarshi (near Kashkadarya) and built his capital city there in 1320s.[24]

In Central Asia, like in other parts of Mongol Eurasia, there were cities which were created and revived for political as well as economic reasons. In turn, cities could not be continuously propped up without the influx of trade which drove much of Mongol prosperity across Eurasia. While we have sparse information relating directly to trade under Central Asian Mongols, we do have the appearance of a large number of coins which point to a monetary cycle and alludes to porous, if not entirely open, borders with the other Khanates. The number of coins which was indeed noteworthy points to the general acceptance of people and the credibility of state finances, and the fact that the coins have been found in numerous regions of Central Asia further attests to their widespread use, implying stability and faith in the government, along with thriving local trade in Central Asia in the 1280s. Overland trade through Central Asia took a beating because of the wars with Yuan China and Ilkhanate Persia but as mentioned above, regional trade within Central Asia still went on. Examples of flourishing cities can be gleaned from well-functioning weaving workshops and quantities of silver coins found in the region. While Transoxiana was under the Ogedeis and Chaghatais, referred to as Central Asian Mongols throughout, other areas which are part of Central Asia in the present day were part of the Golden Horde and still others of the Ilkhanate. Black Sea trade went through Central Asia and was under the Golden Horde’s control. Khiva is one such example and deserves special attention. Part of the Golden Horde, it did exceedingly well as both an entrepot and a supplier throughout the thirteenth and fourteenth centuries. It connected the Golden Horde with Yuan China and in addition to supplying rubies from Badakshan, indigo from Hindustan and rhubarb, porcelain, ginger and silk from China on to the Golden Horde it also produced two kinds of silk of its own: from Urgench (*organium*) and Khwarzm (*corasmisna*) which were much in demand by the Genoese for the European market.[25] The fact that there were numerous Mongol courts and princes allowed for a more flexible approach to the opportunities for trade and the multiplicity of trade routes.

As mentioned above, cities near Chaghatai’s court benefitted from commercial and other activity. Among the most famous cities were: Almaliq, Taraz,

Bukhara, Samarqand and Andijan. Other cities included are Kashgar and the Tarim basin cities along with Kashgar, Yarkand and Khotan.[26] Almaliq became the most important city on the trade route which connected China and Mongolia. It benefitted from having a Chinese community and also attracted the Muslim scholarly community from around Central Asia. It quickly became the hub for economic, cultural and religious activity. Most of the Chaghataid princes continued to live in its vicinity until at least 1260.[27] Yeh lu Chu Tsai mentioned the prosperity of Samarqand and in 1222, Chang Chun and another Chinese traveller, reported early efforts of restoring Transoxiana with experts from China, Tangut and Khitans to deal with Samarqand's agrarian problems. He even reported lavish gardens, plentiful goods in Samarqand's markets and a pleasant city where he spent time in 1221–1222.[28] In 1259 Changde talked of a prosperous Samarqand and the presence of Chinese people in Almaliq. Among the cities of Central Asia, Herat also saw recovery with Ogedei's command of relocating silk weavers to the area in 1239. Sorqoqtani Beki gave 1000 silver ingots for establishment and reconstruction of madrassas in Bukhara and another official, Korguz, ordered recovery work in Tus and Khurasan. For a brief period after 1241, Taraz was mined by German prisoners and produced gold and metal in large quantities (later the city was moved nearer Almaliq). Taraz can be classified as an artisan city like Cinqai and other cities in Northern China which were founded by the Mongols. Taraz and Talas were important under Qaidu. Taraz offered attractive pasturelands[29] and Talas was the site where the Arabs had wrested control over Central Asia from China in the seventh century. In the thirteenth century, Talas was again the focal point of conflict between Yuan China and Mongol Central Asia. It was the seat of Qaidu's enthronement and has been referred to as *sira ordo.*[30] It was most likely here that Qaidu spent considerable time and his famous interview with Rabban Sawma also took place here. Qaidu's court was a mobile court and his closest retinue included Muslim clergymen, physicians, astrologers and poets much like the other Mongol courts across Eurasia.[31] Masud Beg continued as minister under Qaidu who was responsible for the sedentary population. The general level of prosperity in Central Asia can be pieced together from evidence of a regularised monetary policy under Qaidu and Masud Beg which led to the minting of coins with a higher proportion of silver in Utrar, Talas, Khojand and Kanjak. The presence of postal stations across Central Asia connecting to cities of Persia and China further lends credibility to the idea of continuing trade with Central Asia. However, Qaidu's conflict with Qubilai Khan would have impacted the northern Silk Road through Central Asia to China where the bulk of the skirmishes took place.[32]

Bukhara continued to thrive after its initial destruction because of its unwillingness to submit peacefully. The *destruction* of Bukhara (and Samarqand) deserves a caveat; artisans, craftsmen, scholars and able administrators were spared even at that stage to be used and absorbed in other parts of Mongol Eurasia. Immediately after the conquest Yeh lu Ahai ordered reconstruction in Bukhara and later Mahmud Yalavac helped to bring about recovery. The recovery in Bukhara was so swift that it led to a rebellion against the Mongols, under the leadership of a sieve-maker called Tarabi in 1238, which was swiftly put down.[33] Qaidu conducted a census in Bukhara in 1260[34] to regularise taxation which also indicates a certain revival of the town. Bukhara remained an attractive town to plunder in the years following 1260. There are references to Qaidu not being able to guarantee its safety. After 1282 Qaidu and Du'a appointed Masud Beg as administrator, and he revived the town and started minting coins there. Under Masud Beg the collection of revenue from Bukhara and Samarqand was the main source of revenue for the recovery of Alghu's army. This attests to the resumption of agricultural and commercial activity and a recovery of the population which was able to raise the required funds.[35] As we will see later, Maud Beg has been credited with a sophisticated and genteel approach to administration which serves as reason to believe that the collection of taxes and the recovery of Alghu's army and realm were done in a responsible rather than extractive manner. In 1326, Turko-Mongol commanders are said to have had land holdings in major cities like Bukhara pointing to its enhanced status in Central Asia, and in Tarmashirin's time the Mongol court moved to Bukhara for a short period.[36] The military and religious elite owned land in the surrounding region of Bukhara and *waqf* documents attest to the fact that it was well irrigated and home to mosques, reservoirs and other amenities. Wassaf has described Bukhara as a safe, wealthy and prosperous town at the end of the thirteenth century.

In the same vein, Samarqand was revived fairly quickly. It had been and continued to be a great meeting point for goods from India, the Black Sea region and from China and further benefitted from being an oasis city with agriculture in times of trade disruption. It was frequently visited by travellers and was an important city for Christian churches.[37] Samarqand and Bukhara were connected by a journey of six to seven days and Saarkland maintained its status as a great caravan city.[38] After the 1320s Samarqand saw a further rise in prestige and eventually became the capital of Timur and future dynasties. Timur converted Samarqand into a city that would inspire awe and was ranked amongst the richest cities along the Silk Road for a long time.[39] In present day Uzbekistan it still enjoys an important position both for its architecture and its economic and cultural currency.

These policies continued under Qaidu's successor, Du'a. The restoration of Turkistan, Ferghana and Andijan was underway: '… where the development of a flourishing entrepot is implicit in the reference to separate quarters for each of the various ethnic groups'.[40] Andijan continued to prosper throughout the next century and was directed toward the well-being of the sedentary population; but the fact that it lay between the prosperous regions of Jand, Talas and Samarqand might also give an idea of the parts of the Silk Road which were being used in Central Asia in the late thirteenth century.[41] Khwarazm had revived its agricultural production by the fourteenth century, along with Sighnaq and Sawran which became Orda's headquarters. The Chaghatais built Urgench where Gurganj had been and it remains an important city for commerce even today in present day Uzbekistan. Garganj and Khiva were important cities that connected to Bukhara and Samarqand, and onwards to the Caspian and Volga, even under the Khwarezmshah.[42] Khiva was also connected to Hindustan, Tangut territory, Afghanistan and China. Almaliq gained prominence under Du'a once again and became an important city on the trade route through Qara Qocho and on to Beijing and the rest of China. The city also attracted religious building activity and a bishopric was founded there in the 1320s.[43] Kebek instituted reforms to stabilise Central Asia after years of internal warfare between the Ogedeid princes and the Chaghataid princes. The reforms after the 1320s clearly indicate his intentions of reviving cities in Transoxiana through restoration of agriculture and urban centres; trade; administrative re-division along Mongol *tumens*; and redistribution of appanages in the region. He built Qarshi[44] near Nahshab with a fortress which looked toward Khurasan and India, of interest for further expansion to the Central Asian Mongols since at least the 1290s.[45] Qarshi was built along traditional Xiong-nu style and was a place where Chaghataid Khans were buried, including Kebek.[46] Under Kebek other reforms were also instituted especially in the monetary system. He was the first Khan to mint coins in his name. As a result, there was development and reconstruction of cities which usually followed minting of coins in various cities like Andijan, Osh, Bolad, Kashgar and Almaliq to name a few. Further examples include Balkh, Khurasan and Iraq-i Ajam which attained previous levels of prosperity very quickly.

The picture that emerges from this period through careful examination of sources is that Central Asia was no backwater under Qaidu and even the general impression that the Central Asian Mongols were constantly at war with other Khanates and stopped all trade is not accurate. Qaidu's policies and even his wars of conquest were directed toward consolidating his domains which he accomplished by following established Mongol nomadic ways.[47] He had a Central Asian governor (Masud Beg), an eye on trade (local and regional), had instituted monetary policies especially minting coins across cities of Central Asia which drove commercial interaction and paid attention to the growth of cities, whether by supporting trading activities or through workshops and building activities. His immediate successor, Du'a, went even further by negotiating peace with Yuan China which led to a resurgence of trade and exchanges through Central Asia. A further side note to building capital cities is that we should not forget that the Chaghatais continued to have mobile courts and often set up camp outside cities, and that the nomadic Mongols continued to find innovative ways to engage with Eurasia, nomadic and sedentary, while still continuing nomadic practices.[48] The Mongol period was followed by the Timurids which was modelled on Chinggis' Empire and was a period of growth and prosperity in Central Asia, with Samarqand as Timur's glorious capital. In the final judgement of the Mongol century in Eurasia the development and creation of a unified Eurasia deserves special mention and careful analysis.

Ilkhanate cities

The campaign of Iran and Iraq was swift and a prime example of a truly Mongol effort. Hulegu's army was made up of troops from Mongolia, Turkistan and the region of the Golden Horde. There were technical specialist experts at siege warfare from China, the Berkin tribe from the Mongolian steppe which was famous for its mountaineering skills were used against the Ismailis and the army received food from Georgia, Armenia and Central Asia. This campaign was the culmination of Mongol efforts to marshal resources from across Eurasia.[49] The prize was the fall of the Caliphate and access to the resources and trade nodes in the Middle East which brought the Mongols even greater prosperity. As a result of its important position in the Mediterranean trade network at the heart of Islamic lands, the cities were prosperous and promised huge rewards. As in other parts of Eurasia, reconstruction was begun almost immediately after conquest to great success. Buildings in Baghdad were ordered to be restored almost immediately after 1258. Even the libraries of Baghdad survived with accounts of Muslims from Mamluk Egypt journeying there. Khwandmir reports that under the governorship of Khwaja Shamsuddin Muhammd who was appointed by Hulegu, Baghdad began to flourish again, and a sum of 100,000 dinars was allocated for the construction of canals in Najaf among other projects of reconstruction such as bridges and water works throughout the region.[50] So much so that Baghdad created manuscript painting and was a centre of this kind of art form by the 1290s. It continued to serve as a regional centre for trade.

Tabriz was the capital of the northern and eastern territories of Iran under the Mongols as early as the 1230s. Its access to fresh water from Lake Urmiya provided it with enough pastureland, an essential requirement for the Mongol pastoralists and for the armies.[51] It was also at the centre of the east-west caravan routes on the Silk Road. This is where products and merchants from the Caucasus and the Eurasian steppe, forests in the north via Derbend and in the south from the Indian Ocean found their terminus.[52] The revenues from Tabriz were at their peak under the Mongols, and gold and silver measures were standardised as per standards in Tabriz across the Ilkhanate. It was the centre of the Ilkhanate which stretched from the Oxus to Egypt. Italian and European merchants called Tabriz the greatest city in the world because of its location at the crossroads of continental routes. Under Hulegu, Tabriz underwent massive growth and had a colony of Venetian merchants as early as 1263. Under Ghazan Khan and Oljeitu, his immediate successor, Tabriz and other parts of Ilkhanate Persia saw further building of trade infrastructure. Ghazan established a city called Ghazaniya in Tabriz which had *caravansarais*, shops, markets, customs-posts, etc. and became a city which attracted merchants and people alike very quickly.[53] There were 24 *caravansarais*, 1500 shops and countless artisan workshops built in Tabriz.[54] It served as a market for goods from India, Baghdad, Mosul and Hormuz and was frequented by merchants across Eurasia as well as further west from Europe, especially Italians (Genoese and Venetians). Travel between Rome and Tabriz by 1300 was relatively easy and many Mongol Christians travelled to Rome.

Mongol Eurasia connected and allowed merchants, religious leaders and missionaries to travel with ease which led to both a fostering of commercial enterprise but also social connections.[55] For the period between 1290–1340 Tabriz was the most important city for Italian merchants made possible by the presence of the Mongols.[56] As a multi-ethnic city (with Armenians, Nestorians, Jacobites, Georgians, Persians and Tabrizis),[57] it was easy for merchants to be able to communicate and find co-ethnics and co-religionists which in the overall scheme of things helped increase the number of merchants who frequented and made Tabriz a vibrant and exciting city. The city referred to as Rab-i-Rashidi in the suburbs of Tabriz built by Rashid al-Din became a famous centre for scholars and physicians of various ethnicities to interact together, and became the leading centre of Eurasian cultural exchanges, among them medicine, art and literature, in Mongol Ilkhanate.[58] Another city in the suburbs of Tabriz was Maraghah which was chosen as the place to build an observatory by Hulegu who supported the sciences and astronomy. At the behest of Hulegu, many buildings, libraries and the famed observatory were built after 1260 under the directorship of Nasr al-Din Tusi. What followed was a whole new collaborative work between Muslim and Chinese astronomers and scientists, and led to leaps forward in the understanding of astronomical studies in both China and Iran.[59] There were other intimate connections with China as well; Quangzhou in China has gravestones of merchants and craftsmen from Tabriz dating to the early fourteenth century. Persians were found in significant numbers in China,[60] and Persian served as a lingua franca across the Silk Roads, both on land and at sea.[61] Tabriz was an essential part of the Yuan-Ilkhan exchange throughout the Mongol period.

Kashan, a major centre of ceramic production, experienced a resurgence after 1261, and pottery and different kinds of ceramics enjoyed a special position in the Ilkhanate court driven entirely by Mongol demands. In addition to the revival of Kashan's industry, the spread of pottery-making techniques across Mongol Eurasia, especially underglaze painting and the *Sultanabad* style of painting, can also be attributed to Mongol practices:[62] '… Kashan continued to be a major, if not the predominant centre.'[63] Even in pre-Mongol times the spread of pottery-making techniques was common, and after a brief disruption of 15 years, from 1261 onwards these exchanges were not only possible but had further impetus from the establishment of Mongol Eurasia. There were exchanges not only eastward as before, but westward to the Golden Horde where excavations have revealed the use of painting techniques borrowed from the Ilkhanate region. This points to a movement of artists from the Ilkhanate to the Golden Horde, not just Chinese and Persian artists and artisans going back and forth from 'friendly' Mongol regions, but further westward as well.

In addition, the creation of new Hormuz and the thriving port of Kish were also given impetus by Mongol presence in the region. Old Hormuz was abandoned in 1300 and instead the population inhabited the island of Jarun. Kish and Hormuz competed against each other for traffic from the Indian Ocean through the Persian Gulf. While their fortunes went up and down, Kish did very well under the Ilkhans as the main port for goods in the Yuan-Ilkhan connection, and was a hub for goods coming from Arabia and the Indian Ocean. Its fortunes suffered after 1330–1331 when the Ilkhanate was in decline. While Hormuz did well after the the demise of Ilkhans, modern day Kish is an important tourist destination and free trading area in Iran.[64] Ardabil, Ganja, Erzurum, Rayy, Isfahan and eventually Qum were all reconstructed and revived.[65]

Golden Horde

The Golden Horde created new routes and avenues which could bypass troubled areas. Their efforts fostered the birth of new cities and production centres along the northern route of the Silk Road. The Golden Horde did not lie directly on the Silk Road, and thus had to find ways to connect to the larger network of the route in order to be able to earn revenue from mercantile activity. For this reason, the Golden Horde created and founded many towns as craft and supply centres.[66] Golden Horde cities included Sarai, New Sarai, Astrakhan, Urgench, Caffa, Qiram and Machar, which have all been described by Ibn Battuta as flourishing centres of craftsmen, merchants, markets and generally prosperous and safe well into the fourteenth century.[67] They are also attributed with the founding of many small towns as centres of production.[68] As mentioned previously Muscovy became an important city because of its association with Sarai, and port cities on the Black Sea became important trading centres. In addition, Novogorod, Tver, Ustung and Nizhnii Novogorod all continued to be prosperous and grow as a result of burgeoning international trade under the Mongols. Even Kiev which was described by Carpini as having been reduced to nothing is later said to have been visited by many merchants, pointing to either a quick revival or an exaggeration of its complete initial destruction.[69] It has also been argued that the decline of Kiev may have already begun before the arrival of the Mongols and its conquest by the Mongols led to its displacement by Muscovy.[70] Halperin calls the Russian demographic decline under the Mongols and the urbanisation of cities of Russia a paradox.[71] However, Russian cities viewed on a continuum with other Eurasian cities could give an alternative explanation. Most of the cities on the Silk Road saw some degree of revival and in many cases enjoyed prosperity under the Mongols. Consequently, the Russian cities along the Volga River were revived and enjoyed prosperity as a result of renewed trade.[72] The unification of Russia and the surrounding regions was a direct consequence of the creation of the Golden Horde. It forced the grand princes to ally and become vassals to the Mongols which joined the western edges of Asia with the rest of Eurasia. The natural connections of Eurasia once guaranteed by the Mongols made commercial activity and markets much more accessible. The Mongols opened up the south, southeast and parts of the southwest to Russian trade.[73] Commercial activity took the form of both inter- and intra-regional interactions under the tutelage and demands of the Mongol Khans. The interconnections along the Silk Road were brought into stark relief through the creation of Mongol Eurasia.

The Golden Horde promoted trade with Poland-Lithuania, the Hanseatic League, Egypt, Syria, Byzantium, the maritime nations of Genoa and Venice,

Persia and Central Asia.[74] This was no small feat taken by any standards, past or present. Trade between Turkistan and the Eastern Mediterranean was in large part a consequence of the policies of the Mongols. By bringing the region of Russia firmly into the orbit of international trade, the Golden Horde fostered a resurgence of the economy in the larger Russian region and has on occasion been ascribed with providing the momentum for the growth of Russian power in the future. They were in control of the trade of furs and slaves from the Pontic steppe to the Mamluks, a major source of revenue for them.[75] The Eastern Slavic region and the Pontic steppe were already integral to trade in the region but with the arrival of the Mongols they were connected with more lucrative markets and additionally the Mongols created new markets for goods for consumption and trade. Cities like Novogorod, Tver and later even Muscovy could make huge profits from mercantile activities because merchants were able to travel and participate in much larger markets than before; they were now part of the caravan continental trade routes. Russia was connected with China and Persia through a network of Mongol courts along the way, and through Central Asia, historically the lifeblood of the Silk Road.

According to Morgan, '[Arguably] the major lasting Mongol legacies were the rise of the previously not important city of Moscow …'.[76] In the Golden Horde, the Khan passed on the responsibility of collecting taxes to the Muscovy princes. The Khan bestowed the title of Grand Prince and that office gave the holder authority and power over other princes in Rus.[77] Moscow benefitted in at least two ways from Mongol presence in the region, first because the Mongols weakened the traditional bearers of power in the region, refugees from surrounding cities came to Moscow and this in turn increased the population of the city; second, the Mongols' administrative structure which the Muscovites later borrowed, provided them with a sophisticated taxation and administrative system which helped fill up their coffers.[78] Communications within Russia even after the Mongols depended on the *jam* system. During the period of Golden Horde rule, the Muscovite princes managed to outmanoeuvre Tver for a favoured position with the Khan in Sarai and remained important from the fourteenth century, later going on to unify Russia. Muscovite princes also sent troops on Mongol campaigns which gave them a share of the loot.[79] With the shift away from Novogorod as a transit route, Moscow and Ustung became hubs through which the fur trade was carried out. While Novogorod did not enjoy the same preferential treatment as Muscovy did, it retained its positon, especially in the trade with the West. Since, Alexander Nevskii submitted peacefully, Novogorod was not sacked and continued to flourish throughout the thirteenth and fourteenth centuries. It remained the entry point into Russia for the Hanseatic League merchants and had monopoly over Baltic trade.[80]

Among the cities built by the Mongols, Sarai occupies a special place. It was built on the Lower Volga, near Astrakhan and has been referred to as a 'travelling city'. William of Rubruck described Sarai as a bustling city which was always followed by *bazaars*. The trade along the caravan routes east and south of Sarai was bigger than trade going through even Russia at that time.[81]

Important cities in the Golden Horde connected to Sarai including the Bulgars who were important merchants in this region.[82] The city was enlarged and came to be referred to as New Sarai under Batu's successor, Berke, who ordered mosques and buildings to be constructed according to the Egyptian style and the city grew rich as a result of being the capital of the Golden Horde and a centre of mercantile activity.[83] Russian princes along with all other vassals of the Golden Horde in the thirteenth century had to travel to Sarai to pay allegiance and give tribute to the Mongols. Sarai came to represent the centre of fur trade and was frequented by travellers and merchants from the west and the east. John of Carpini, William of Rubruck and later Genoese merchants along with Pegolotti all traversed across the Golden Horde, paying homage to the Khan and moving deeper into Eurasian territory. Ibn Battuta travelling from Egypt described and verified Pegolotti's assertions about prosperous cities of the Golden Horde in the fourteenth century; especially Berke's New Sarai which he described as prosperous, multi-cultural and full of buildings and mosques with flouring markets aplenty and safely connected to Urgench in Central Asia which was under the Chaghatais in the fourteenth century.[84] Archaeological evidence from Sarai and New Sarai reveal a high level of urbanisation with influences from Iran, Egypt and Syria.[85]

The cities on Crimea were the result of the development of the Black Sea trade and led to new players like the Genoese and the Venetians who entered Mongol controlled transcontinental trade. The opening of this trade route gave merchants access to Khwarezmian markets which were part of the Golden Horde and through them to China which allowed for both the Mamluks and the Southern Europeans to predominantly partake in the slave trade but also to other goods and products which were sourced from the Orient and in demand in Europe. For these reasons, the Genoese and the Venetians along with other Italian and Catalan towns got involved in overland trade, especially after 1291 when Acre fell to the Mamluks and signalled embargoes on trade with Muslim countries. The Genoese benefitted greatly despite paying huge penalties and taking huge risks in going against papal embargoes in trading with the Mamluks. The Ilkhans and the Golden Horde, through their activities and control of the slave trade essential to the Mamluk state, created conditions in which the Genoese became the forerunners in trade going westward from Mongol domains. The Genoese traders were allowed to establish trading stations in Soldaia (1274), merchant quarters in Caffa and Tabriz and consulates in cities like Sivas. A number of documents ranging from: *yarlighs* (edicts), *otul* (application requests) and *yop* (endorsement of request) were given to traders in the Golden Horde. In addition, Tana and Caffa were given immunity charters which encouraged trade with the Golden Horde.[86] The Genoese were allowed to operate from Soldaia and were charged a fixed rate of three per cent of the value of the merchandise, less than other merchants, especially the Venetians. Even in the 1380s when the Genoese were quite powerful, they still sought treaties with the Golden Horde to keep operating in the Crimea.[87] The Genoese were involved with the slave trade from the Golden Horde to Alexandria, and enjoyed a position of pre-eminence in the Straits and on the Black Sea. They had relationships with both the Ilkhans and the Golden Horde since the 1280s. The papal embargoes against trading with the Mamluks after the fall of Acre in 1291 may have prompted the Genoese to increase their presence in transcontinental trade going through Mongol domains. Venetians were also involved with trade with the Mongols, especially the Ilkhans and there were Venetian colonies in Tabriz throughout the end of the thirteenth and early fourteenth centuries.[88] Under Janibeg of the Golden Horde, the Venetians finally returned to the Crimea and replaced the Genoese in Soldaia and Solkhat, in exchange for two per cent to three per cent import tax,[89] later raised to five per cent. In 1265 the Genoese traders got privileges to operate in the Mongol realm and soon had trading posts in Caffa and Sudak.[90] In the wars between the maritime nations of Venice and Genoa, control over the Black Sea trade was a point of contention and points to the importance of this trade route.

As a consequence, cities like Caffa experienced their golden age in the thirteenth and fourteenth centuries because of their interaction with the Golden Horde.[91] An insignificant port city, by the end of the thirteenth century Caffa attained the position of most important port on the northern Black Sea trade route; one of the key developments of Eurasian trade under the Golden Horde in Mongol Eurasia.[92] By 1316, eye witness accounts from travellers reported Caffa as a sprawling town and fortified city with a harbour which could accommodate 200 ships.[93] It was an important port for the West as it exported grain from across Eurasia into Europe.[94] The city of Tana at the mouth of the Don was also an important city for the Genoese and was the easternmost trading port in the Black Sea. It was a hub for goods arriving from the Eurasian steppe, forests and caravans arriving from Transoxiana and Khwarezm.[95] Venetians also set up a colony in Tana and were involved with collecting taxes and the local bureaucracy. The hides that the Venetians bought in the Golden Horde were essential for Venetians to become the hub of leather manufacturing for Europe, something they are famous for still. The sea trade of Genoese merchants in 1293 was three times larger than the revenue of the Kingdom of France in the same period.[96] The Genoese not only had quarters in Tabriz and Caffa but had a consulate in Sivas as well.[97] The flourishing of Black Sea trade sparked a whole new trade route which impacted new players and brought Europeans much closer to the action in Eurasia. Famous cities of Italy today – Venice and Florence – and Black Sea cities – Caffa, Tana and Soldaia – saw increased activity and prosperity in response to the routes created by the Mongols. There is little doubt as to their global presence today which is intimately connected with their importance in Eurasian trade in partnership with the Mongols.

The rise and fall of the golden period of Siena also coincided with Mongol power.[98] Siena and Venice, rivals in Italy, continued to play significant roles in trade with the Golden Horde. When Siena managed to push Venice out of Crimea, Venetians set up colonies in Tana. Under Mengu-Temur (1267–1280) Italian colonies of Crimea were founded.[99] Siena at the western end of the Mongol realm participated in Mongol Eurasian trade. The trade not only delivered textiles but also led to movement of labour which even included women artisans who were involved in the production of the Tatar cloth, *nasij*. These women artisans found themselves in production centres in China and Persia which were manufacturing hubs in Mongol Eurasia.[100] Sienese ways of political thinking and governance have also been linked to their interaction with Mongol Eurasia which is said to have brought openness and inclusiveness in their domains.[101] In comparison with other art in Italy, art in Siena often used Persian and Chinese motifs from their interaction with the Ilkahante which after 1260 was intimately involved with Mediterranean trade and had cultural interactions with Syria and the Mamluks along with Tuscany, Florence, etc.[102] Italian art at the time included various elements of Mongol Eurasian features, from motifs to dancers and other symbols which were incorporated by artists in frescos and other cultural representations. Franciscan Spirituals ascribed softer images to the Mongols which indicated the Mongol tolerance of religions, especially when compared with the policies of the Pope who was restrictive with other religions and within Christendom.[103] Cultural renditions of the period put Siena at the centre of a world which was inhabited by relations and influences from Mongol Eurasia as much as with relations with Northern Italy and other parts of the Mediterranean.

Yuan China

The destruction of Northern China by the Mongols has been discussed at length by historians and authors, including the adverse effects on a severely depleted population. Over time these claims have been qualified with errors in census taking and other problems in discerning actual figures. There is no doubt that Northern China went through a period of hardship but after 1260 with Qubilai Khan elected as *Qaghan*, cities of Northern China underwent a period of rapid recovery. The inclusion of officials and bureaucrats from across Eurasia into China reflected a comprehensive plan for economic and political administration of China under the Mongols. As a sedentary society which was predominantly agricultural, Qubilai instituted policies to renew agriculture in his domains which included a series of reforms and tax reliefs for peasants who were given sops and exemptions. Along with tax rebates, infrastructure for storage (58 granaries were constructed) and cessation of agricultural lands for grazing of animals which belonged to nomads were significant measures toward reconstruction and rehabilitation of all sectors of the economy.[104] Peasants whose mulberry trees and silkworms had been destroyed in natural disasters in 1261 were also given tax exemptions. An important organisation introduced by Qubilai in 1271 was the institution of *she* which organised peasants into 50 households under the supervision of Chinese officials and created rewards for increased production. It also helped with the education of children of peasants and even set up charity granaries to help families in hard times.[105] Yunnan province also saw development under the Mongols. A southwestern province of China with a largely Muslim population, under the governance of Sayyad Ajall Shams al-Din, it saw recovery of agriculture, forestry and ordered irrigation projects which were developed there and are still in use today. Trade was improved and traditional cowry shells from the region began to be traded in the wider region.[106] The prosperity of cities can also be linked with the development of industry and art. The Mongols settled artisans and other skilled craftsmen across Eurasia for the establishment of workshops and markets. These population movements helped the rise of cities and towns across Eurasia. An aspect related to this is the development of drama in Chinese cities under Qubilai which further provides evidence of the efforts of the Mongols towards comprehensive development. According to Rossabi, '[T]he Yuan was indeed a period of flourishing cities and for many Chinese the Yuan drama was the apogee of Chinese theatre'.[107] As part of building activity in the Yuan, the construction of theatres and the profession of actors took on a whole new dimension, with the writing of various plays under Qubilai's patronage. Mongol patronage of the arts further points to the development of urban centres and steps away from a heavily military discourse on the impact and legacy of the Mongols.

The capital cities of the *Qaghan* did exceedingly well as their growth was guaranteed by the establishment of the Mongol court and the presence of the person of the *Qaghan.* Among them Khan Baligh and Beijing deserve special mention. Qubilai was first sent to Northern China by his brother Mongke in the 1250s. Qubilai set up his summer residence in Khan Baligh (Shangdu, Jandgdu, Xanadu) which was built according to positive omens on the site of an older capital which had enjoyed prosperity.[108] Qubilai's winter capital, Beijing, gained prominence on a grand scale as a consequence of his policies. After the Yuan, other than a short period of 50 years, it has remained the centre of political activity in China. Qubilai Khan commissioned a Muslim engineer to build Beijing in 1265 and made it his winter capital. Rashid al-Din in his description of Beijing calls it a populous city with innumerable towers and buildings. It was referred to as the *Great Capital* by Marco Polo with the palace of Qubilai. It had numerous fruit and gardens,[109] was a commercial hub for the north and was home to a large population. Qubilai chose this city, more north than other Chinese capitals of the past, due to its relative closeness to Mongolia.

Other than cities, Qubilai extended the Grand Canal in order to secure the supply of food and water for Beijing, which spurred the growth of cities along the way.[110] The rivers around Khan Baligh and Beijing were both expanded and received goods from cities like Zaitun, Machin and Khingsang via ships. Qubilai even built a highway from the canal to Machin which was paved all the way along and made transport of goods much easier. The 40-day route was fully populated and Qubilai built villages, temples and markets to make the road attractive, accessible and convenient.[111] His successor, Temur Qaghan (1291–1307), built another summer capital in Kemin Fu which was near Beijing. Kemin-Fu was connected to hunting grounds, nearby cities of Simali (inhabited and built by Samarqandis) and generally enjoyed favour of the *Qaghan* and the general population.[112] Cities in and around Honan, modern day Peking and Hohsi, were given tax exemptions when paper money was introduced to relieve some of the hardships caused by warfare and natural disasters in 1261–1262. In general, the Mongol army and administration was restrained by Qubilai Khan in its demands for revenues and labour in order to rehabilitate the economy.[113] In addition to the main cities, garrison cities sprung up in Northern China especially during the conflict with the Central Asian Mongols under Qaidu in the 1280s. These towns were fortifications which came up as a way to defend Qara Qorum and other important cities along with postal stations which were being targeted by Qaidu and his forces. The garrison cities housed permanent troops and led to the establishment of military-agricultural colonies with access to organised grain supply routes. Predominantly used for defence, these garrisons also served to initiate attacks against the Central Asian Mongols.[114]

Grand Canal Cities in Yuan China

The costs and hurdles to maintain the Grand Canal which dated back to the seventh century were huge and the Mongols often suffered losses, but they tried to build connections for China's north-south trade by extending it to Beijing. However, Qubilai's refurbishment of the Grand Canal provided the necessary infrastructure for connecting Northern and Southern China into an integrated region.[115] The main commercial hubs in Yuan China were centred on the transport of goods from north to south via the Grand Canal which received a lot of attention from Qubilai Khan. Provinces of Jiangnang, Jiangxi and Linqing were commissioned with workshops and continued to play an important role throughout the Yuan and Ming periods. Linqing represented the northern most terminal on the Grand Canal and became the '… link between the southern economy and the northern state'.[116] Once it gained prominence under the Yuan, it remained important, merchants collected licences there and it became one of two preferred routes for transporting gran from the south to the north.[117] Eventually Linqing became a sub-prefecture in 1489 indicating its rise as an important city. Artisans flocked there from the Chenghua area to produce tiles and bricks for projects in Beijing. The Grand Canal was a waterway and Linqing became a hub of ship building, ferries and other boats as well as textile merchants who built shops there.[118] Linqing along with four other cities was made into a government granary where grain from all over the southern provinces was brought to be stored. Jiangdezhen in Jiangxi served as the centre for porcelain production under the Yuan.

In general, Qubilai's attention to maritime trade was a response to the inclusion of the Southern Sung to his domains, though it has also been understood as an alternative way to compensate for loss of trade through Central Asia. The need for recovery of the Sung domains included the same measures which had been used in the north. These measures included the creation of *she*, agricultural households; tax exemptions and waivers; and an impetus for maritime commerce for which various superintendencies were established.[119] The Mongol presence in Northern China had already caused migration to the maritime provinces of Southeast China which came to house half of the Chinese population. As a result, the six Maritime Provinces grew in size and attracted attention from Qubilai after 1279, especially since two-thirds of the tax-paying population of China came to reside there.[120] Hangchow, a port city, which grew to prominence and became part of an integrated system under the Mongols, owed its increased status and prosperity to the unification of China under the Yuan. It attracted foreign merchants, established markets with abundant kinds of products and has been variously described as one of the jewels of China and a remarkable city with a huge population. It housed artisans, manufacturers and ten markets across the city. The merchant cities were rich and prosperous and had Chinese and Muslim merchants as well as those of other ethnic affiliations. In the 1340s, Ibn Battuta reports people of various professions residing in the city, from carpenters to seamen, caulkers, archers and footsoldiers.[121] Along with Hangchow, the port city of Ch'uan-chou also did exceedingly well, aided in part by connections with cities like Te-hsing, An-fu, Te-hua and Ching-te-chen which served as important sites of ceramic production and exported their wares to Ilkhanate Persia and to the southeast from here.[122]

Summary

To summarise then, the Silk Road under the Mongols experienced a golden age. The reconstruction of the cities on the Silk Road began as soon as the period of conquest was over. Trade was important and was a main source of revenue for the Mongols. It was essential to have stability across caravan routes which were connected over long distances across Eurasia. The Mongols spurred production through creating demand, provisioning for workshops and establishing markets which required a general level of safety across the region. In addition, they also created new routes and thus gave birth to new cities and commercial hubs as per their own vision and necessities. The demand for pasturelands for grazing animals as well as hunting and other nomadic pursuits gave rise to capital cities in the Caucasus, in outlying regions near cities like Baghdad, Beijing and Almaliq. The presence of numerous big and small Mongol courts allowed for a proliferation of production centres which gave rise to markets and created more spaces for mercantile activity which furthered urbanisation. These conditions gave rise to urban centres and spurred reconstruction efforts of those centres which had been impacted in times of conquest and war. As mentioned above Eurasian cities of note in China, Central Asia, Persia and the Caucasus and further afield closer to Europe all saw mushrooming and growth. The destruction caused by the Mongols did indeed lead to certain cities falling into disrepair, however, this is also true of other empires and states and not only in medieval times but in the present day as well.

Mongol impact on world history has been a work in progress. The last decade or so has seen strides by various scholars on subjects ranging from trade (commodity exchange), technology, art and printing, along with the legacy of Mongol rule in China, Iran, Iraq, Central Asia and Russia, not to mention their rivals in Egypt, Syria, India and Japan. David Morgan's overview of the political implications of Mongol rule in the unification of Russia and China, and the shaping of their national identity, is a fascinating observation on the overall global impact on two of the world's most important economies today.[123] Central Asia can trace its various tribal groupings to Chingissid times. Whether it was Timur or the later Shaybanids and the Kazakh Khanates, they all owed their legitimacy to Chinggis Khan and his *yasaq*. The impact of the Mongols on the Arab and Persian Middle East and Central Asia is undeniable. Japan, India and parts of the southeast of Asia were also differently impacted by the creation of Mongol Eurasia. The inclusion of Italian maritime empires in Eurasian trade gave rise to an increase in Europe's knowledge of the world and gave rise to the first moment of contact between China and Europe.[124] A study of the Mongol period can go a long way towards understanding the historical context of Eurasia as it is shaping up today. The next chapter delves into trade and economic relations in Mongol Eurasia and helps paint a picture of the multiplicity of ways in which the Mongols impacted trade from the kinds of commodities being exchanged, to the discovery and use of new routes, co-opting and forming relationships with new groups even beyond the immediate Eurasian region and how the internal conditions of the Mongol Khanates in large part defined those modes and kinds of exchanges.

Notes

1 Morgan 2006, p. 426
2 Masuya 2013, p. 248
3 Cunliffe 2015, p. 425
4 Jackson 2017, p. 222
5 Kaplonski 2000, p. 257
6 Biran 2013, p. 271
7 Biran 2013, p. 270
8 Jackson 2017, p. 208
9 Carr 2015, pp. 127–128
10 Allsen 2001, pp. 122 and 126
11 Jackson 2009, p. 57
12 Allsen 2001, p. 140
13 Jackson 2017, p. 416
14 Rachewiltz 2004, p. 988
15 Ratchnevsky 1991, pp. 99–100
16 Kaplonski 2000, p. 268
17 Biran 2013, p. 265
18 Biran 1997, p. 103
19 Biran 1997, p. 109
20 Jackson 2017, p. 218
21 Jackson 2017, p. 219
22 Biran 2013, p. 261
23 Biran 2013, p. 265
24 Biran 2013, p. 269
25 Adshead 1993, p. 94
26 Biran 1997, pp. 102–103
27 Biran 2013, p. 262

28 Hookham 1962, p. 36
29 Biran 2013, pp. 263–268
30 Yellow court
31 Biran 1997, p. 97
32 Biran 1997, p. 110
33 Hookham 1962, p. 36
34 Biran 1997, p. 110
35 Boyle 1971, p. 261
36 Hookham 1962, p. 40
37 Bretschneider 2000, (Vol. II) p. 58
38 Abu-Lughod 1989, pp. 157, 180
39 Biran 2013, p. 279
40 Jackson 2017, p. 207
41 Biran 1997, p. 105
42 Cunliffe 2015, p. 421
43 Biran 2013, p. 270
44 Bretschnieder 2000, (Vol. II) p. 61
45 Jackson 2009, p. 57
46 Biran 2013, p. 272
47 Biran 1997, p. 105
48 Biran 2013, p. 273
49 Allsen 1987, pp. 219–220
50 Thackston 2012b, p. 59
51 Rossabi 2010, p. 98
52 Ciociltan 2012, p. 49
53 Hambly 1969, p. 113
54 Ciociltan 2012, p. 136
55 Praznik 2010, p. 185
56 Di Cosmo 2005, p. 403
57 Ciociltan 2012, p. 48
58 Allsen 2001, p. 144
59 Allsen 2001, pp. 162–163
60 Rossabi 2010, pp. 101–102
61 Yingsheng 2010, p. 95
62 Watson 2006, p. 342
63 Watson 2006, p. 345
64 Kauz 2006, pp. 51, 67
65 Jackson 2017, pp. 178–179
66 Jackson 2017, p. 207
67 Hambly 1969, p. 120
68 Jackson 2017, p. 207
69 Kaplonski 2000, p. 258
70 Kaplonski 2000, p. 266
71 Halperin 1985, p. 84
72 Halperin 1985, pp. 85–86
73 Ischoboldin 1973, p. 16
74 Halperin 1985, p. 28
75 Ciociltan 2012, p. 46
76 Morgan 2006, p. 434
77 Vasary 2009, p. 79
78 Halperin 1985, pp. 89–90
79 Halperin 1985, p. 78
80 Halperin 1985, p. 81
81 Halperin 1985, p. 30

82 Jackson 2017, p. 216
83 Marshall 1994, pp. 201–202
84 Ciociltan 2012, p. 110
85 Hambly 1969, p. 118
86 Vasary 2007, pp. i, xii
87 Di Cosmo 2005, p. 396
88 Aubin 1983, p. 59
89 Ischboldin 1973, pp. 51–52
90 Martin 1978, p. 416
91 Vasary, 2009, p. 77
92 Ciociltan 2012, p. 157
93 Ciociltan 2012, pp. 183–184
94 Jackson 2017, p. 216
95 Ciociltan 2012, p. 101
96 Abu-Lughod 1989, p. 11
97 Aubin 1983, p. 57
98 Praznik 2010, p. 177
99 Vasary 2009, p. 77
100 Praznik 2010, p. 179
101 Praznik 2010, p. 188
102 Praznik 2010, p. 191
103 Praznik 2010, p. 216
104 Rossabi 1988, p. 120
105 Rossabi 1988, pp. 120–121
106 Rossabi 1988, p. 202
107 Rossabi 1988, p. 161
108 Boyle 1971, p. 274
109 Boyle 1971, pp. 274–275
110 Rossabi 1988, p. 132
111 Boyle 1971, pp. 275–276
112 Boyrle 1971, p. 276
113 Rossabi 1988, pp. 117–118
114 Biran 1997, p. 90
115 Brook 2010, pp. 110–111
116 Brook 2010, p. 113
117 Rossabi 1988, p. 189
118 Brook 2010, pp. 113–114
119 Rossabi 1988, p. 187
120 Gipouloux 2011, p. 76
121 Abu-Lughod 1989, pp. 335–340
122 Rossabi 1988, pp. 169–170
123 Morgan 2006, pp. 425–436
124 Morgan 2006, pp. 433–435

5 Trade and economic relations in Mongol Eurasia

> The Mongol conquest of China,
> most of Southwest Asia, and eastern Europe
> created a new empire of unparalleled power and extent.
> It united the eastern and western parts of Eurasia
> Into a single political order, facilitating
> the exchange of people, trade, and ideas.[1]

The previous chapters have laid out the basis of Mongol Eurasia as a geographical place and a philosophical construct. The rise of Chinggis Khan and the rise of a united Eurasia under his descendants created a unique space which relied on providing interconnections, exchanges and contact. It included disparate regions, religions, peoples and political systems. Steppe traditions, Mongol institutions, religious policies and the construction and revival of cities as political and commercial centres contributed to the Mongol endeavour in Eurasia. The Mongol transformation of Eurasia and the Silk Road remains singular, unqualified and lasting. The impact of Mongol policies on the political systems and military has already been discussed. The third aspect of the economic transformation of Eurasia under the Mongols is the focus of this chapter. The chapter is divided between a discussion on trade in the economic system of the nomads, followed by economic relations in Eurasia, between and within the Khanates based on the use of established trade networks and the creation of new routes; and finishes with a discussion of a description of the diversity of goods traded along the Silk Road under the Mongols. The network of trade relations includes the special place of manufacturing in Mongol Eurasia. The Mongols as the true heirs of steppe tradition accorded a prominent place for artisans and skilled craftsmen in all four Khanates. The tradition of amassing the skilled population in court to express majesty, honour marriages, alliances and other important social events, was an old steppe custom which was passed down to the Mongols.[2] It also helps make a much stronger case for Mongols as producers. The Mongols established a large number of workshops which earned *kingly incomes.*[3] By far, Allsen's work on *Culture and Conquest in Mongol Eurasia* and his wider research on trade under the Mongols, Yuan-Ilkhan exchanges and Mongol agency have been of the greatest help in the conceptualisation of this chapter. The attempt here is to highlight the varied and composite ways in which the Mongols attended to trade under *Mongol* unification: symbolic and physical. The unique underpinning of trade relations which looked beyond divisive lines of religion as discussed in Chapter 3 and the place of merchants in the administrative-bureaucratic complex of government analysed in Chapter 2, along with the reconstruction of cities, commercial hubs and investment in infrastructure described in the previous chapter, all point to the complex and layered relationship the Mongols had with trade. As we shall see, Mongol expansion was along the east-west trade routes and the building blocks of Mongol Eurasia were merchants, artisans and other professional people. They occupied a special place in Mongol courts and government across Eurasia. The Uyghurs of Eastern Turkistan along with other Turkic groups like Onggud and Kipchaqs were established merchant communities with access to commercial networks on the Silk Road going back centuries and it was to these people that the Mongols naturally turned as their influence expanded.

Mongol Eurasia was home to Chinggis Khan's descendants, princes and *khatuns*, along with close allies who were all stakeholders in this vast system. The commercial activities of the Mongols centred on traditional forms of pastoralism and trade. A note on pastoral nomadism is important at this point to lay the groundwork to understand the Mongolian economy. Pastoralism refers to raising livestock with migrating seasonal patterns based on the resources and availability of grassland on the steppe. The livestock included sheep, goats, horses, cattle, camels and yaks. Nomads move according to the availability of fodder and the Khans had summer and winter camps (capitals) even when they moved to sedentary regions. The steppe pastureland was common property; wealth was determined by the number of animals in the herd which were also considered private property. Winter pastures were essential and determined the number of animals which would survive over a period of time.[4] Personal wealth also included a retinue of people and troops attached to family members. As discussed in Chapters 1 and 2, the Mongols divided all wealth through the appanage system which created the notion of *corporate sovereignty* and made stakeholders and joint owners out of the Mongol Khans and imperial family.[5] In a similar way, Chinggis Khan made the soldiers in his army stakeholders in any military campaign by assigning a portion of the spoils of war to them. This created space for personal gain in the continued successes of the empire. While pastoralism was restricted to nomadic groups, with the absorption of sedentary populations the Mongols also had access to agricultural revenue and institutional frameworks were put in place to govern them. Institutions in the subject regions were set up to take censuses and register people in order to regularise taxation and accumulate knowledge of the resources of the expanding territories under the Mongols. In most cases the Mongol governors administered through local officials. In addition to the revenues from land, trade and mercantile activity was a main source of revenue and wealth for the Mongol Khans. It is not surprising, coming as they did from the steppe, that they were aware of the importance of trade. As mentioned above, nomads at the crossroads of exchange had always been the drivers and purveyors of commercial activity. The interest and intimate relationship of the Mongols and trade was only further solidified with the inclusion of merchants from Central Asia who had voluntarily submitted to the Mongols (Uyghurs, Kipchaqs) as early as 1216 and had thus become essential to the Mongol state. As the closest allies of Chinggis Khan and his descendants, merchants exercised influence on policy in lasting and impressive ways. As a consequence, the priorities of the Mongol economic system after conquest were: the resumption of trade and the revival of cities and commercial networks discussed in the previous chapter. Another important institution that played a significant role in achieving this aim was the *jam* which guaranteed free flow of information for political purposes and was vital for caravan trade on the Silk Road. As has been mentioned in Chapter 4, Mongol conquest undeniably brought destruction and stoppages in trade and movement. However, the bywords of Mongol policy in every region after conquest were *order, stability and recovery*[6] which resulted in rapid revival of cities like Bukhara, Samarqand, Merv and Almaliq discussed in the previous chapter, along with the establishment of new cities like Sarai, Hangchow, Qarshi and others which were on the main trading routes. These cities provided the necessary infrastructure in terms of markets, storage facilities and workshops for burgeoning trade relations under Mongol rule.

The Mongols established an *unprecedented transcontinental empire*[7] on the crossroads of the historic Silk Road and bolstered trade across the territory, from port cities of Italy to the extremities of Korea in ways which had never been seen before. The *Mongol worldview* and system, with individual Khans, princes and *khatuns* guaranteeing this global enterprise, created an economic community of unparalleled report. Mongols created institutions and administrative structures to ensure that trade would continue seamlessly throughout their vast territory. They offered the three most important aspects of trade, even today: 'protection, capital and market[s]'.[8] Very often the extent and impact of influence of the Mongols in the trade complex is described in terms of them only as mediators and not actors. It falls into the larger category of viewing Mongol history through a sedentary lens. It creates a hierarchy of positions and firmly places nomads in the position of the receiver and gives sedentary societies power over the nomads. However, the Mongols exemplified a political and social system which was adaptable but leaves little doubt about the instrumental role they played in the exchanges that ensued. Nomadic empires have always been at the centre of exchanges and Mongols were not exceptions to this rule. On the contrary, the Mongols expanded all kinds of exchanges and determined the nature of things which were transmitted in proactive ways. Mongol appetites determined the kind of goods that were traded. The policies they instituted magnified the volume of trade and spurred commercial activity in innumerable regions of Eurasia. The variety and scale on which commodities were produced, consumed and circulated under the Mongols was unparalleled.[9] While it is difficult to comment on exact figures, there is evidence of large volumes being traded. For example: a fire in Baghdad is said to have led to the destruction of 'Chinese cloth and wares valued at 100 tuman'.[10] Others similarly point to *substantial* volumes passing through Mongol domains. The conveyance of this kind was not limited to trade, resources for conquest and development followed a similar pattern. The Mongols were able to impact movement across Eurasia in multifarious ways. So much so that under Mongke in the 1250s, for instance, '[M]anpower, economic resources, or technological know-how available in one part of the domain could promptly be mobilized and deployed to meet a need in some other part of the far-flung empire'.[11] The Mongols with their conquest of all of Eurasia were able to convert this geographical landscape into a macro-economy of unmatched influence. They not only marshalled a variety of Eurasian communities to participate in trade across the continent but also engaged with Christians and others from further afield who had limited access to Eurasia. In this way, the Mongol complex was served by an elaborate structure of political, social and economic ties.

As remarkable as the overland trade was under the Mongols, there was also maritime trade which attracted the resources of the Khans. Mongols of Yuan, the Golden Horde and the Ilkhanate all played a significant role in encouraging maritime trade in their regions. Mongols' efforts at overland trade through their building of Mongol Eurasia into an interconnected region should not discount their role in maritime trade of the period. Sea trade was significant in the thirteenth and fourteenth centuries.[12] According to Martinez the three major routes for trade which were all heavily used under the Mongols were as follows: the first was maritime and under Mamluk control through Egypt but was part of the Golden Horde network because of good relations between them; the second an overland trade route which connected through the Persian Gulf and was under the Ilkhans; and lastly, the Mongol Silk Road which connected Eurasia to China and India through Central Asia, Golden Horde and Ilkhanate Persia.[13] Chinese shipbuilding techniques including the invention of the magnetic compass and the fixed stern rudder,[14] especially in Southern Sung were well developed, and trade on the South China Sea, Indian Ocean all the way to the African coast passing through the Red Sea and the Persian Gulf was all possible and was taking place.[15] In addition to maritime trade in the South China Sea and the Mediterranean, the Golden Horde stimulated Black Sea trade and encouraged Volga River trade. If anything, the opening of the Black Sea route by the Golden Horde which connected China with the Mediterranean was one of the most significant aspects of the Silk Road under the Mongols.[16] For the Ilkhanate, trading with Yuan China, the ports of Hormuz and Kish were of prime importance especially in times of hostilities with the Mongols of Central Asia.[17] Qubilai Khan invested time and effort in securing access to grain for Beijing through the Grand Canal. The Mongols, as has been discussed in previous chapters, never destroyed anything completely, especially in matters regarding economic and mercantile activities. The language of competition between overland and maritime trade which is part of any discussion about European hegemony in the East was not as clear-cut under the Mongols. On the contrary, even during the time of the so-called *dark ages* in Central Asia, trade continued and even increased between Central

Asia and China.[18] The fur trade on the northern Silk Road also increased.[19] The binary understanding from the way latter day Europeans participated in trade with Asia does not accurately tap into the complexity of the relationships which existed in Eurasia. The Mongols responded in a variety of ways to the conditions that existed and arose and the development of waterways was another strategy which was in use. In addition, as with all other resources that they came to control, the navies of China and Persia gave them access to markets and technologies which they put to use in efficient ways.

The Mongols were not remiss in creating a commiserate system which could respond to the disparate regions and goods flying across Eurasia in the thirteenth century. Nomads had been interacting with sedentary societies for centuries and that historical experience in combination with the knowledge of merchants who were central to the Mongol enterprise made regularising exchanges a fairly accessible task. Regularising commercial interaction was at the forefront of these endeavours and was achieved by Mongke in the 1250s under the governorship of Mahmad Yalavac. Under Mongke, all regional Khanates had a reserve to transact government business and guarantee payments. It will come as no surprise to anyone that silk was the most convertible currency on the Silk Road and was used as a stop gap measure between different currencies. Other than fabrics, the two main currencies in circulation in Mongol Eurasia were: coins and paper money. While coins were popular in Central Asia and the Middle East, Yuan China dealt predominantly in paper money. Beginning in the 1250s the coinage in Central Asia was expanded by increasing the number of places where coins could be minted. Mints were established in Herat, Bukhara, Utrar, Mosul and parts of the Transcaucasus region.[20] China was unable to supply as much silver and thus paper money was almost exclusively used for all economic transactions. Qubilai Khan fixed the paper money to silk and silver ingots. By 1280 all business transactions had to take place in paper money in Yuan China and this practice continued as late as the 1340s. Paper money stirred economic growth because foreign exchange rates could be maintained and mercantile activity grew even more robust.[21] Travellers and traders across the Silk Road have left accounts of conversions between silver and gold, for example, one silver ingot was equivalent to 75 gold dinars.[22] However, silk and other luxury fabrics were used in transactions and a portion of taxes was also collected in fabrics across the Mongol Khanates. In Russia in 1240 fur was part of the taxes that were collected by the Golden Horde. Silk and fur were easily transportable and were obviously valuable. One of the most detailed descriptions of convertibility across Mongol Eurasia has been supplied by Pegolotti who describes his journey from Tana to China. His account explicitly lays out markets where merchants can easily sell goods (Urgench) and get silver in return which is then converted into *balishi* (paper money) in Kassai before reaching China where the money can buy bales of silk for the return journey.[23] In Merchant Guides the presence of a comparison of weights and measures in cities of Alexandria, Apulia with the cities of the Levant, Cairo, Tabriz and others point to lively trade with Christian groups like the Genoese and Venetians with their counterparts in Mamluk and Mongol realms. Transfer of money between Tabriz and Caffa, for instance, was an ordinary matter by 1280s.[24]

The aforementioned sections provide the context against which this chapter is set. The complexities of Mongols as harbingers of commercial activity, as consumers and producers, requires examination in order to see how trade on the Silk Road thrived. This chapter describes and sheds light on the various ways in which the Mongols encouraged production, whether as consumers or in the form of workshops which were set up across Eurasia and brought workers and raw materials closer to each other. The goods produced were essential to the economy, filled the coffers of the Mongol court and were also used as gifts for diplomatic missions and for forging new alliances. The economic activities of the Mongols were not made up of raiding their newly acquired populations but rather of creating an apparatus which enabled them to build a long-term relationship with the region. The nature of conquest and the relationships within the Mongol imperial family brought different aspects of trade to the fore. The Mongols universally encouraged trade by creating demand for goods and by providing capital and infrastructure. They determined what kind of trade passed through their territory and what was produced within their regions. The different societies that were brought into closer contact than before also influenced what was being traded. The list of what the Mongols demanded after conquest sheds light on the knowledge they had about the kinds of goods available in a particular region, and is both impressive and extensive.[25] In all this the Mongols were assisted by their institutions which gave them the tools to harness the knowledge about Eurasia in the most effective manner. Their reservoir of knowledge with every conquest increased and information was used to create functional order immediately. The next section provides a picture of Mongol Eurasia and the trade routes they came to dominate and expanded as a result of bringing raw materials and workshops closer to markets.

Trade routes

The Silk Road represented a multiplicity of trade routes and has been in existence since at least the second century. It has been described as 'an international highway which connected China with the West and served as a conduit of [goods] technological innovations, religious ideas and cultural achievements'.[26] Usually divided between northern, middle and southern routes, the Silk Road begins in China and goes through cities of Central Asia like Kashgar, Merv, Aksu, Ferghana, Samarqand, Semirechye and Bukhara and ends up in India, the Mediterranean and Syria. Over centuries, especially from the seventh century, the Silk Road(s) were under the control of Turkic *Qaghans* who possessed wealth and attracted embassies and caravans from far afield. These routes and cities responded to social and civil conditions which led to parts and branches doing well while others declined only to resurface with the rise of other Turkic groups. Mongol control for the first half of the thirteenth century led to the resurgence of all three major routes simultaneously. They were secured for travelling from end to end.[27] Even during the course of the thirteenth century the Silk Road continued to transform and change form, due mainly to the rivalries between the Khanates. While some roads fell into disrepair, other completely new routes were brought into circulation. This resembled the steppe environment which is a constantly evolving entity. Mongol courts 'defined the choice of itineraries by diplomats and merchants'[28] and dictated the route thus taken. Set within this context we can piece together how Mongol Khanates continued to trade even during times of conflict.

Famously, the Polos travelled from Venice to Acre, passed into Tabriz via land routes and reached the port of Hormuz; from there they travelled further through Herat, Balkh through the Pamir Mountains, reaching the Tarim basin in Central Asia, onwards through Khotan, Dunhuang, crossing the Gobi Desert to China and Xanadu. The journey took them four years from 1271 to 1275, when they got to meet Qubilai Khan.[29] Mediterranean traffic, chief among it spices and silver, passed through Tabriz to Northern India and through Samarqand (Central Asia) on to China.[30] Tabriz's presence at the crossroads of three rivers made it the most important city in the northern and eastern parts of Persia as it not only served as a hub of commercial activity but also had pastureland which was very attractive for the Mongols. There are contracts drawn up by Federico di Piazzalunga in 1274 for Genoese merchants pointing to frequent trade and visits by the Genoese in Ilkhanate domains. Furthermore, there is evidence that Ghazan's reforms of the late 1290s spurred commercial activity in the Ilkahante by streamlining mercantile activities. His reforms made merchants more accountable and initiated a sense of profit sharing which indicated a long-term perspective on development. The regulation of trade-related policies also included ensuring prices of goods from Persia were competitive on the Mediterranean market through moderating taxes and cutting out middlemen by allowing merchants to go to the source for raw materials and transport them across Ilkhanate Persia. This was done to ensure larger profits which could be shared with the local population not directly involved with commercial activity and to mitigate simmering tensions with merchants.[31] As a result, under the Ilkhanate, Tabriz flourished and became a hub for manufacturing silks and textiles along with being a remarkable entry point for international trade. Later, Marco Polo accompanied a princess from Yuan China to Ilkhanate Persia, an official naval expedition through Malacca, the Indian Ocean and up to Hormuz, a journey of two years. The Polos went further through Persia, Anatolia and Trebizond overland and sailed to Constantinople and on to Venice which they reached in 1295.[32] Marco Polo's account of Mongol Eurasia is a comprehensive account of the expanse and scale of Mongol lands and continues to be a reservoir of information about the Mongol Khanates. Over the years various allegations have been made about the veracity of his account and the importance he accords himself but it remains an important source for western European knowledge on the Mongols in the thirteenth century.

The Golden Horde in particular deserves special attention. Their impact on Eurasia was perhaps the longest lasting because they developed the Black Sea trade emporia which connected the east and the west. They created new trade termini, like Caffa, Tana, Trebizond and Ayas to name a few. The Golden Horde's impact on the fur trade is as important as the silk trade from China under the Yuan. The agency of the Golden Horde is noteworthy because they singlehandedly changed the trade network for the northern principalities and developed north-south trade which provided them with vast quantities of fur and other products from northern forests.[33] The establishment of the Golden Horde capital, Sarai, made it the main entrepot for fur and more than compensated for routes no longer in use. This north-south trade route included expensive furs from the Pechora river basin. These furs were sold to the court in Sarai and also connected with the larger network of east-west trade.[34] They revived the lucrative trade under Bulgar control which had been disrupted in the eleventh and twelfth centuries as a result of the general chaos on the steppe. The ability of the Russians to transport fur further south was greatly hampered because of declining powers of Kiev and the reduced demand for luxury goods from Constantinople.[35] The Golden Horde not only reinstated this trade but was able to provide the necessary stable conditions to expand the fur trade well beyond its extent in previous centuries. Trade through Russia not only included luxury items but archaeologists have dug up vast quantities of everyday goods like glass, beads, shells, etc. in villages across Russia, indicating a thriving trade in items which would have been characterised as bulk commodities.[36]

The Golden Horde controlled trade from Central Asia through the lower Volga and Black Sea to European markets.[37] The Sarai–Cairo–Tabriz triangle and the northern most overland route connected the Golden Horde with Yuan China through the major city of Khiva in Central Asia which continued to thrive and provide revenues and wealth from trade not only for the Golden Horde and Yuan China but also for Central Asian Mongols. It is important to make one qualification here. Central Asia as defined under the Mongols was divided between three Khanates in the latter half of the thirteenth century, the Chaghatais and Ogedeis (referred to as Central Asian Mongols), the Golden Horde and the Ilkhanate. Cities like Nishapur, Merv, Bukhara, Samarqand, Urgench, Khiva, Utrar, Balqasun, Almaliq, Kashgar, Taraz, Khurasan[38] and many more, as discussed in the previous chapter continued to attract investment, trade and reconstruction activity by the Khanates. In other words, during the conflict between Yuan China and the Central Asian Mongols under Qaidu, mentioned previously, cities of the former Khwarezmshah like Bukhara, Samarqand and even Merv suffered but not Khiva and Urgench which were part of the Golden Horde, or for that matter parts of Eastern Iran like Khorasan and parts of modern day Afghanistan which fell under Ilkhanate control but in the historical context were part of larger Central Asia. Any discussion of the Central Asian Mongols tends to limit the extent of Central Asia and boxes the borders of the Mongol Khanate as all of Central Asia. This was clearly not the case and as seen above and in the next section, both the Golden Horde and the Ilkahanate continued to do exceedingly well throughout the thirteenth and fourteenth centuries. Even the cities under Qaidu and Du'a (Ogedei and Chaghatais' descendants) were central to trade especially in commodities like horses and slaves which were primarily sourced from Central Asia. The state of Central Asia's economic situation is complicated by these factors. In addition, until the end of the thirteenth century they were the primary trade partners of the Mamluks in Syria and Egypt as well. Trade from Sarai to Azerbaijan, Tabriz and the Caucasus was another network which was exploited by the Golden Horde through Genoese intermediaries.[39] Europe, having undergone a revolution in manufacturing, relied on the east for raw materials like fur, silk and cotton, which was supplied through Golden Horde domains.

The Italians were deeply involved in trade with the Mongols and were the western-most points of Mongol control. In 1265 the Genoese traders got privileges to operate in the Mongol realm and soon had trading posts in Caffa and Sudak. Cities like Caffa experienced their golden age in the thirteenth and fourteenth centuries because of their interaction with the Golden Horde. They were predominantly involved in the fur trade. The Golden Horde was the access point to luxury furs which found its way to India, China, Central Asia and Europe.[40] Due to the war between Genoa and Venice, older routes through Baghdad to Anatolia, and Acre, Tyre and Tripoli became unusable. To replace the loss of these routes Sarai and Tabriz became flourishing markets for goods arriving from across Eurasia. Other routes included; linking Tabriz to Khurasan and Transoxiana; towards the Persian Gulf, through Basra and Shiraz; Hormuz to India and China. Tana and Caffa connected to Egypt and Syria. Black Sea trade offered alternative routes for Europe to continue trading with India and the Far East especially in lieu of papal embargoes of trade with the Muslim Levant after 1291. The demand for spices and grains in Europe from the Far East along with fur remained the main commodities to be traded.[41] Even after the Black Death which impacted trade and exchange along the Silk Road, Black Sea trade and overland Eurasian trade expanded rather than contracted. This was a result of demand for cheap grains, foodstuffs, slaves and lumber in Europe which lasted well into the middle of the fourteenth century. Furthermore, the Black Death had led to the decimation of labour which in turn spurred demand for slaves from the east, especially since in many cases the means of production and factories required labour for manufacturing.[42] The decline of luxury goods was replaced by cheaper commodities as the spending ability of rich merchant houses of Venice and Genoa were affected. A change in the consumption patterns of a Europe transformed by the Black Death changed the nature of trade from the east but did not end it. With the change in commodities, profits were also impacted and eventually trade slowly passed into the hands of non-Mongols, mostly Muslims who had been the traditional leaders of trade before the Mongols in the Middle East. While this impacted trade between the Muslims and the Christians because of resurgence of old divisions, the Russia–Central Asia–China commerce continued well into the eighteenth and nineteenth centuries.[43]

In Yuan China, the Grand Canal was revived (a seventh century creation) under Qubilai's efforts. It connected the north and south trade in China. The Grand Canal flowed from North Zhili, and it was extended from the Yellow

River to Beijing. The cities along the Grand Canal benefitted from connecting the southern agricultural economies to northern markets. Cities like Linqing, Jiangxi and Jiangnang all profited from being on the route and became artisanal hubs, commercial centres and important cities under the Yuan, something that continued under the Ming and further down the centuries. The development of intra-regional trade was bolstered and China found a means to integrate its economy under the Yuan. The introduction of paper money which was backed by grain surplus also helped the economy and the currency maintained its value throughout the Yuan period which made commercial activity less risky.[44] Maritime trade under the Yuan was primarily directed through the southeast of China and as a result port cities like Shanghai, Ningbo, Quangzhou and Hangchow all did exceedingly well trading with Japan, Vietnam and Malacca. Qubilai Khan imposed a government monopoly on maritime voyages in 1284, and monitored all maritime activity.[45] Qubilai had ambitions in the southeast and traders and ships were sent to Southeast Asia for fostering relations. The southeast coast was also used to transport much needed grain to the north from the south of China which in the 1280s was a successful and safe route.[46] This led to shipbuilding activities in the Yangzi delta for ships going to Ryukyu, Malacca and Singapore, along with Japan.[47] Yuan China was crucial in overland trade through Central Asia with Beijing as a terminus, and the Indian Ocean sea trade with the important cities of Canton, Zaytun and Hangchow as termini and was a 'formidable power in an increasingly integrated world system'.[48]

Ilkhanate maritime trade through the Persian Gulf also deserves special attention; after 1260 when the Central Asian Mongols were fighting with the Yuan and the Ilkhans, maritime trade was an essential component of contact between Yuan China and the Ilkhanate Persia. The port cities of Hormuz and Kish, rivals for the position of most important city reveal a sea route to China through the Indian Ocean. The commodities which were most likely traded from Kish (between old Hormuz and Siraf) included horses, pearls, rosewater, flowers, quicksilver, silver bullion, madder and cinnabar among others which are supposed to have arrived there from Arabia. However, considering its connections with India, it can be safely assumed that Kish had commodities from India as well.[49] There is also evidence that the rise of Hormuz (on the Jarun Island in 1300)[50] and the offices of Kish in Mongol dominions under Ilkhanate Persia were in response to Mongol activity in the region. After 1330–1331, Kish declined and Hormuz was the winner in the Persian Gulf.[51] Overall these efforts indicate a comprehensive strategy towards creating conditions for movement of goods in Mongol Eurasia. The growth of cities and production centres along the way shows the attention the Mongols paid to creating and reviving connections for the benefit of economic activity. Essentially rather than a fractured, disconnected relationship between overland trade and maritime trade, Yuan China connected the land and sea trade in ways which challenged the competition between them which is continuously used to explain the rise of European naval powers at the expense of overland trade through Central Asia from the sixteenth century onwards.[52]

Another aspect of exchange under the Mongols was achieved through the movement of peoples and the establishment of workshops across Eurasia. The continuation of an old steppe tradition, the Mongols were attracted to specialists of all varieties and divided populations along lines of their professions. Consequently, not only did these people offer their skills for the consumption of the Mongols but were essential in accumulating and promoting wealth and culture in Eurasia. Simply put, '[T]he various Chinggisid branches, dispersed throughout Eurasia, completed for these specialists who were vital to their efforts to tap into the economic and cultural wealth of the settled zones of the empire'.[53] Artisans, in particular, were a group nearly on a par with the merchants in the Mongol state. The movement of peoples in response to the presence of raw materials and markets was part of the interconnected network forged by the Mongols across Eurasia. As a result of the importance of merchants and trade, artisans as the creators of products, especially luxury goods, were prized and constantly in demand. The prevalence of merchants and artisans in Mongol Eurasia also secured the position of Central Asians (Muslims and otherwise) who formed the majority of these two groups especially in the first part of the thirteenth century. Far from the picture of desolation and destruction which is often conjured up with regards to Central Asia under the Mongols and beyond, it was Central Asian personnel and artisans who did exceedingly well and served in the most important roles under the Mongols. As we shall see, seen through a Mongol prism the economic system thus created saw Eurasia as a single unit and thus regional disparities were of little concern. While the Khans and princes of the Khanates did exhibit rivalries and jealousies, the principle of shared patrimony meant that Eurasia was a shared resource. The next section considers Mongol agency through the treatment of artisans and the establishment of manufacturing workshops across Eurasia.

Artisans and manufacturing under the Mongols

The Silk Road is often described as a thoroughfare for goods travelling from China to Europe, with the cities on the way, especially those of Central Asia and the steppe merely acting as spectators. A further look into Mongol Eurasia reveals that far from being bystanders, nomads and Central Asians were the drivers of manufacturing and commodity exchange. The Mongol Khans were not only consumers of products but were heavily involved in setting up production units in their domains.[54] Manufacturing fuelled by the spread of artisans across Eurasia garnered much in the way of spreading markets across Eurasia which were connected and spurred trade on the Silk Road. The creation of workshops, the movement of artisans from one region to another, resettlement of groups of peoples depending on the need for goods or placing them closer to raw materials in Mongol Eurasia is alluded to without providing a context. These policies and actions stemmed from old steppe traditions and served to legitimise rule in Turkic Qaghanates over centuries. The Mongol pre-occupation with skilled craftsmen was a product of at least 2000-year-old traditions.[55] Artisans represented a source of prestige for the Mongols. The custom of collecting and showcasing artisans and skilled peoples in the courts of the Khans to celebrate marriages, alliances, founding of capitals etc. was an age old practice which was passed down to the Mongols and continued to be a sign of wealth, access and power for steppe political elite which is best surmised in the following statement: 'the accumulation of talented individuals was a display designed to create an aura of majesty'.[56] The Timurids continued this tradition forward; Timur is famous for collecting artisans and other skilled people to celebrate his victories in his capital Samarqand in the early fifteenth century. The Mongols, much like the Chinese and the Persians, were discerning in their understanding of artisans and as a consequence an impressive differentiation existed in the categories of artisans which have been reported in censuses.

The movement of people under the Mongols has attracted much derision. This is similar to the pronouncements in relation to the destruction of cities with no mention of the subsequent revival and reconstruction. The impact of deportations on populations under the Mongols ignores state sponsored projects which required labour or migrant workers. One cannot argue with the fact that the Mongols were exacting on populations but they also created opportunities for people who served under a new system and benefitted from it. Mongol policies when considered from a historical perspective of nomadic traditions and set within a context of a global market system which was spread over a large geographical area tell a different story. Economic migration was not a Mongol creation and it did not stop with them either. The Mongol state was like a big corporation of the time and there were instances of voluntary migration as well as involuntary movement of peoples. Economic migration is a matter of concern today. Globalisation in the late twentieth to early twenty-first centuries echoes these very aspects of an integrated world economy which creates mobility but is also a consequence of limited opportunities. This is indeed topical and poses as many questions and concerns today as it does when revisiting Mongol Eurasian economic conditions.

Interestingly, the Silk Road as populated with manufacturing centres, especially across Central Asia, is seldom discussed in terms of nomads as producers. References to the destruction of cities, including centres of commercial activity like Bukhara, Samarqand, Utrar, Merv etc. exist, which while accurate, fail to show Mongol attempts at reconstruction shortly after. Resources, administrators and postal stations were organised fairly quickly and most of these cities resumed their place in commercial activity. There is, however, the accusation by contemporary historians that these cities, for example, Bukhara, never resumed their former glory. We are forced to accept these statements because we do not have written evidence to prove otherwise, but we need to raise questions based on the fact that Bukhara was rebuilt and resumed its place on the Silk Road soon after Mongol conquest. As for Samarqand and neighbouring cities, they were also rebuilt, Samarqand of course went on to become important and central enough to become the capital of the Timurids in the fourteenth century. Bukhara and Samarqand have remained important throughout the centuries since the Mongols and these cities continue to play an active role even today.

The commissioning and establishing of manufacturing workshops across Mongol Eurasia is a less known fact, though it is well described in historical sources of the time, such as in the *Yuan shih*, Rashid al-Din's *Jami al tawarikh* and in later histories such as the *Tarikh-i Harat*. Mongols not only formed the demand for certain products but also created the necessary infrastructure to produce those goods across the territory of Eurasia. They followed the demand and supply model of economics which entailed first and foremost access to resources and production centres peopled by artisans who could manufacture finished products. For example, Allsen in his thesis on cloth and the importance of luxurious cloth for the Mongol princes and royal family has provided a rich historical account of the *nasij* or '*Tatar*' cloth. *Nasij* production was undertaken by numerous artisan workshops throughout the Yuan; three of these workshops were peopled by West Asian artisans, in Besh Baligh (connected to Herat which was also famous for its gold brocades), the city north of Peking called Hsin-lia and Simali which had Samarqandi weavers, along with Hangchow which was the site of a Civil Artisans Superintendency.[57] Artisans enjoyed a special status in Mongol Eurasia much like merchants, as discussed earlier. Artisans were spared from Utrar, Ghazna, Tus, Samarqand, Khwarezm, Urgench, Merv, Mosul and Aleppo, cities across Central Asia, Iraq and Syria throughout the thirteenth century. There are references to the sack of Samarqand where everyone other than artisans and religious leaders were spared and relocated to other parts of Eurasia, mostly further east, into China.[58] In Merv 400 artisan households were spared.[59] Centres of arms manufacturing across Eurasia were built and served the Mongol Khanates. There is mention of arms manufacturing in Bukhara and Samarqand[60] and the Yuan shih talks of Chinese workshops which produced a variety of weapons including swords, shields, arrows, bows, armours and spears.[61] Set against the backdrop of the place of Central Asia in Mongol enterprise this deserves remark. Movement of artisans from Central Asia remained an important aspect of the exchange between the Yuan and Central Asia after 1220.

According to the Yuan shih, artisans were divided into four categories, civil, military, *jam* and government artisans. References to these can be found in *Jami al tawarikh* as well, though they are less precise. Artisans were enrolled into censuses from as early as Ogedei and Guyuk's reigns. Mongke's reign identified and utilised artisans across the Eurasian space and organised them for use much more efficiently. Following the pattern of the patrimonial economy of the steppe, artisans much like the rest of the population, along with animals, were portioned off and divided among princes and *khatuns* of the royal family. In this way, artisans were relocated and moved to different parts of Mongol Eurasia. These were then divided along categories; the military artisans attended to the need of the military, civilian artisans participated in society, specific artisan activities paid for the upkeep of postal stations and government artisans were permanently attached to court workshops which prepared gifts and met the requirements of the court.[62] In Ilkhanate Persia, workshops were called *kar-khanahs* and artisans there were called *karigars*; in Chinese they are referred to as *kuan-chang*. In Ilkhanate Persia the office of chief artisans was named in each urban centre. Hulegu appointed Ibn Darrus immediately after the sack of Baghdad in 1258 and Mengu Bolad was appointed as chief craftsman in Tabriz.[63] The government artisans enjoyed privileges and were often exempt from taxation, especially in Qara Qorum. Qubilai is attributed with setting up numerous institutions and offices for the protection of artisans from exploitation in China and they were offered extra rations, jewellery and other goods that would keep them in prosperous conditions.[64] There are references to court workshops in Herat, Nishapur, Tus, Baghdad and Isfahan after the conquest of Iran. These cities were old hubs of manufacturing and commercial enterprise before Mongol conquest. Baghdad had been the most important city under the Abbassid Caliphate and retained its position in Mongol times as well. Herat in Afghanistan also retained its position, though later accounts of the fourteenth century refer to the relocation of artisans from 300–1000 households from Herat to Besh Baligh (the Uyghur summer capital) in 1221. A portion of them were moved back to Herat in 1236.[65] After 1260, artisans were moved from Central Asia to China as part of Qubilai Khan's patrimony as *Qaghan*. In Yuan China artisans were administered by Civil Artisan Superintendency and the Gold Brocade Office, which were further controlled by a Clothing and Brocade Bureau under the Bureau for Empress' Administration. In the cities of Hsin-ma-lia (Simali) and Hangchow for instance, important manufacturing cities populated with foreigners (mostly Central Asians) from Samarqand and neighbouring cities, there was a vibrant ethnic mix in the population which led to cross cultural and technology transfer in textile manufacturing.[66] Besh Baligh, Hsin-ma-lia and Hangchow, the three most important civil artisan colonies in Mongol Eurasia were peopled by Central Asians. They were created fairly early on in Chinggis and Ogedei's times. They mixed with local Chinese populations and provided ample quantities of gold brocade or tartary cloth for the Mongol court at Qara Qorum and later in Beijing. The Chinese cities were at a distance of not more than 180 km from Beijing and continued to be active in the 1270s and 1280s.[67] There were workshops and specialised workshops created in commercial centres of Jiangnang and Jiangxi provinces on the Grand Canal. The Jiangxi workshops specialised in porcelain kilns, and there were tile kilns in Linqing.[68] The exchange was not only in the direction of China but Chinese craftsmen were found in Samarqand and Zandan as early as 1221/1222 when Li Chihchang visited Samarqand soon after its conquest. The Upper Yensei region, which had reserves of gold and other metals and where Kyrgyz were famous for mining these metals and as metalworkers, also had populations of Chinese workmen weaving thread from gold, gauze and silk. Cinqai, an important general under Chinggis Khan and later the prime minister or *darugachi* under Ogedei and Guyuk was asked the relocate an agricultural colony and a colony of artisans in the upper reaches of the Altai. The city referred to as Cinqai Balqasun was located between Chinggis Khan's base camp in Northern Mongolia and the area of operations of Turkistan. Balqasun or Bai Baliq was populated by Chinese craftsmen and it became a centre for goldsmiths and jewellers. These artisans were relocated back to China in the 1260s as part of Qubilai's policies.[69] These contacts created opportunities for interaction which led to the creation of new techniques in textile production and were in demand by Mongol courts across Eurasia and beyond. According to Allsen, these workshops not only produced textiles and clothing but also sold these items, and secured large incomes in exchange.[70] Other than textile manufacturers, there were metalworkers, artisans who made saddles, bows and quivers for military use, as well as iron and copper and ceramic-makers. The production of ceramics was regulated, and along with registration of artisans, all kilns were registered and taxes were levied on them. Most of the trade in ceramics went to Iran and to the southeast through port cities in China.[71]

The Mongol desire for fabrics led to the development of centres across Eurasia in order to produce fabrics and textiles such as silk, rayon, cotton, brocades and many others; 'As the principal consumer of such goods [textiles], the state took an active role in the creation and staffing of manufacturing facilities and in production, and distribution'.[72] The demand for these textiles was rampant and can be seen through the wide variety of luxury goods made out of them. For example, the headgear of women was a symbol of status in the nomadic world and as the empire grew headdresses (especially in the court) reflected the variety of cloth available for purchase.[73] Along with headdresses, girdles were important and with the expansion of the empire included fabrics which were not used before. Shoes for ceremonial purposes were also made out of gold brocade. Luxury goods were important symbols of prestige and respect in nomadic political culture.[74] They were a political currency which was used to reinforce the principle of generosity for securing allegiance and loyalty. The redistribution of wealth was the means through which the Mongol Khans continued to keep the nomadic population and most importantly the Mongol military content. In other words, cloth was akin to gold in other economies. Gold and silver were especially in limited supply in Yuan China and silk replaced them in the Mongol period, much like the US dollar in modern day economic terms. The manufacturing of textiles was another way to increase wealth in Mongol Eurasia, much like mining more gold or printing more paper currency. This made the artisans and court workshops even more important to the Mongols, since part of their wealth was being created through the production of cloth. The role of the state in production is not new especially in sedentary societies. The Mongols were no exception to this rule despite being nomadic. Infrastructure and manufacturing on the scale that Eurasia required was only possible with the involvement of the state and the Mongols provided that much needed investment. This naturally leads into a discussion of what was being traded in Mongol Eurasia both as a result of what was available and what the Mongols wanted.

Types of goods and commodities

One of the most striking features of Mongol Eurasia and trade under their aegis was the sheer quantity of goods and products available in the markets across

Eurasia. In other words, one of the major achievements of the Mongols was how Eurasian markets came to represent the pinnacle of commercial activity because they attracted the highest quality and quantity of goods from across the Eurasian space. By connecting near and far flung cities and regions of Eurasia, and by demanding a wide variety of goods, the Mongols stimulated volumes of trade. The landscape created by the Mongols in terms of mercantile activity facilitated and burgeoned trade of everyday as well as exotic goods in quantities that could satisfy Mongol courts across Eurasia. Time and again, whether it was Italian merchants or travellers, Persian and Central Asian merchants or Chinese travellers, the quantity of goods available inspired amazement and awe in all observers across the board. Trade in Mongol Eurasia can be divided into four categories: luxury items (easily transportable, like silk, gems, precious items, furs); silver and gold which was traded by all four Khanates; and the Golden Horde also traded in slaves and bulkier items like grain and foodstuffs including dry fruits, caviar etc, especially going east to west.[75] After 1260, the two routes which connected Eurasia with South Asia were reopened, one which was based out of the Mediterranean and the other one connected East, West and South Asia which went through present-day Central Asia. Political unification under the Mongols kept profit margins high as a result of lower duties and risk in contrast to the Mediterranean route.[76] Chief among the goods available in massive quantities and of huge value were textiles. Account after account of tribute demanded by the Mongol courts starting from Chinggis Khan down to the end of the fourteenth century refers to gold brocades, cloth and fabric. For example: 'From the Uyghur of Turfan, who submitted voluntarily in 1209, Chinggis required tribute of gold brocade (*nachit*), damasks (*dardas*), silks and satin; three years later the Tangut state of Kansu attacked following which it sent the Mongols woollen garments'.[77] After the annexation of Koryo,[78] Mongols demanded textiles and pelts[79] among other things.[80] Textiles included chiffon, silk gauze, silk brocade, embroidered materials, damask, pongee and ramine cloth.[81] Rubruck in his account says that the Mongols acquired furs from the north (Russia, Siberia), silks from the east (Cathay) and cotton, silks etc. from Persia as well.[82] Furthermore according to Rubruck, there was a lively trade from China to Russia to Iran etc. in furs, textiles, mead, wine, dried fruits, nuts, grains etc. This was true even under Mongke whose administration regularised commercial activity and imposed taxes on merchants.[83] In the late 1250s Chinese silk was being traded in Genoa, Lucca and Tuscany from Armenia through Tabriz in Ilkhanate Persia.[84] In Transoxiana the kinds of goods being traded included 'agricultural products (fruits, grains), animals (horses, camels, tigers, leopards), jade, jewels, furs, medicinal herbs, textile, wine and slaves, and there existed a commercial infrastructure of loans, hospices, road maintenance, post-stations and load animals for hire'.[85] Horses and slaves remained the most important commodities to be traded from Central Asia all through the Mongol period. Alan Christian cavalry in the Yuan army continued to receive horses from Central Asian Mongols well into the fourteenth century. Steppe horses could not be bred in China and were bought from cities like Besh Baligh and Derbend, which along with Sarai appear prominently on a Korean map of the time period.[86] The Ilkhanate army also received horses from Central Asia.

According to Marco Polo, clothes signified different characteristics, value and class of the princes in a Mongol court.[87] Gifting of expensive clothing was normal practice in the Mongol court, as far back as Chinggis Khan's time and lasted all through the end of the Yuan and Ilkhanate in the fourteenth century. The method of acquisition included: trade, taxation/tribute, court-sponsored production and booty.[88] Chroniclers have reported the demand for cloth by the Mongols from nearly all their conquests: satin from the Chin capital, satin and clothing from Khurasan and Ganja and beautifully coloured tents were taken from Rum in 1243.[89] From Baghdad a huge booty of textiles and garments along with gold, pearls and other precious metals was taken. According to Allsen, cloth remained an essential item of booty in every expedition.[90] It is easy to understand why this would have been the case, one of the main reasons for the Silk Road's name is because silk remained the main exchangeable currency in Eurasia. It was easily transportable, merchants and people on the Silk Road understood its value and it remained an essential commodity used in exchange throughout the period. Tatar cloth became synonymous with the Mongols and attests to its value under the Mongols who encouraged its consumption and increased its value by using it themselves. Taxation included a portion paid in silk, '[In] 1263 for example, the silk fibres received totalled 425 tons and in 1328 the figure reached 655 tons'.[91] Fur, fine cotton and even linen from Europe was in high demand in Mongol Eurasia. The gifting of clothing was a cornerstone of nomadic statecraft, as the single most exchangeable currency at the time, cloth signified wealth and as a consequence, power and prestige. The extension of nomadic traditions was visible in the acceptance of clothing as remuneration as well, 'nomadic leaders when selling their military services to sedentary powers often took payment in cloth and clothing'.[92] All this cloth had to be fashioned into articles which the nomads could wear and exhibit. This needed artisans and workshops which have been discussed in the previous section and vouch for the ways in which the Mongol economy functioned. The aspects of control and consumption which were most important to the Mongols remained nomadic in origin and impacted the development of the Eurasian economy.

Other commodities in high demand were precious gems of all varieties; these were found in large quantities in Tabriz which was connected to China and India through Central Asia and the sea respectively. There are accounts of the availability of high quality spices like ginger and cinnamon along with indigo, coral, woollen cloth etc.[93] Markets in Yuan China were prosperous and full of rice, wheat, meat, wine etc. and people lived by 'trade and industry'. As late as 1488, a Korean official on the same route as Marco Polo described Chinese cities and people as luxurious, markets full of silks, gauze, jewels, rich merchants etc. The prosperity of the Yuan Chinese markets which were flooded with goods under the Mongols paints a picture of a thriving polity in China under Mongol rule.[94] Chinese goods like ceramics, silks and copper were being exported from port cities of Ch'uan-chou and Fuchou in Southeastern China and stones, exotic animals, spices etc. were flowing into the country.[95] The thriving trade between Yuan China and Ilkhanate Persia can be verified by looking at the amount of Persian goods which could be found in Chinese markets and Chinese goods in the markets of Persia. Part of this trade also included foodstuffs and gave rise to a new Eurasian elite cuisine which was a conglomeration of Turkic, Mongol, Chinese and Persian influences. According to Buell, 'Mongols set in motion a profound but little studied change in the habits of much of a continent, one whose influence persists even to the present'.[96] This is evidenced by cooking techniques and the kinds of spices and foodstuffs which were being used well into the seventeenth century in Mughal kitchens in India.

The markets were full of rich merchants and goods and often surprised travellers.[97] According to the account of Odorico of Pordenone, Tabriz generated more revenue than all of the French domains at the time.[98] According to Pegolotti, there was a brisk trade of wax, iron, tin, spices, pepper, ginger, saffron, silk, cotton, various types of furs, linens and pearls in Tana; while in Caffa grain was an important commodity which was going west through that port.[99] A Genoese notary, Lomberto di Sambuceto, in Caffa in 1289–1290, left a register of goods exported from the steppe and the Taiga region which includes: slaves, fleece, hides, wheat, barley, millet, wax, salt, cheese, fish and silk.[100] These contracts do not only provide us with information on the variety of goods but also point to contact between Crimea and Central Asia. Russian merchants brought fur, honey, linen, European metals, timber and slaves to Bulgar down the Volga.[101] The slave trade between the Pontic steppe and the Near East was further bolstered under the Mongols. The Golden Horde extended this trade to the Mamluks and supplied slaves from the Kipchaq steppe to Egypt, where the bulk of the military and even the ruling class were made up of slaves from the Mongol Eurasian steppe.[102] The Ilkhanate was involved with the slave trade but in their case, Indians, mostly from Kashmir were being traded with the Mamluks.[103] The Persian Gulf was also connected with Canton, the longest route in use before the sixteenth century and the advent of modern routes.[104] As has been mentioned earlier, the Mongols very often sought talent across the Eurasian space and shifted talent to wherever it was needed. In the case of maritime trade, the Ilkhans and the Golden Horde closely partnered with Italian merchants like the Genoese and Venetians in their bid to ensure activity on the seas. Along with Tabriz, the Chaghataid Mongols in Central Asia developed Andijan in Ferghana as a main centre of production. Khiva, in Central Asia, which fell under the control of the Golden Horde, was an entrepot and a supplier of silk, ginger and rhubarb from China, indigo from Hindustan[105] and rubies from Badakshan. In addition, it also exported two varieties of silk which were produced there: Urgench and Khwarezm.[106]

Exchanges between the Mongol Khanates fell into the following categories: tribute which included exotic animals for the hunting parks in the Yuan; government trade funded by the state treasuries; private merchant trade which included merchants which had their transportation costs covered; revenues from allocated territories and even movable property like sheep, cattle and camels.[107] One of the main reasons for conflict between the Yuan and their Central Asian cousins and the Golden Horde was the flouting of these exchanges especially the last one. Qaidu (Ogedeid), Baraq (Chaghatai) and Berke (Golden Horde) were not paid their dues from their territories in Northern China and in Persia. However, from the accounts of European travellers, we can piece together a brisk trade between the Golden Horde and the Yuan through parts of Central Asia which were part of the Golden Horde. The markets of China were accessible through the Black Sea for government sponsored trade and private trade. This was the principal route used by the Genoese merchants in the second half of the thirteenth century. Relations with the Central Asian Mongols were essential not only because most of the overland trade went through Central Asia since antiquity but also because along with Mongolia, Central Asia was a source for horses necessary for the Mongol army. In order to continue using light cavalry Yuan China needed a constant supply of horses. Once Qaidu cut off the supply, the impact on the Yuan army was huge and led to a move towards using more heavy cavalry. The peace embassy sent by Du'a to Temur Oljeitu Khan in 1304/1305 was as important for Yuan China as it was for the Central Asian Mongols. Resumption of trade, especially of horses for the Christian Alans in the Yuan army was a direct consequence of the cessation of conflict between the Yuan and the Central Asian Mongols.[108] Its impact on the Ilkhanate army was similar and could be attributed to the change from light to heavy cavalry in Persia as well.

The Yuan-Ilkhan exchange has attracted a lot of attention principally because they have left us with sources which can be used to verify the exchanges between them in the thirteenth and fourteenth centuries. Both China and Persia were established empires with long histories of political and social influences. The Ilkhans and the Yuan also remained closer because they supported each other: militarily and diplomatically and derived legitimacy from each other. In addition, the differences between the Mongols and their subject populations give a far clearer picture of influence and exchange than in Central Asia where the Mongols and Turks shared a common heritage. The same is true for the Golden Horde where the Mongols remained in a largely steppe environment and ruled Russia through vassals. Contact between the Yuan and the Ilkahante brought two ancient civilisations closer together.[109] Among the list of commodities and exchanges that took place between the Yuan and Ilkhanate were silk and jewels; military and other technologies; agricultural practices and products; geographical information and cartography, among much more. Rashid al-Din has left us agricultural manuals which show an extensive exchange of trees, fruits, medicines, foodstuffs and even cotton, the growing of which was encouraged under the Yuan and rice which was personally encouraged by Ghazan Khan to be grown in Iran.[110] In addition to these, paper and porcelain require special attention because of the revolutionary changes they brought with them and the rise of global alterations of the use of these technologies. While the quantity may have been limited, the transfer of the technology of the use of paper went westward from China under the Mongols. The main centre for bookmaking in Yuan China was in the Jianning prefecture, in the Fujian mountains, in the city of Jianyang. The industry required a whole host of craftsmen: scribes, engravers, binders, calligraphers, copyists, printers and cover-makers.[111] Manuscript writing in the Ilkhanate can be directly attributed to Yuan-Ilkhan exchange and the production of paper in China. Under Ghazan Khan after 1290 there was a move towards the circulation of paper money in Iran as well, but this was less successful. Not only was paper transferred to the Middle East, but there was also an improvement in paper manufacturing under the Mongols which enabled large-folio manuscripts. Rashid al-Din's ateliers mentioned earlier were prominent examples of the use of this technology. Even religious *Sufi khanqahs* used paper when they commissioned manuscripts in this period.[112] There is a clear connection between the Ilkhanate court and the influence of Chinese styles in Persian painting and art. This is evident from the observation that art produced in places far away from the Ilkhanate court, for example, in Shiraz and Isfahan, showed less Chinese influences. In other words, the extent of Mongol influence and control in areas dictated such interactions and the consequent developments within Eurasia.[113] Porcelain, another Chinese invention, was produced in Jingdezhen, Jiangxi province. It was located near reserves of china-stone from which porcelain was made and shipped its products down the Yangzi delta to connect with commercial centres.[114] In response to the demands of the Persian elite during the Yuan period, the production of white and blue porcelain began in Jingdezhen, which continues to be a centre of production even today. The prefecture was brought under government procurement in 1278 and was an integral part of the provincial government by the end of the thirteenth century. The growth of the province which served internal as well as external markets, as far afield as Iran, was a consequence of the Mongol presence in Eurasia. The Mongols created new markets for producers across Eurasia. They facilitated the inclusion of a wide array of provinces to become part of a global network of economic interaction. In addition, archaeological evidence proves that Chinese goods have been found in Iran in fairly large quantities, allowing one to speculate that the exchange of goods between Iran and China during the latter half of the thirteenth century and the first half of the fourteenth century were indeed noteworthy. The contact between Iran and China led to the development of the import of cobalt into China and the creation of white and blue porcelain.[115] By the end of the thirteenth century Muslim weavers in Tabriz were copying Chinese techniques and themes which may have existed prior to the Mongols arrival but was encouraged and promoted by the Mongols of the Yuan and the Ilkhans.[116] The quantity and opportunities for such exchanges increased in a Eurasia which was more connected than before.

While the aforementioned interactions across Eurasia under the Mongols cover the bulk of relations, the previous chapters lay out the complex and deep ways in which the Mongols and the Khanates impacted nearly all aspects of Eurasian exchange. According to Bosworth the Mongol period represented even among the Turkic nomadic Qaghanates by far, 'a unique moment in history [arose] for the interchange of ideas and of aspects of material culture'.[117]

The Mongols represented the very diverse elements of the steppe and of Eurasia put together and fashioned a hybrid system. The Mongols could accommodate disparate aspects of Eurasia and its regions without diluting their independence. As a precursor to modern day globalisation it deserves attention and reiteration not only for a better understanding of Eurasia but of the world in general. Standing as the bridge between the east and west, Eurasia under the Mongols succeeded in generating a mutually connected world system. As mentioned previously, seen through the prism of a specifically nomadic tradition, the dichotomies often seen in the Westphalian understanding of political and economic relations are minimised and the possibilities of co-existence are highlighted. Modern day globalisation of the twenty-first century similarly boasted of the ease with which people, goods and ideas could travel from one part of the world to another.

Eurasia, a contiguous landmass, with the historical Silk Road passing through it connecting cities and peoples, was a fertile breeding ground for the Mongols. There have long been questions regarding why the Mongols were so successful; historians and academics have answered the question differently over the centuries. The success of the Mongol enterprise has predominantly been associated with the military and the techniques, strategies and innovations in warfare. However, conquest was only the starting point; the Mongols were successful at governing this vast space for over a century. The Mongol legacy lasted even beyond that. Their political genius is no less significant as they were able to combine and fashion policies across Eurasia which were harmonised. The *Mongol worldview* originated in the conditions of the steppe and the immediate life experiences of Chinggis Khan. Steppe tradition with its own ideology of control and governance was at the heart of Mongol Eurasia, which represents a significant unit of history.[118] The Mongol Khans were astute leaders who were militarily brilliant, economically savvy and had an eye for talent. Overland trade with its seemingly natural restrictions were overcome and while the Mongol Khanates were in power remained open to trade. Far from interfering with mercantile activities, the Mongols created avenues for increasing commercial activities, they charged low customs duties and did not impose restriction on movement based on religion. They sponsored trading expeditions and merchants, paid travel costs, incurred risks on large caravans and helped flood markets in their regions with goods from all over Eurasia. Mongols not only created demand for products by attracting all kinds of traders and goods, but through their personal interests and willingness to pay for goods even above the asking price ensured that merchants would choose to come to Eurasia over other parts of the world. Everything from infrastructure within cities to the creation of workshops for production and inter-city connections on the Silk Road made Eurasia a beacon for commercial activity. Through their activities the Mongols managed to bring new players and participants into the international market; Genoese, Venetians and other Europeans managed to find their way into the heart of Eurasia with the establishment of the Golden Horde in Sarai. Iran and China were brought in closer contact and the transfer of goods, peoples, ideas and technologies was easy and in abundance. Relationships within the Mongol Khanates played a role in these connections, and as in the case with the Golden Horde and Ilkhans, their enmity and competition gave rise to a new trade emporia: Black Sea trade.

Summary

In summary, the Mongols were able to achieve that which had been impossible until then. The Silk Road as represented by numerous differentiated networks of roads and passages through which trade took place belies the reality of Mongol Eurasia. The Mongols in world history represent connections but not content. This chapter challenges that idea and shows how the Mongols spurred production as much as they did trade and encouraged manufacturing of numerous products based on what the Mongol state required and demanded. They adapted and innovated a system which was open, diverse and inclusive which formed the underpinnings of a *Mongol worldview* essential to controlling Eurasia. Chinggis Khan and his legacy, whether on the steppe or on the larger map of Eurasia under his grandsons, created a new world in a familiar form. The reorganisation of tribes and the creation of a *suprastate*, which could accommodate local forms of government,[119] was made possible under the Mongols. They managed to create an interconnected state in the form of Mongol Eurasia which attracted loyalty from disparate peoples. This perspective helps formulate an analytical lens which can then be used in the modern day to see processes and events unfolding in Eurasia today. China, Russia and Central Asia can forge relationships which come out of Mongol ideas of *corporate sovereignty* which has to do with the connectedness of Eurasia as a source of wealth and operate on the principle of comprehensive development. Stepping away from the *zero-sum game* would imply the possibility of benefit for China, Russia *and* Central Asia. In simple terms, '[Qualitatively], their [Central Asia] interconnections are much higher than any other economic community';[120] there is no reason why this same principle cannot ring true for larger Eurasia as well and include Russia and China. As we shall see in the next chapter, the new and exciting projects and initiatives in this region echo the rhythms of the past.[121]

Notes

1 Barfield 1989, p. 198
2 Allsen 2001, pp. 201–202
3 Allsen 1987, p. 214
4 Barfield 1989, pp. 20–25
5 Barfield 1989, p. 204
6 Manz 1994, p. 29
7 Allsen, 2001 p. 14
8 Allsen 1989, p. 109
9 Brook 2010, p. 186
10 Allsen 2001, p. 43
11 Allsen 1987, p. 219

12 Vinokurov and Libman 2012, p. 33
13 Martinez 2009, pp. 101–104
14 Cunliffe 2015, p. 466
15 Cunliffe 2015, p. 445
16 Vinokurov and Libman 2012, p. 33
17 Kauz 2006, p. 61
18 Adshead 1993, p. 179
19 See Di Cosmo 2010
20 Jackson 2009, p. 61
21 Abu-Lughod 1989, pp. 334–335
22 Allsen 1987, pp. 182–184
23 Ciociltan 2012, pp. 105–107
24 Aubin 1983, p. 57
25 Allsen 2002, p. 29
26 Baipakov 2000, p. 221
27 Bosworth and Asimov 2000, p. 29
28 Baipakov 2000, p. 222
29 Cunliffe 2015, p. 443
30 Abu-Lughod 1989, p. 145
31 Cioclitan 2012, pp. 136–137
32 Cunliffe 2015, p. 445
33 Martin 1978, p. 401
34 Martin 1978, p. 405
35 Martin 1978, pp. 403–404
36 Halperin 1985, p. 81
37 Martin 1978, p. 401
38 Baipakov 2000, p. 222
39 Ciociltan 2012, p. 95
40 Martin 1978, pp. 410–416
41 Aubin 1983, p. 63
42 Martinez 2009, pp. 105–106
43 Manz 1994, p. 39
44 Brook 2010, pp. 110–114
45 Brook 2010, p. 220
46 Rossabi 1988, p. 189
47 Brook 2010, p. 219
48 Abu-Lughod 1989, pp. 346–347
49 Kauz 2006, p. 63
50 Kauz 2006, p. 51
51 Kauz 2006, pp. 52, 61, 64
52 Abu-Lughod 1989, p. 347
53 Allsen 2001, p. 210
54 Allsen 1997, p. 36
55 Allsen 2001, pp. 200–201
56 Ibid.
57 Allsen 2002, pp. 40–44
58 Allsen 1997, pp. 31–32
59 Allsen 1987, p. 213
60 Biran 1997, p. 86
61 Biran 1997, pp. 86–87
62 Allsen 1997, p. 32
63 Allsen 1987, pp. 214–215
64 Rossabi 1988, p. 122
65 Allsen 1997, pp. 39–40

66 Allsen 1997, pp. 42–44
67 Allsen 1997, pp. 44–45
68 Brook 2010, p. 109
69 Ratchnevsky 1991, p. 100; Allsen 1997, p. 35
70 Allsen 1987, pp. 213–214
71 Rossabi 1988, p. 169
72 Allsen 2002, p. 36
73 They included velvet, buckram, gold embroidery, pearls and bird feathers; Allsen 2002, pp. 17–18
74 Allsen 2002, p. 103
75 Martinez 2009, pp. 100–101
76 Maritnez 2009, p. 103
77 Allsen 2002, p. 28
78 Korea.
79 Otter and Marmot pelts were prized by Mongols; Henthorn 1963, p. 201
80 Henthorn 1963, p. 203
81 Skilled textile industry of Koryo; Henthorn 1963, p. 205
82 Allsen 2002, p. 29
83 Allsen 1989, p. 109
84 Praznik 2010, p. 179
85 Biran 2009, p. 62
86 Adshead 1993, p. 92
87 Allsen 2002, p. 20
88 Allsen 2002, p. 27
89 Allsen 2002, pp. 27–28
90 Allsen 2002, p. 28
91 Allsen 2002, p. 37
92 Allsen 2002, p. 55
93 Jackson 2017, p. 216
94 Brook 2010, p. 106
95 Rossabi 1988, p. 122
96 Buell 1999, p. 205
97 Brook 2010, p. 107
98 Jackson 2017, p. 216
99 Jackson 2017, p. 216
100 Ciociltan 2012, p. 102
101 Martin 1978, pp. 412–415
102 Jackson 2017, p. 212
103 Jackson 2017, p. 214
104 Vinokurov and Libman 2012, p. 37
105 India
106 Adshead 1993, p. 94
107 Allsen 2001, p. 50
108 Adshead 1993, p. 92
109 Spuler 1971, pp. 28–29
110 Allsen 2001, pp. 120–126
111 Brook 2010, p. 202
112 Jackson 2017, p. 235
113 Ibid.
114 Brook 2010, p. 206
115 Wood 2003, p. 116
116 Jackson 2017, p. 227
117 Bosworth 2000, p. 29
118 Christian 1994, p. 173

119 Manz 1994, p. 31
120 Islamov 1994, p. 217
121 Phrase borrowed from Siddharth Saxena who used it in a Symposium to celebrate 25 years of Independence of Kyrgyzstan in October 2016 at Jesus College, University of Cambridge

6 Echoes of the past in present day Eurasia

> The Chinggisid era in world history was a major step towards Eurasian integration and expanded the world or a larger world-consciousness to realms in North Africa and Southern Arabia, beyond the range of Mongol control.[1]

The Mongols initiated a process of transformation and change of the landscape of Eurasia and in doing so created the idea of the Eurasian continent as a connected and integrated landmass for posterity. The Silk Road which connected Eurasia before the Mongol period underwent a mammoth change; it was politically unified for the first time in history. Under Mongol control Eurasia saw a period of protracted trade and social and cultural interactions between its diverse inhabitants. The *Mongol explosion* sparked the beginning of a *continuous world history* and Mongol Eurasia represented an *embryonic world order* based on coexistence.[2] Having discussed the ways and means through which this was achieved helps unravel the mysteries of medieval Asia. The Mongols paved the way towards incorporation without supplanting existing habits, customs and traditions. The creation of Mongol Eurasia which accommodated its unparalleled diversity in political and social structures and economies was an innovative strategy that bore fruit. The Mongol federal structure of governance inherited from the steppe allowed for political unity and a foundation for cultural transmission across Eurasia. Mongol agency evidenced from institutions and an administrative framework which was set up in order to fully exploit Eurasian resources through emphasising and using the natural connections of this landmass are testament to the *Mongol worldview*. The Mongol state amalgamated three aspects in its governance in Eurasia: nomadic social and cultural norms, Chinggissid innovations and the indigenous and/or local traditions of the subject peoples. Time and again the historic continuity, common ancestry and shared political heritage based on steppe models[3] best describe Mongol governance of Eurasia, which leaves no doubt about a particularly *Mongol worldview* which made all this possible.

The economic prosperity witnessed under the Mongols was a combination of the Mongol political system, the Mongol military and Mongol cultural habits which represented inclusiveness and flexibility. As seen in Chapter 2, a combination of steppe traditions and institutions led to the formation of a system which increased economic and commercial activity in Eurasia. The three requisites of successful trade are: infrastructure, investment and logistics, all of which were developed in profound ways under the Mongols. The creation of infrastructure was the foundation for the Mongol transformation of Eurasia. The Mongols established workshops, storage facilities, *caravansarais*, markets and postal stations for the use of merchants, diplomats, couriers and monetarily invested in trade. The special place of merchants, artisans and religious institutions guaranteed a steady flow of information, goods and people across Eurasia. The Mongols had access to old and established commercial networks through these groups. By connecting Eurasia and offering a welcoming environment for traders, irrespective of religions and ethnicities, the Mongols were able to overcome the traditional limitations on the Silk Road. The Mongols were in the 'business of moving goods, animals and people over extended distances'[4] to the effect of unprecedented contact. Political unity on the steppe requires a *geopolitical formlessness*[5] which is different from other world systems. The strength of steppe politics was derived from the federal nature of its governance which was cognizant of migration, mobility and flux. These principles were applied to wider Eurasia to achieve interconnections which could accommodate political, social and economic diversity. The Mongols opened the Silk Road to a cross-section of groups by making overland trade attractive through building infrastructure, minimising risks and increasing margins of profit and prestige attached to the profession of mercantilism.[6] They impacted the quality, quantity and range of markets, goods and services across the board. As a consequence of their policies they were able to engineer the development of a *regional international order*[7] in Eurasia. Markets and the volumes of goods had an influence on profit margins which in turn led to the creation of more markets that furthered commercial activity. There were at least three kinds of activities which propelled trade in this period: tribute and taxes in kind demanded by the Mongols; private trade; and government sponsored trade with capital and support furnished by the Khans, princes and the Mongol imperial family. The appearance of Mongol courts across Eurasia brought with them workshops and markets which reduced the distance between raw materials and manufacturing centres and also attracted merchants from a variety of places to make their wares available in many more places than before. A new kind of common market arose that was based on patterns of consumption and dissemination of the Mongols and the new Eurasian elite. The opportunities thus created brought Eurasia into stark relief and made large scale exchanges and transmissions based on pan-regional connectivity possible. The main achievement of the Mongols was the transformation of Eurasia's economies into a macro-economic reality. As early as the end of the 1250s, the Mongols were able to marshal resources from one end of Eurasia to the other.[8] This would not have been possible without the construction of an integrated system.

The quintessential place of trade and its related aspects for the Mongols and other nomadic groups is not in dispute. Mongol history from the beginning is filled with examples that corroborate that assumption. The immediate cause for the conquest of Khwarezm (Transoxiana/Central Asia) in 1219 was the massacre of Chinggis Khan's trade embassy to Utrar in Turkistan by the local governor which was both a challenge to his authority and detrimental to trade in the region. The conquest of Khwarezm sparked westward conquests and within a period of three years all of Central Asia came under the sway of Chinggis Khan. Trade continued to be associated with political embassies and missions to other empires and resumption of trade after every conquest was among the first steps undertaken by every Khan and/or prince. Merchants filled the ranks of the *Qaghan*'s offices: governors, financial advisers, scribes and so on and represented a key Mongol institution as described in Chapter 2. If there was any doubt that the Mongols did not consciously set out to unify Eurasia or that the shared Chinggissid inheritance of this landmass was key to success, the peace embassy of 1304/1305 which ended the conflict between Yuan China and the Central Asian Mongols, and the subsequent letter to King Philip IV of France in 1305 by Oljeitu (Ilkhan), abrogates it in no uncertain terms. The embassy clearly invokes Chinggis Khan and the inheritance of the Mongol princes and princesses as a consequence, the importance of the caravan trade across the Silk Road and the significance of unification for everyone. Mongol unity in Eurasia with its insistence on Mongol and nomadic steppe traditions and the place of trade as a major revenue stream were anything but an accident. As is expected, individuals and their personalities played an essential role in how events unfolded, however, protracted warfare and the effects of non-cooperation for trade made the princes and Khans mindful of the legacy of Chinggis Khan and his immediate successors. These ideas lasted well after the death of Chinggis Khan and his sons and continued on through until the middle of the fourteenth century. That these ideas percolated further, especially in the figure of Amir Timur who fashioned himself on Chinggis Khan but never called himself Khan because he was not directly related to Chinggis; or the later Uzbek and Kazakh Khanates which sought legitimacy through the Chinggissids remains noteworthy. The Mongol impact on Eurasia runs deeper than even the influence on ruling families because the political entities in modern Eurasia in many ways took shape under the Mongols. Central Asian Turkic tribal identity is only partially altered from the time of the Chinggissid reshuffle of tribes on the steppe,[9] modern China echoes Qubilai Khan's political unification of China in the thirteenth century and Moscow's prominence in Russia was a direct consequence of Mongol rule. These are remarkable feats at any time, that they resonate even today make them even more significant.

The paramount place for a Eurasia connected across borders is easily traced back to the Mongol epoch. Guaranteed, initiated and driven by the Mongol Khans who were kings, military commanders, investors, consumers and strategists able to see the immense potential of the region, it is indeed an achievement worth retelling. Today's world is an expanded version of Mongol Eurasia which included China, the Middle East, Central Asia and Russia and was connected to Europe, Africa and the Indian Subcontinent. All the elements of a modern economy were present: manufactured goods, surplus in production, modes of mobilising and organising labour, along with mechanisms for setting prices, trade contracts, investment, credit facilities and the like.[10] In addition, mechanisation, large scale production and marketing of textiles were taking place in Eurasia on a grand scale and there was a 'gradual flow of goods and information across the landmass'.[11] Eurasia has remained connected in parts through the efforts of Central Asian Khanates and Tsarist Russia, which followed by the Soviet Union continued to engage in a largely borderless exchange of goods and movement of peoples. The end of the Cold War sparked a crisis in the region and for the first time since the Mongols in the thirteenth century Eurasia was divided along hard borders. In the early 1990s these borders were almost insurmountable for trade or any exchange of peoples, ideas and technologies. Since then the countries of Central Asia, Russia and even China have been working through bilateral and multilateral organisations.[12] Now, more than 25 years after the collapse of the Soviet Union, the emergence of mostly stable sovereign nations of Central Asia and the economic miracle in China are changing the landscape of Eurasia. Central Asia, the centre that is treated like a periphery because of its lack of inherent flexibility and disparity, is developing new relationships with its neighbours, Russia and China, by entering into regional organisations and groupings which give them an equal platform. The Eurasian Economic Union and the One Belt One Road (OBOR) initiative point to a recommencement of interactions which enjoyed prominence under the Mongols in the thirteenth century, in subsequent Khanates, in Tsarist Russia and finally, in the Soviet Union. Russia in many ways has had a more continuous relationship with Central Asian countries and shares a far more recent Soviet past with the region which continues to carry on the legacy of institutions of the Soviet Union. The immediate memory of exchanges sans borders is still very much alive but is associated closely with an imperial-coloniser relationship rather than more positive exchanges. The complex relationship between Russia and the Central Asian countries remains a point of contention fraught with remnants of old unequal relationships. Conversely the relationship between Central Asia and China stretches back centuries, but was circumvented soon after Mongol power waned and eventually was directed by Moscow in Tsarist Russian and Soviet times. China's intentions towards Central Asia have been pigeonholed by a European colonial discourse which reflects the Russia-China relationship rather than China and Central Asia. However, despite these obstacles in forging future relationships, the countries of Eurasia are making a concerted effort to revive connections and enter into closer partnerships. At the heart of this lies the promise of opportunities that connectivity in this region offers for all countries. The immediate past of the region can be counterbalanced with a longer historical lens which incorporates the Mongol era.

Chinese scholars, unlike Sovietologists in the 1960s, tended to consider the Mongols in the history of China as a progressive force for breaking barriers and fostering economic prosperity. So, it comes as no surprise that China's activities in the present day resemble connectivity which evokes images of Mongol Eurasia.[13] The bulk of overland trade in the thirteenth century was transported from east to west through Central Asia. With China's OBOR initiative, trade to and through Central Asia can pass effectively and to everyone's benefit. The relationship between China and Russia also requires Central Asia. China's focus on developing infrastructure projects and relationships with the countries on the historic Silk Road is in line with a thinking dating back centuries. The main reason the Mongols were able to successfully connect Eurasia was the syncretistic nature of their policies.[14] Mongols were agents of exchange and were able to fully support circulation of ideas, peoples, technologies and goods. In doing so they created the conditions for transcontinental exchanges.[15] Mongol Eurasia was different from Eurasia before but accommodated diversity, and if anything, even expanded it. This is even more important today because with the formation of hardened identities which are promoted through borders and the creation of nations, the possibility of maintaining cultural differences while still interacting intimately surely acts as a further incentive. The memory of a unified Eurasia under the Mongols with its economic prosperity and cultural diversity can serve as a positive example of working towards a common goal while still being distinct. The historical continuum of Eurasia starting with the Mongols makes it possible to envision the benefits of an integrated Eurasia for one-fifth of the world's population.

This brings us to the finer details of the countries that make up Eurasia today and the importance of individual players: big and small, in Eurasia 2.0 following in the footsteps of Mongol Eurasia. Much of the discussion regarding Eurasia in today's parlance centres around China and Russia who dominate regional discourse both within and without. The central part of Eurasia, the Central Asian countries of Kazakhstan, Uzbekistan, Kyrgyzstan, Turkmenistan and Tajikistan tend to be viewed as mere spectators of events unfolding in the region. The place of Central Asians within Mongol administration is undeniable. Seen through a snapshot of history the Mongols and Central Asians might appear distinct but their shared heritage is undeniable. It was not in the least surprising that Central Asians played an important role in either the Mongol military[16] or political structure. Much like Central Asia's position at the beginning of Mongol expansion, and the importance of the Central Asian multi-lingual elite in state building and administration in the thirteenth century, Central Asia's 'centrality has allowed it to be alternatively a point of diffusion and a point of convergence'.[17] Mongols and Turks on the steppe were not fixed units of identity but rather negotiated identities which were constantly evolving. The steppe was home not only to the Mongols but also to Turkic tribes which lived across Central Asia. This shared heritage allowed Central Asians to understand and convey Mongol principles of governance. The make-up of Central Asian tribal entities today date back to Mongol times because these groups were part of the milieu of the steppe. The environment in which Chinggis Khan rose to power was one of shifting alliances which had constantly changing tribal formations. The constant reorganisation of tribes in Central Asia as late as the 1320s and then again under Timur all point to the fluidity of these groups. Flexibility can be interpreted as unstable but also as an opportunity for negotiation.

The dichotomies concerning Central Asia as centre (Marija Gimbutas) and as periphery (Colin Renfrew) persist,[18] just as they persevere for the Mongols as destroyers and at the same time as the providers of safe conduit across the Silk Road. Seen through the lens of history, Central Asia has steadfastly remained at the centre of world institutions and religions in both passive and active ways: Buddhism, Islam and (Nestorian) Christianity; philosophies and science (Avicenna and al-Khwarezmi to name a few); and served as the supplier of goods and services (slaves, horses, multi-lingual administrators) to China and the subcontinent, as well as to Iran, Iraq and as far as Egypt and even Europe. The decentralised nature of Central Asia has relegated its population and achievements to be remembered as either through religion (mainly Muslim) or as nomads (part of the Mongols). Successfully written out of history as agents the region is perceived as a passage at best. Central Asia continues to be recalled in terms which imply its subservient position, not as innovators, creators or producers of ideas, goods and services. Colonised first by the Russians and subsequently being incorporated into the Soviet Union has further pigeonholed Central Asian countries as sources of raw materials at worst and a thoroughfare to better and more profitable markets at best. Never the endpoint, always the passage, Central Asia's flexibility to be able to adapt and seamlessly merge with world systems has continued to dictate its position in world history. Even after being referred to as the *pivot of history* by Mackinder,[19] Central Asian countries see themselves as constantly being acted upon and not as actors.

The current discussion on Eurasia threatens to be overtaken by the same weakness unless the history of Eurasia can be understood as first and foremost a nomadic enterprise which brought disparate systems in close contact with each other. Mongol expansion was underscored by Central Asian elite that had the knowledge and experience of government and business so essential to the Eurasian enterprise. Not only do the previous chapters focus on institutions, including religious policies, and trade throughout Eurasia, they also provide the multifarious ways and means through which the Mongol hierarchy activated, achieved and encouraged exchange of nearly every variety. Within that system, the groups that did well were the ones who were willing to take risks and work in the new world order. The Central Asians had obvious advantages: geographical proximity, experience, multi-lingual skills, and they were intimately immersed in ancient commercial networks in the east and the west on the Silk Road. The lessons of the history of Eurasia under the Mongols transgress nations and groups and bring to light the cooperative nature of the region that cut across borders, ethnic groups, religions and political systems. The history of Central Asia as part of Eurasia has been one of adaptation to different world influences, and through all that the region has remained distinct, with separate lineages, dynasties, policies and even goals. The Central Asians have managed to combine nomadic, sedentary, Islamic, Tsarist Russian and even Soviet influences and yet remain distinct.[20] Just like the shared heritage with the Mongols on the steppe enabled Central Asians to be at the centre of interactions, they now have the lived experience of Russian and Soviet institutions. This in conjunction with their centuries old interactions with China give them a unique agency in the Eurasian space. The distance, be it logistical, political or economic, between Russia and China can effectively be reduced through Central Asia. Connections, and not separation, have been at the heart of Eurasia since the people of Inner Asia broke physical, religious and social barriers. These aspects are as relevant today as they were in Chinggisid times.

The Mongol drive towards creating a trade infrastructure and a market system across Eurasia, guaranteed by their military prowess and political authority, created an unparalleled system. Infrastructure, regularised customs duties, markets, currency convertibility, state guarantees and subsidies, financial and other investment, insurance and visa-free travel across the length of Eurasia cut across regions and was delivered equally across the landscape. As a consequence, Central Asia has remained connected with Russia and China since Mongol times. The Timurids, Uzbek and Kazakh Khanates and following them the Khanates of Bukhara, Kokand and Khiva were not closed off from each other and coming from the steppe imbibed Mongol principles of state formation, governance and interaction. The Tsarist Russian Imperial drive, while being negative and destructive to the local Khanates, governed the region of Central Asia as one political unit, Turkistan, and minimised the presence of borders in the region. The Soviet Union was yet another drive towards the deletion of borders, and while there are mixed feelings in the region of Central Asia about the impact of the Soviet Union, it did create physical infrastructure in the region and connected remote parts with the economy of Moscow through the 70 years of its existence. The post-independence period, from 1991 to present times, has witnessed one of the first instances of hardened borders, which has separated families and peoples coexisting for centuries. The negative effects of the economies of Central Asia being separated from each other are still impacting the countries of the region. Many attempts at regional organisations, economic and political, have been made, initially to no effect but they are finally coming to fruition. Organisations like the Commonwealth of Independent States and the Shanghai Cooperation Organisation along with other regional initiatives have tried in their own ways to engage with political and economic conditions of the region. As mentioned in the introduction, the aspects of globalisation today and under the Mongols in the thirteenth century are almost identical: a professional class, trade, generosity and reciprocity, cosmopolitanism, technology and innovation, multilingual citizenry, open religious policies, maximum exploitation of resources and a flexible system that can accommodate multiple political cultures. Under the Mongols these aspects were underwritten by the Mongol Khanates with a well-informed and able bureaucracy. Today, the global world order is guaranteed by international organisations, regional and multilateral groupings and other such mechanisms.

Within this context, the formation of the Eurasian Economic Union with Russia and Kazakhstan as the main drivers and the latest Chinese initiative of the OBOR which goes even further than the immediate region and encompasses the whole of the Silk Road, including countries in Southeast Asia as well, much like Mongol Eurasia, are proving formidable and are set to redefine the rules of development, trade and Eurasian relationships. One cannot escape the notions of the Westphalian state and sovereign rights of independent countries within the context of a largely Eurocentric understanding of political and economic relations. However, if we step back, as we have done here, and consider the historical underpinnings of Eurasia we can see that the region has a lot in common and can benefit from overall development which bridges connections and builds parity in the region. The world economic system initiated by the Mongols and continued by the Europeans from the sixteenth century, encouraged and built further by the Americans after World War II, requires comprehensive redevelopment and recasting. It is not enough for the global system to open borders and make wealthy nations still wealthier. There is need for a more inclusive development which translates into real infrastructure (building roads, bridges, ports and banking institutions) in order to provide for widespread development across regions. The European and Western knowledge economies have built a world system which maintains them as forerunners at the cost of keeping other economies dependent on them. This has proven unsustainable by the recent and continuing financial crises. A large part of the world's population remains unable to benefit from the present system while still being affected by global developments. The new initiatives from China, Kazakhstan and Russia are well within the existing world economic system and by using the framework of the global economy have begun to bring in a Eurasian perspective which indicates comprehensive development. By investing in infrastructure development across the Eurasian space there is a trend towards connecting economies which have remained behind and to provide mutually beneficial exchanges which have the potential to bring economic benefit to the wider region. As landlocked countries, Central Asian economies suffer from a lack of access to maritime trade, however, as seen in the thirteenth century, the Mongols overcame that problem and created a whole new system of markets and used innovative strategies like reducing customs duties and risk, guaranteeing caravans over long distances and establishing workshops for production closer to markets, to make overland trade competitive and profitable. The Mongols used all possible avenues to encourage overland and sea trade. When they came across blockades because of infighting and rivalries, they found new routes and created markets and trading systems to compensate for those losses. Eurasia requires resources and skills from across the region to function in a seamless manner and overland trade is an important aspect of this integration. Central Asia is at the heart of overland trade and occupies a central position in any discussion on Eurasian cooperation. Central Asian societies have continuously renegotiated their position in this framework and have historically been the *movers and shakers* of the Eurasian economy since time immemorial. The time is ripe now to harness strategies which stretch back centuries but are relevant even today. The Mongol century can provide answers in innovative strategies which were used by a cross-section of people to engage with a world which had hitherto been opaque. With 25 years of independence of Central Asian countries, booming prosperity in China, resurgent economies of Russia and Kazakhstan, and the increased global presence of Asian economies like India, Korea and Singapore, we are presented with new alternatives to regional development.

The Eurasian Economic Union emerging from the countries of the former Soviet Union and the OBOR initiative by China point to a sea change in the way that trade, development and relationships in the region will be conducted in the future. The aim is to connect Asia, Europe and Africa in order to revive the old Silk Road in new and exciting ways and for the economies of these regions to enjoy the benefit of global trade in the world's richest continents. The OBOR initiative, previously called the Silk Road Economic Belt was unveiled in 2013 includes a land-based Silk Road Economic Belt and the twenty-first century Maritime Silk Road. It aims at connecting Eurasia through six corridors: Western China to Eastern Russia, Northern China with Eastern Russia, the China-Mongolia-Russia corridor, the China-Central Asia-West Asia corridor, the China-India Peninsula, the China-Pakistan corridor and the China-Bangladesh-India corridor.[21] In addition, there is a Maritime Silk Road which will link China to the Mediterranean. In its entire vision, it hopes to include 60 countries and is expected to have an estimated investment of $8 trillion over a period of time. It includes half the world's population, 30 per cent of the global economy and is seen as a stimulus package for trade rather than just a development project. China has established financial institutions like the Asian Infrastructure and Investment Bank (AIIB, 2016) and the Silk Road Fund (2014) with members from across Eurasia and the world in order to provide for the financial needs of infrastructure development in the region and beyond. Funding is set to be primarily carried out through preferential debt financing and equity. The Chinese government has pledged funds from its foreign exchange reserves and its largest state-owned banks. It has already invested by giving out loans and through other aid, to build transport networks: roads, railways, ports; power-plants, oil and gas pipelines and refineries; information technology and telecoms; and other forms of financial infrastructure to reinvigorate Eurasian trade. The OBOR is directed towards developing the less developed regions within China as well, especially Western China which borders Central Asia. China's immediate neighbours in Central Asia are of prime importance. China has initiated talks with Kazakhstan to integrate it with the *Nurly Zhol* programme[22] in order to create a joint partnership with countries of Central Asia. One of China's key goals is to stimulate trade, improve connectivity, reduce transportation and transit costs, make overland trade cost effective (especially in the transport of raw materials) and connect inland countries in Eurasia with the larger markets of China and Russia in more intimate ways. In all this China has stressed the importance of partnerships, not only in its membership, for example, of the AIIB but it is also encouraging Public Private Partnerships. It wants to engage governments, private funds and companies to participate in these wide-ranging projects. This kind of engagement allows for both Chinese and foreign companies to come into closer contact with each other. The riskier investments will be guaranteed and/or subsidised by the Chinese government in face of political or social turmoil. China intends on investing $150 billion every year in projects across Eurasia. The initiative is designed to stimulate medium- and long-term growth in the region and beyond.

The OBOR is an initiative which fully encapsulates the rising power of China in the world and funding began in 2016. A few years earlier, the Russia-Central Asia space was already experiencing a resumption of connections through the Eurasian Economic Union which was first established as the Customs Union in 2010 and included Russia, Kazakhstan and Belarus. In 2015, it was renamed the Eurasian Economic Union and Armenia and Kyrgyzstan joined the group. The main goal was to create a customs-free zone which would bolster trade and exchange between the countries by reducing trade barriers and allowing for freer movement of goods and peoples. The concept of Eurasianism was pioneered by President Nazarbayev of Kazakhstan who proposed the idea of the Eurasian Economic Project soon after Kazakhstan gained independence in 1991. Furthermore, '[T]he ideology of Eurasianism was officially recognized in Kazakhstan, and one of Kazakhstan's leading universities – the Eurasian National University in Astana – was named after Lev Gumilev'.[23] Nazarbayev has even been called the father of Eurasianism and his vision of the economic space embraces economic pragmatism and states that the driving forces are 'economic interests and not abstract ideas and slogans'.[24] Nazarbayev's vision is driven by innovation and technology and is set apart from its Russian counterpart by stressing the importance of Central Asia's will and desire to be part of, or indeed to lead, such a project.[25] In the lead up to the creation of the Eurasian Economic Union in the early days of 2012, while analysing the impact of the Customs Union, Kalra and Varadzhakov pointed out that if

> … the Customs Union continues to move in a positive direction, it has the potential to develop into a significant step towards greater integration in the region. It is well placed to help provide a counter-balance to China by increasing the bargaining power of Kazakhstan as key to the transportation of Chinese goods into Europe. Kazakhstan is already important to China as a resource base for oil and wheat but by becoming a transit point it catapults Kazakhstan as an actor in the region. China is also one of the most important trading partners of Belarus, it ranked as the fifth foreign trade partner in 2009. The territory of Russia and Kazakhstan can form the transportation link between Western China and Europe which has been stressed by both President Medvedev and President Nazarbayev.[26]

Seen in conjunction with each other, the OBOR takes up where the Eurasian Economic Union leaves off and singles out Kazakhstan in Central Asia and Western China as the first areas for infrastructure development.

Both these initiatives have attracted attention and as with many non-Western endeavours, there is suspicion and trepidation concerning the motivation and reach of these programmes. When the Customs Union (Kazakhstan, Russia and Belarus) was established in 2010 there were accusations and fear of a revival of the Soviet space and Russian hegemony. It was also seen as a threat to trade to other players like the European Union from countries in the region and abroad. Kazakh businesses and private citizens viewed it as a move to dilute their sovereignty. However, the figures have shown that since 2010 the Kazakh economy has done well and has benefitted from a more relaxed trade environment. In a similar vein, the OBOR has been viewed as China's outreach programme and a means to increase its soft power around the world. The initiative has been variously seen as a rival to American supremacy and depending on the relationships between neighbours seen as an impending threat to regional security sometime in the future. Even the countries within Eurasia, especially countries like Kazakhstan in Central Asia, India in South Asia and others have raised the spectre of Chinese power and the aspirations of China to become a new superpower. From the projects that the OBOR has funded it is difficult to see China as working unilaterally, if anything the projects are set to improve connectivity and give significant returns to China only in the long term. For example, rail networks linking Southeast Asia through Cambodia, Laos, Vietnam, Myanmar, Thailand, Malaysia and Singapore; construction of a combined cycle power plant in Saudi Arabia through a joint partnership between Siemens and the Shandong Electric Power Construction 3rd Company; and recently in May 2017 India was approved a loan to build 'The Power for All' programme by the AIIB[27] among other such grand projects. Sceptics who have raised concerns over whether any of these projects will come to completion should look to the rail network established in Kenya financed by Chinese loans and the China-Myanmar pipeline which is now operational and which will be essential for China's crude oil imports which will help in its production of refined products to be exported abroad.[28]

The opportunities that the OBOR is offering are not limited to companies and governments within Eurasia but also to companies and governments beyond the region. The membership of the AIIB is global and includes many countries from Europe and South America. Siemens is doing well in winning contracts and one of the key aspects of the way funding will be made available is to encourage Chinese and non-Chinese companies to interact and work together. China's growing position in the world will allow for guarantees and increase the possibilities of partnerships within China as well which is a market many Western companies still want to break into. Experts and analysts have offered numerous theories to explain China's motivations and have pinpointed overcapacity in steel and manufacturing in China as one which requires outlets to ease pressure on the domestic economy. Indeed, the OBOR and its emphasis on building infrastructure and exporting Chinese steel and related technologies are all designed to benefit China, but that does not preclude advantages for other domestic economies in the region. In actual economic terms, this allows for a more positive outlook and makes stakeholders out of a larger cross-section of players. China has openly admitted it is not in a position to finance all the projects even within China. Western provinces of China need to catch up with other more prosperous southern provinces within the country. As a result, the immediate developmental projects are directed to the western regions of China and projects in Central Asia. This clearly indicates a view toward reducing gaps in China and connecting to its neighbours to re-activate avenues of growth and economic benefit in traditional Eurasia.

After 1991, the newly formed sovereign states of Central Asia found themselves trying to connect with a wider world, including the countries within the region. The rebuilding of connections within the region mostly came to naught in the period following independence. Although trade in the region has increased, it is not as seamless as it was in Soviet times. However, the creation of the Eurasian Economic Union and the more recent initiative (OBOR) of China signal a new direction for Eurasia and beyond. These two initiatives are first and foremost economically driven and highlight the natural connections in the region which are not being utilised properly because of a lack of infrastructure. Recalling the Mongol period of the thirteenth century, one of the first things that the Mongols did was to build infrastructure on the Silk Road which connected Beijing to Korea, Persia, parts of Russia and beyond. Similarly, both the Eurasian Economic Union and the OBOR are development projects which focus on infrastructure and legal frameworks to navigate this vast geographical space with diverse populations, ethnicities, religious affiliations, customs and traditions. All of these point to a well thought out and planned strategy to connect Eurasia in essential ways which over centuries have been overshadowed by differences and political turmoil both home grown and imported from outside. The natural connections of the larger region have long been superseded by European understandings of the region and their economic demands and needs. Seen in the larger historical perspective, China's initiative and to some extent the Eurasian Economic Union, reflect something deeply ingrained in the region which can be traced back at least to the thirteenth century. There is a growing understanding especially in response to world politics today that we live in an interconnected world and while a global perspective includes a much wider region, the Eurasian region is a microcosm of that same process and is inhabited by the majority of the world's population. The region was connected and developed as a cohesive whole until European hegemony dismantled its compositeness and transformed Eurasia in ways which focused on differences rather than commonalities.

The OBOR harks back to the ancient Silk Road and scholars and journalists have talked at length about the positive currency that China is trying to associate its strategy with by associating with it. China's use of the symbolism of the Silk Road is in line with other initiatives which over the last decade countries in Central Asia, Japan and even the United States have tried to create. The origins of the Silk Road stretch back to the Han dynasty; however, it was not until the thirteenth century that a truly Eurasian project in the form of Mongol Eurasia took shape. It was the Mongols of the thirteenth century that brought to light the interconnectedness of the region and made possible, through their practices and policies, a unique moment in history which continues to impact the world. This was the moment at which the Silk Road became the highly lucrative, heavily travelled and profitable route it has come to represent. The mythic nature of the Silk Road, while useful in building grand projects, needs to be revisited as a tool which was used by a vast portion of the population. It supplied everyday essentials along with luxury goods as a commonplace aspect of life in Eurasia. The adjectives most closely associated with the East continue to be words like *mysterious* and *dangerous* which evoke distance and unfamiliarity even for people who inhabit the region. This reinforces old concepts of colonialism and backwardness which came to represent the countries of China, Central Asia, Russia and beyond. By challenging established opinions about the Mongols, Eurasia can be revisited in a way that highlights its uniqueness. Considering modern day happenings, the Mongol century provides the basis for rethinking, reimagining and reinventing notions of interaction. By considering an alternative worldview which had its roots in steppe tradition Eurasia can escape the overwhelming realist interpretation of geopolitics. Central Asia does not need to balance the power of Russia and China, it can mediate and negotiate its position based on its constant role as part of the fabric of Eurasia. To summarise, Eurasia is a contiguous landmass with enormous potential for economic and cultural development. There is an urgent need to disengage with the discourse of great games and geopolitical balancing. A historical perspective on Eurasia can go a long way to unleash our imaginations in the region and without.

Notes

1 Di Cosmo *et al.* 2009, p. 4
2 Adshead 1993, p. 5
3 Buell 1994; Mott 2015; Jackson 2017
4 Allsen 2009, p. 144
5 Mott 2015, p. 11
6 Twitchett *et al.* [1994]1998, pp. 295–296
7 Mott 2015, pp. x, xiv, 3
8 Allsen 1987, p. 219
9 Golden 1992, p. 292
10 Abu-Lughod 1989, p. 8
11 Goody 1997, p. 112
12 For example: Commonwealth of Independent States, Shanghai Cooperation Organisation, Organisation for Security and Cooperation in Europe and Organisation of Islamic Cooperation
13 Ratchnevsky 1991, p. 212
14 Di Cosmo *et al.* 2009, p. 3
15 Allsen 2001, p. 193
16 Adhsead 1993, p. 53
17 Adshead 1993, p. 27
18 Adshead 1993, p. 28
19 Mott 2015, p. 4
20 Manz 1994, p. 20
21 PwC's Growth Market Centre 2016

22 Kazakhstan's Program for the Future initiated by President Nazarbayev. For more information see Nazarbayev 2014
23 Eurasian Doctrine of Kazakh President Nursultan Nazarbayev, see Biryukova 2013
24 Ivanov 2011
25 See Saxena and Kalra 2015
26 Kalra and Varadzhakov 2012, p. 6
27 Asian Infrastructure and Investment Bank 2017
28 The Independent 2017

Epilogue

As has been discussed so far, Eurasia as a geographical concept has existed since time immemorial. The physical connectivity of Eurasia is best depicted through the ancient Silk Road which signified a complex network of roads and waterways to connect the different regions of Eurasia, from China through Central Asia, Iran and Iraq to Russia and the surrounding regions. In the previous chapters I have touched upon the first moment of the physical connectivity of the Eurasia region which was unified by the Mongol Khans in the thirteenth century. The regions of Eurasia were brought closer to each other and the Mongols provided infrastructure for a more uniform and regulated way of conducting trade and other exchanges along the Silk Road. The Mongol Khans brought a sense of unity to policies and practices across this vast territory and created unprecedented prosperity along the Silk Road. They connected parts of Eurasia which had hitherto been intermittent and limited. In the run up to the establishment of Mongol Eurasia, merchants had traversed the immense network of the Silk Road(s) and had built relationships along the way which allowed for mercantile activity in the form of micro-economies. The Mongols scaled those exchanges by building a composite macro-economy through policies which connected distant regions and minimised costs and risks. The Eurasian experience could thenceforth include movement across the full expanse of the Silk Road.

The establishment of Mongol Eurasia with its four subdivisions: Yuan China, Ilkhanate Persia, the Golden Horde and the Chaghatais and Ogedeis in Central Asia began to be ruled according to steppe traditions of joint patrimony. They shared common goals and aspirations, economic activity based on trade being among the most important. The formation of Mongol Eurasia which connected and represented a contiguous region underwent development along similar lines. As has been described in Chapter 2, the institutions introduced by the Mongols were cognizant of local conditions. They were able to lay the groundwork for essential infrastructure which connected the region and made information free flowing and accessible throughout the region. The Mongols provided security and safety, investment for trade and manufacturing, fiscal and monetary infrastructure which extended markets and thus created a much larger network of demand and supply to greater success than ever before. In addition, the Mongols exploited all possible avenues for trade: land and maritime. The Khanates created multiple manufacturing hubs and markets that led to increased economic activity in all the regions of Eurasia.

The formidable ways in which overland trade competed with maritime trade created a new understanding and agency among the peoples of Eurasia. The possibilities offered by the Mongols felt almost limitless and allowed new players like the Venetians and the Genoese to enter the region. Maritime trade and waterways continued to play an important role and the Mongol Khans spent resources and energy on making sure that maritime and waterways trade flourished as well. The particular political and economic structure of the steppe engineered changes in the wider Eurasian economic structure. Mongol Eurasia was the formation of a new world order and has been variously called the first moment of globalisation and even a precursor to the European century which arose in the sixteenth century.[1] The world which we inhabit today is still guided in a large part by the principles and economic system which was first introduced by the Mongols and carried forward by the Europeans. Capitalism, industrialisation and market driven economies as European constructs of the sixteenth century remain the building blocks of modern economies. With the growth of Europe, the East, especially Eurasia came to be seen as a kind of backwater and a place where natural resources were found in abundance but whose inhabitants were perceived as backward and traditional, unable to utilise that wealth. They needed the benevolent hand of European masters to bring them into the modern world. European colonialism introduced an unequal system which worked on principles alien to Eurasia. The downward spiral of the biggest economies in the world in the seventeenth and eighteenth centuries is testament to the failure of a disconnected Eurasia. European dichotomies replaced what had existed before and led to the collapse of Central Asian, Chinese and Indian socieities. World Wars I and II brought the colonial order to a close and with that the American century, as the second half of the twentieth century came to be called, began. The culminating point of this process was the collapse of the Soviet Union in 1991 which was the final word on the triumph of capitalism. The moment of absolute globalisation was achieved with the post-Soviet space now part of the 'capitalist' world order. Beginning in 2016 that global order has been challenged and that too from within; with the United Kingdom's Brexit vote to opt out of the European Union and the election of Donald Trump as President of the United States the world in 2017 looks poised to turn its back on globalisation. However, the processes of globalisation are reverberating on the continent where it first took form. With the Mongols as the frontrunners in the history of Eurasia is replete with models of global outreach. The history of the world seen through a uniquely Eurasian lens can help understand regional shifts. President Xi Jin Ping in China's inaugural address at *Davos* in 2017 has declared the importance of globalisation for a stable and prosperous world order. The theme of the Davos Economic Forum, *Responsive and Responsible Leadership*, which was fully supported by China's leadership, leaves little room for conjecture. China is committed to the global vision of the world and is acting accordingly.[2] In the historical continuum of Eurasia this clearly represents a continuation of the natural order.

Notes

1 Abu-Lughod 1989, p. 4
2 Shujie 2017

Appendix 1

Key words

Basqaq	Officials
Biceci	Scribes
Darugachi	Governor
Ilkhan	Subordinate Khan
Jam	Postal stations
Khatun	Princesses/Female title
Ordo	Horde
Paizas	Visas/Tablets
Sharia	Muslim customary laws
Tamgha	Imperial seal/Taxation on stamped goods
Tumen	Decimal units
Ulus	Four Mongol Khanates
Yasaq	Chinggis Khan's legal code/Mongol customary laws

Appendix 2
Golden lineage

Qaghans and Khans[1]

Chinggis Khan 1206–1227
Ogedei Qaghan 1229–1241
Chaghatai (died 1244/1245)
Jochi (died 1227)
Tolui (died 1232/1233)
Toregene Khatun (Regent) 1241–1246
Guyuk Qaghan 1246–1248
Oghul Qaimish Khatun (Regent) 1248–1251
Mongke Qaghan 1251–1259
Qubilai Qaghan 1260–1294 (Yuan China)
Temur Qaghan 1294–1307
Qaishan (1307–1311), Buyantu (1311–1320) and Yesun Temur (1323–1328)

Chaghatai Central Asians

Chaghatai
Yesu Mongke 1246–1251
Qara Huegu 1245–1246
Orghina Khatun (Regent) 1251–1252
Mubarak Shah 1252–1260
Alughu 1260–1266
Baraq 1266–1271
Du'a 1282/3–1307
Konchek, Kopek/Eljigidei and Dore Temur 1307–1331
Tarmashirin 1331–1334

Ogedeis

Qaidu 1271–1302

Jochids (Golden Horde)

Batu 1225–1255
Sartaq 1255–1256
Berke 1257–1267
Mengu Temur 1267–1280
Tode Mengu 1280–1287
Tole Buqa 1287–1290
Toqta 1290–1312
Ozbeg 1312–1341
Janibeg 1342–1357
Berdibeg 1357–1359

Ilkhanids

Hulegu (died 1265)
Abagha 1265–1282
Arghun 1284–1291
Gaikhatu 1291–1295
Ghazan 1295–1304
Oljeitu 1304–1316
Abu Said 1316–1335
Sadi Beg Khatun 1338–1339

Note

1 Jackson 2017, Appendix 2 Tables 1–4

Appendix 3

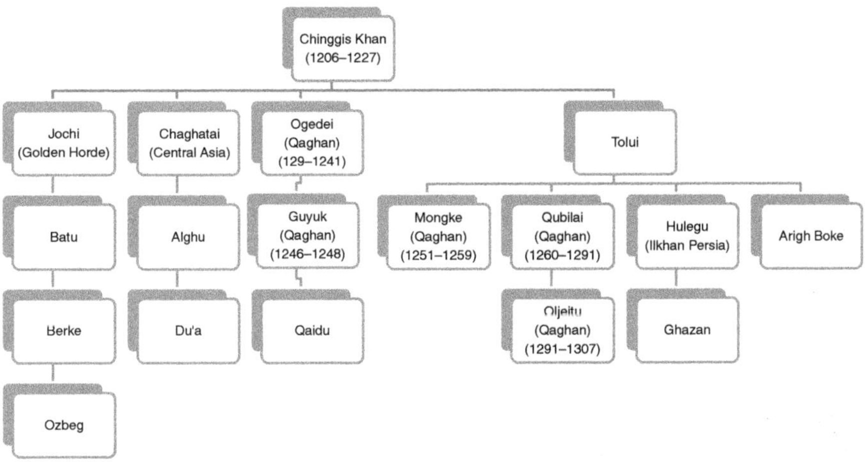

Appendix 3.1 Genealogy chart.

Appendix 4

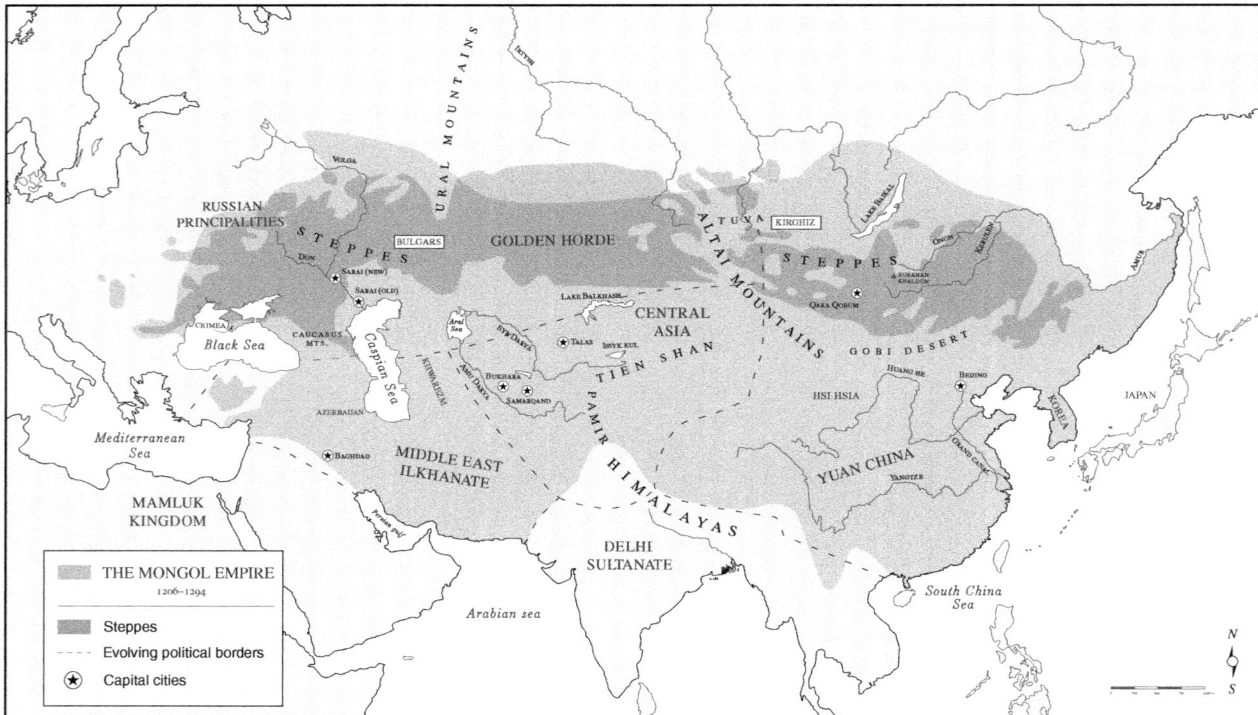

Appendix 4.1 The Mongol Empire in the thirteenth century: Yuan China, Central Asia (Chaghatais and Ogedeis), Golden Horde and the Ilkhanate.

Appendix 5

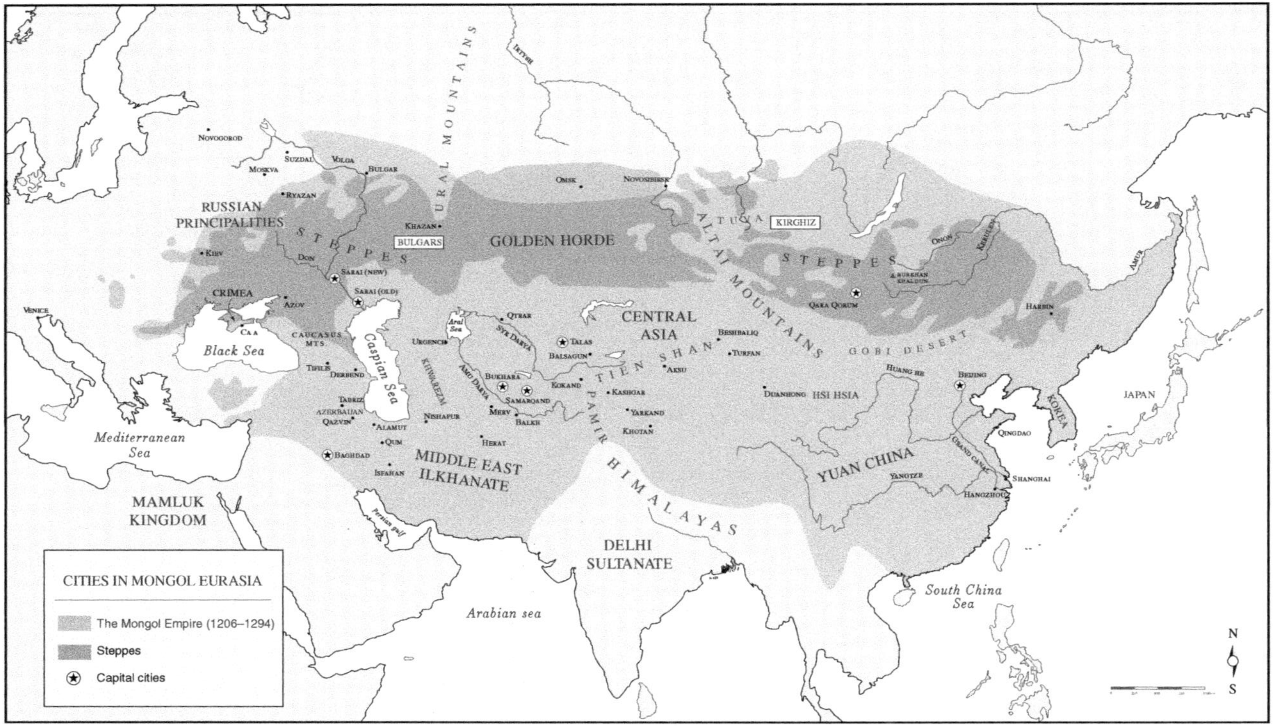

Appendix 5.1 Important cities in Mongol Eurasia: capital cities, trading cities, port cities and garrison cities.

Appendix 6

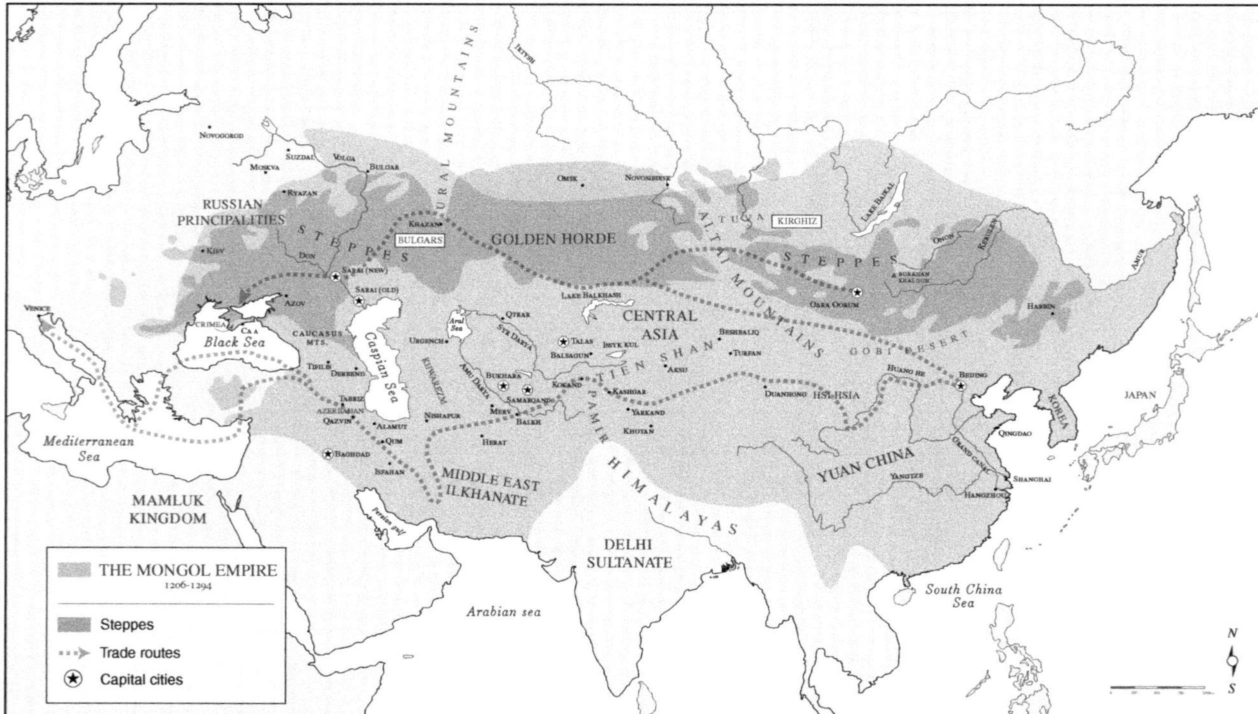

Appendix 6.1 The Silk Road(s): trade routes linking Yuan China with the Ilkhanate (Middle East) through Central Asia; Yuan China with the Golden Horde and Europe through Central Asia.

Appendix 7

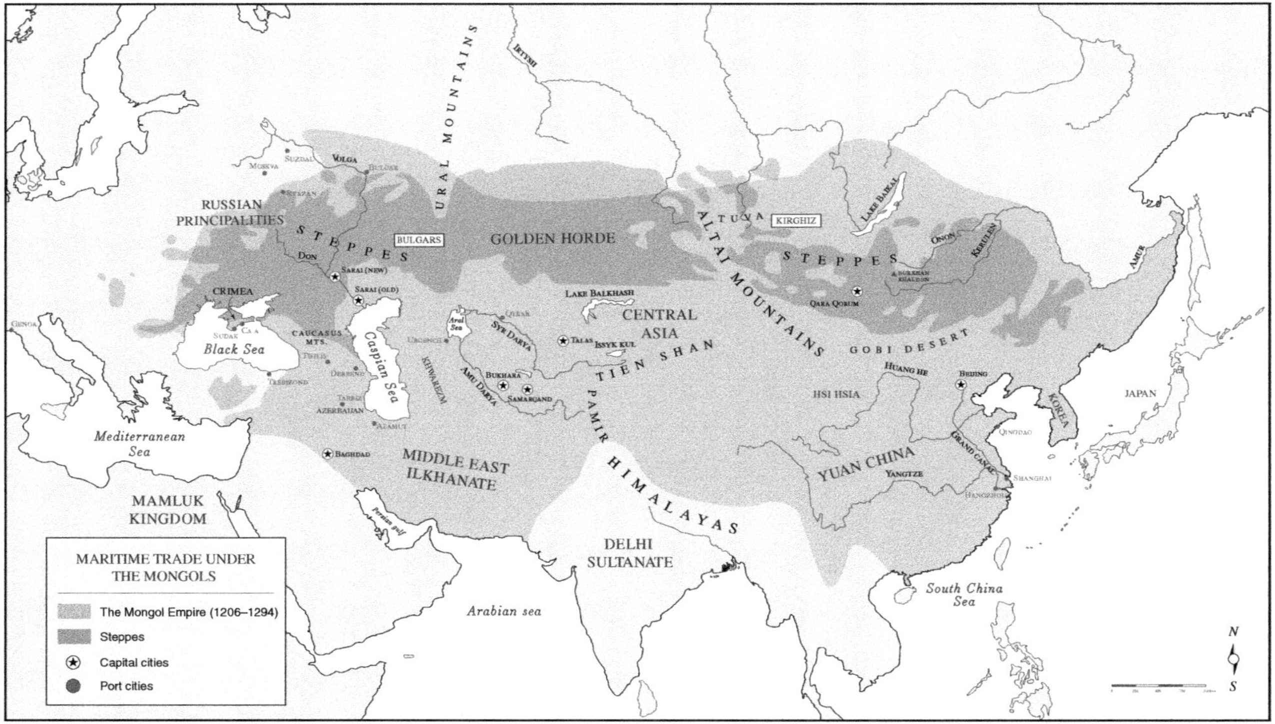

Appendix 7.1 Maritime trade in Mongol Eurasia: waterways, rivers and sea trade.

Bibliography

Abu-Lughod, J. *Before European Hegemony The World System* A.D. *1250–1350* (Oxford, United Kingdom: Oxford University Press, 1989)

Adshead, S. A. M. *Central Asia in World History* (London: Macmillan Publishing, 1993)

Aigle, D. *The Mongol Empire Myth and Reality: Studies in Anthropological History* (Boston, United States: Brill, 2014)

Alam, M. and Subrahmanyam, S. *Indo-Persia Discoveries in the Age of Discoveries 1400–1800* (Cambridge, United Kingdom: Cambridge University Press, 2007)

Allsen, T. *The Mongols in East Asia, Twelfth-Fourteenth Centuries: A Preliminary Bibliography of Books and Articles in Western Languages* (Sung Studies Research Aids, I., Sung Studies Newsletter, 1976)

Allsen, T. *Mongol Census Taking in Rus, 1245–1275* (Harvard Ukrainian Studies, Vol. 5, No. 1, 1981) pp. 32–53

Allsen, T. 'The Yuan Dynasty and the Uighurs of Turfan in the 13th Century' in *China Among Equals: The Middle Kingdom and its Neighbours 10th–14th Centuries* (ed.) M. Rossabi (Berkley and Los Angeles, United States: University of California Press, 1983) pp. 281–310

Allsen, T. *The Princes of the Left Hand: An Introduction to the History of the Ulus of Orda in the Thirteenth and Early Fourteenth Centuries* (Archivum Eurasia Medii Aevi, Vol. 5, 1985–1987) pp. 5–40

Allsen, T. *Guards and Government in the Reign of the Grand Qan Mongke, 1251–1259* (Harvard Journal of Asiatic Studies, Vol. 46, No. 2, 1986) pp. 495–521

Allsen, T. *Mongol Imperialism: The Policies of the Grand Qan Mongke in China, Russia and the Islamic Lands 1251–1259* (Oakland, United States: University of California Press, 1987)

Allsen, T. *Mongolian Princes and their Merchant Partners, 1200–1260* (Asia Major, Third Series, Vol. 2, No. 2, 1989) pp. 83–126

Allsen, T. 'The Rise of the Mongolian Empire and Mongolian Rule in North China' in *The Cambridge History of China: Volume 6, Alien Regimes and Border States* (eds) D. C. Twitchett, H. Frank and J. K. Fairbank (Cambridge, United Kingdom: Cambridge University Press, 1994; online edition, 1998) pp. 321–413

Allsen, T. *Commodity and Exchange in the Mongol Empire: A Cultural History of Islamic Textiles* (Cambridge, United Kingdom: Cambridge University Press, 1997)

Allsen, T. *Ever Closer Encounters: The Appropriation of Culture and the Appropriation of Peoples in the Mongol Empire* (Journal of Educational Multimedia and Hypermedia, 1/1, 1997) pp. 2–23

Allsen, T. *Culture and Conquest in Mongol Eurasia* (Cambridge, United Kingdom: Cambridge University Press, 2001)

Allsen, T. 'The Circulation of Military Technology in the Mongolian Empire' in *Warfare in Inner Asian History (500–1800)* (ed.) N. Di Cosmo (Leiden, The Netherlands and Boston, United States: Brill, 2002)

Allsen, T. 'The Eastern Steppe: Mongol Regimes after the Yuan (1368–1636)' in *The Cambridge History of Inner Asia: The Chinggissid Age* (eds) N. Di Cosmo, A. J. Frank, P. Golden (Cambridge, United Kingdom: Cambridge University Press, 2009)

Amitai, R. *Mongols and Mamluks: The Mamluk-Ilkhanid War 1260–1281* (Cambridge, United Kingdom: Cambridge University Press, 1995)

Amitai, R. *The Mongols in Islamic Lands Studies in the History of the Ilkhanate* (Franham, United Kingdom: Ashgate, 2007)

Amitai, R. *Holy War and Rapprochement: Studies in the Rlations Between the Mamluk Sultanate and the Mongol Ilkhanate (1260–1335)* (Turnhout, Belgium: Brepols, 2013)

Amitai, R. and Biran, M. (eds) *Mongols, Turks and Others* (Leiden, The Netherlands: Brill, 2005)

Amitai, R. and Biran, M. (eds) *Nomads as Agents of Cultural Change: The Mongols and their Eurasian Predecessors* (Honululu, United States: University of Hawai'i Press, 2015)

Amitai, R. and Morgan, D. (eds) *The Mongol Empire and its Legacy* (Leiden, The Netherlands: Brill, 1999)

Arberry, A. J., Bailey, H., Boyle, J. A., Gray, B., Lambton, A. K. S., Lockhart, L., Avery, P. W. (eds) *Cambridge History of Iran 5 The Saljuq and Mongol Period* (Cambridge, United Kingdom: Cambrudge University Press, 1968)

Arnasson, P. and Wittrock, B. *Eurasian Transformations, Tenth to Thirteenth Centuries: Crystallisations, Divergences, Renaissances* (Leiden, The Netherlands: Brill, 2004)

Asian Infrastructure and Investment Bank. *AIIB Approves First Loan to India for $160 Million to Support Power Sector* www.aiib.org/en/news-events/news/2017/20170503_001.html, 2017 (Accessed 9 June 2017)

Atwood, C. P. *Encyclopaedia of Mongolia and the Mongol Empire* (New York: Facts on File, 2004)

Aubin, J. (Tr. Eliyahu Ashtor) *Levant Trade in the Late Middle Ages* (Princeton, United States: Princeton University Press, 1983)

Ayalon, D. *The Great Yasa of Chinggis Khan: A Re-examination* (Studia Islamica, 38, 1973) pp. 107–156

Ayalon, D. *Outsiders in the Lands of Isla: Mamluks, Mongols and Eunuchs* (London: Variorum Reprints, 1988)

Baipakov, K. 'The Silk Route across Central Asia' in *History of Civilizations of Central Asia Volume IV* (eds) C. E. Bosworth and M. S. Asimov (Paris: UNESCO, 2000) pp. 221–242

Banbridge, M. (ed.) *The Turkic Peoples of the World* (London: Kegan Paul International Ltd., 1993)

Barfield, T. *The Hsiung-nu Imperial Confederacy: Organization and Foreign Policy* (The Journal of Asian Studies, Vol. 41, 1981) pp. 45–61

Barfield, T. *The Perilous Frontier Nomadic Empires and China* (Cambridge, United States: Basil Blackwell Inc., 1989)

Barthold, V. V. *Four Studies on the History of Central Asia* (Leiden, The Netherlands: Brill, 1956)

Bawden, C. (Tr.) *The Mongol Chronicle of Altan Tobci* (Wiesbaden, Germany: O Harrossowitz, 1955)

Beazley, R. *The Texts and Versions of John de Plano Carpini and William de Rubruquis* (London: Hakluyt Society, 1903)

Bell-Fialkoff, A (ed.) *The Role of Migration in the History of the Eurasian Steppe, Sedentary Civilizations vs 'Barbarian' and Nomad* (London: Macmillan, 2000)

Bergel, Y. 'Turko-Mongol Influences in Central Asia' in *Turko-Persia in Historical Perspective* (ed.) R. Canfield (Cambridge, United Kingdom: Cambridge University Press, 1990)

Bira, Sh. 'Historiography among the Mongols' in *History of Civilizations of Central Asia Vol IV* (eds) C. E. Bosworth and M. S. Asimov (Paris: UNESCO, 2000) pp. 156–160

Biran, M. *Qaidu and the Rise of the Independent Mongol State in Central Asia* (London: Curzon Press, 1997)

Biran, M. *Chinggis Khan* (Oxford, United Kingdom: Oneworld, 2007)

Biran, M. 'The Mongols in Central Asia from Chinggis Khan's Invasion to the Rise of Temur: The Ogedeid and Chaghatai realm' in *The Cambridge History of Inner Asia* (eds) N. Di Cosmo, J. A. Frank, P. Golden (Cambridge, United Kingdom: Cambridge University Press, 2009)

Biran, M. 'Rulers and City Life in Mongol Central Asia 1220–1370' in *Turko-Mongol Rulers, Cities and City Life* (ed.) D. Durand-Guerdy (Leiden, The Netherlands: Brill, 2013) pp. 257–285

Biran, M. *Nomads as Agents of Cultural Change: The Mongols and Their Eurasian Predecessors* (ed.) R. Amitai and M. Biran (Honululu, United States: University of Hawai'i Press, 2015)

Biryukova, N. *Eurasian Doctrine of Kazakh President Nursultan Nazarbayev: 'Thinking Space'* www.geopolitica.ru/en/article/eurasian-doctrine-kazakh-president-nursultan-nazarbayev-thinking-space#.UzDCbvl_tyM, 2013 (Accessed 09 June 2017)

Bosworth, C. E. and Asimov, M. S. *History of Civilizations of Central Asia IV* (Paris: UNESCO, 2000)

Bosworth, C. E. and Asimov, M. S. *History of the Seljuks* (London: Curzon Press, 2001)

Boyle, J. A. (Tr. from the text of Mirza Muhammad Qazvini) *The History of the World Conqueror 2 Vols. (by Ata Malik Juvaini)* (Manchester, United Kingdom: Manchester University Press, 1958)

Boyle, J. A. *The Journey of Het'um, King of Little Armenia, to the Court of the Great Khan of the Mongke* (Central Asiatic Journal, 9, 1964) pp. 175–189

Boyle, J. A. (Tr. from Persian of Rashid al-Din) *The Successors of Ghenghis Khan* (New York: Columbia University Press, 1971)

Boyle, J. A. *The Mongol World Empire 1206–1370* (London: Variorum Reprints, 1977)

Bretschneider, E. *Medieval Researches from Eastern Asiatic Sources Vol I and II* (London and New York: Routledge, 2000)

Brook, T. (ed.) *History of Imperial China* (Cambridge, United States: The Belknap Press of Harvard University Press, 2010)

Buell, P. *Sino-Khitan Administration in Mongol Bukhara* (Journal of Asian History, Vol. 13, No. 2, 1979) pp. 121–151

Buell, P. 'The Role of the Sino-Mongolian Frontier Zone in the Rise of Cinggis-qan' in *Studies on Mongolia, Proceedings of the First North American Conference on Mongolian Studies* (ed.) H. Scwartz (Bellingham, United States: Center for East Asian Studies, 1979) pp. 63–76

Buell, P. *Kalmyk Tanggaci People: Thoughts on the Mechanics and Impact of the Mongol Expansion* (Mongolian Studies, Vol. 6, 1980) pp. 41–59

Buell, P. *Early Mongol Expansion in Western Siberia and Turkestan (1207–1219): A Reconstruction* (Central Asiatic Journal, Vol. 36, No. 1/2, 1992) pp. 1–32

Buell, P. 'Chinqai (1169–1252): Architect of Mongolian Empire' in *Opuscula Altaica, Essays Presented in Honor of Henry Schwarz* (eds) E. H. Kaplan and D. W. Whisenhunt (Bellingham, United States: Center for East Asian Studies (Studies on East Asia, 19), 1994) pp. 168–186

Buell, P. 'Mongolian Empire and Turkicization: The Evidence of Food and Foodways' in *The Mongol Empire and its Legacy* (eds) R. Amitai and D. Morgan (Leiden, The Netherlands: Brill, 1999) pp. 200–223

Budge, E. W. W. (Tr. from the Syriac) *The Monks of Khubilai Khan, Emperor of China or the History of the Life and Travels of Rabban Sawma Envoy and Plenipotentiary of the Mongol Khans to the Kings of Europe and Markos who as Mar Yahbh-Allaha III became Patriarch of the Nestorian Church in Asia* (London: The Religious Tract Society, 1928)

Burger, G. (ed.) *Hetoum A Leytell Cronycle, Richard Pynson's Tr. (*c.*1520) of La Fleur des histories de la terre d' Orient* (Toronto, Canada: University of Toronto Press, 1988)

Canfield, R. (ed.) *Turko-Persia in Historical Perspective* (Cambridge, United Kingdom: Cambridge University Press, 1990)

Carr, M. *Merchant Crusaders in the Aegean 1291–1352* (Woodbridge, United Kingdom: Boydwell Press, 2015)

Chambers, J. *The Devil's Horsemen: The Mongol invasion of Europe* (London: Cassell, 1988)

Chan, H-L. *China and the Mongols: History and Legend under the Yuan and the Ming* (Aldershot, United Kingdom: Ashgate, 1999)

Chan, H-L. and De Barry, W. T. (eds) *Yuan Thought: Chinese Thought and Religion Under the Mongols* (New York: Columbia University Press, 1982)

Chen, Y. *Western and Central Asians in China under the Mongols: Their Trasnformation into Chinese (translated and annotated)* C. Hsiang-hai and L. C. Goodrich (Los Angeles, United States: Monumental Serica, University of California, 1966)

Ch'en, P. *Chinese Legal Tradition under the Mongols* (Princeton, United States: Princeton University Press, 1979)

Ch'i-ch'ing, H. *The Military Establishment of the Yuan Dynasty* (Cambridge, United States: Harvard University Press, 1978)

Ch'i-ch'ing, H. 'Mid-Yuan politic' in *The Cambridge History of China: Volume 6, Alien Regimes and Border States 907–1368* (eds) D. C. Twitchett, H. Franke, J. K. Fairbank (Cambridge, United Kingdom: Cambridge University Press, 1994; online edition, 1998) pp. 490–560

Christian, D. *Inner Asia as a Unit of History* (Journal of World History, Vol. 5 No. 2, 1994) pp. 173–211

Christian, D. 'Silk Roads or Steppe Roads? The Silk Roads in World History' in *Silk Road Studies IV Worlds of the Silk Roads: Ancient and Modern* (eds) D. Christian and C. Benjamin (Turnhout, Belgium: Brepols, 2000)

Christian, D. and Benjamin, C. (eds) *Silk Road Studies II Worlds of the Silk Roads: Ancient and Modern* (Belgium, Turnhout: Brepols, 1998)

Christian, D. and Benjamin, C. (eds) *Silk Road Studies IV Realms of the Silk Roads: Ancient and Modern* (Belgium: Brepols publishers, Turnhout, 2000)

Ciociltan, V. *The Mongols and the Black Sea Trade in the Thirteenth and Fourteenth Centuries* (Leiden, The Netherlands: Brill, 2012)

Cleaves, F. W. *A Chancellery Practice of the Mongols in the Thirteenth and Fourteenth Century* (Harvard Journal of Asiatic Studies, Vol. 14, No. 3/4, 1951) pp. 493–526

Cleaves, F. W. *Darugha and Gerege* (Harvard Journal of Asiatic Studies, Vol. 16, 1953) pp. 237–259

Cleaves, F. W. *Secret History of the Mongols* (Cambridge, United States and London: Published for the Harvard-Yenching Institute by Harvard University Press, 1982)

Crump, J. *Chinese Theatre in the Days of Khubilai Khan* (Tucson, Unites States: University Arizona Press, 1980)

Cunliffe, B. *By Steppe, Dessert and Ocean* (Oxford, United Kingdon: Oxford University Press, 2015)

Dardess, J. *From Mongol Empire to Yuan dynasty: Changing Forms of Imperial Rule in Mongolia and Central Asia* (Monumenta Serica, 30, 1972–73) pp. 117–165

Dardess, J. *Conquerors and Confucians: Aspects of Political Change in Late Yuan China* (New York: Columbia University Press, 1973)

Dawson, C. (ed.) *The Mongol Mission: Narratives and Letters of the Franciscan Missionaries in Mongolia and China in the Thirteenth and Fourteenth Centuries* (New York: Sheed and Ward, 1955)

De Nicola, B. *Women in Mongol Iran: The Khatuns, 1206–1335* (Edinburgh: Edinburgh University Press, 2017)

DeWeese, D. *Islamisation and Native Religion in the Golden Horde: Baba Tukles and the Conversion to Islam in Historical and Epic Tradition* (Philadelphia, United States: Pennsylvania State University, 1994)

DeWeese, D. 'Mongols as Vectors for Cultural Transmission' in *The Cambridge History of Inner Asia: The Chinggissid Age* (eds) N. Di Cosmo, A. J. Frank, P. Golden (Cambridge, United Kingdom: Cambridge University Press, 2009)

Di Cosmo, N. *Ancient Inner Asian Nomads: The Economic Basis and its Significance in Chinese History* (The Journal of Asian Studies, Vol. 53, No. 4, Association for Asian Studies, 1994) pp. 1092–1126

Di Cosmo, N. *State Formation and Periodization in Inner Asian History* (Journal of World History, Vol. 10, No. 1, 1999) pp. 1–40

Di Cosmo, N. (ed.) *Warfare in Inner Asian History* (Leiden, The Netherlands and Boston, United States: Brill, 2002)

Di Cosmo, N. 'Mongols and Merchants on the Black Sea Frontier' in *The Thirteenth and Fourteenth Centuries: Convergence and Conflicts in Mongols, Turks and Others* (eds) R. Amitai and M. Biran (Leiden, The Netherlands: Brill, 2005)

Di Cosmo, N. *Black Sea Emporia: Reassessment of the Pax Mongolica* (Journal of the Economic and Social History of the Orient, Vol. 53, No. 1/2, 2010) pp. 83–108

Di Cosmo, N., Frank, A. J. and Golden, P. (eds) *The Cambridge History of Inner Asia: The Chinggissid Age* (Cambridge, United Kingdom: Cambridge University Press, 2009)

Durand-Guedy, D. (ed.) *Turko-Mongol Rulers, Cities and City Life* (Leiden, The Netherlands: Brill, 2013)

Endicott-West, E. *Imperial Governance in Yuan times* (Harvard Journal of Asiatic Studies, Vol. 46, No. 2, 1986) pp. 523–549

Endicott-West, E. *Merchant Associations in Yuan China: The Ortoy* (Asia Major, Third Series, Vol. 2, No. 2, Academia Sinica, 1989) pp. 127–154

Farquhai, D. 'Structure and Function in the Yuan Imperial Government' in *China under Mongol Rule* (ed.) J. D. Langlois Jr (Princeton, United States: Princeton University Press, 1981) pp. 25–55

Fitzherbert, T. 'Religious Diversity under the Ilkhanid Rule *c.*1300 as Reflected in the Freer Bal`ami' in *Beyond the Legacy of Ghenghis Khan* (ed.) L. Komaroff (Leiden, The Netherlands: Brill, 2006) pp. 390–406

Franck, I. and Brownstone, D. M. *The Silk Road: A History* (London: Facts on File Publication, 1986)

Franke, H. *Sino-Western Contacts under the Mongol Empire* (Journal of the Hong Kong Branch of the Royal Asiatic Society, 6, 1966)

Franke, H. *From the Tribal Chieftain to the Universal Emperor and God: The Legitimation of the Yuan Dynasty* (Munich, Germany: Verlag der Bayerischen Akademie der Wisserchaften, 1978)

Frankopan, P. *The Silk Roads: A New History of the World* (London: Bloomsbury, 2015)

Gabriel, R. *Subotai the Valiant* (Santa Barbara, United States: Praeger Publishers, 2004)

Giploulox, F. *The Asian Mediterranean* (Cheltenham, United Kingdom: Edward Elgar Publishing Ltd., 2011)

Golden, P. *An Introduction to the History of the Turkic Peoples* (Wiesbaden, Germany: Otto Harrassowitz, 1992)

Golden, P. *Turks and Khazars: origins, Institutions and Interactions in Pre-Mongol Eurasia* (Farnham, United Kingdom: Ashgate Variorum, 2010)

Goody, J. *The Theft of History* (Cambridge, United Kingdom: Cambridge University Press, 1997)

Grousset, R. (Tr. Denis Sinor and Marian MacKellar) *Conqueror of the World* (Edinburgh and London, United Kingdom: Oliver and Boyd, 1967)

Grousset, R. (Tr. Naomi Walford) *The Empire of the Steppes: A History of Central Asia* (New Brunswick, United States: Rutgers University Press, 1970; paperback edition, 1991; eighth paperback edition, 2002)

Gumilev, L. N. (Tr. R. E. F. Smith) *Searches for an Imaginary Kingdom* (Cambridge, United Kingdom: Cambridge University Press, 1987)

Haldou, P. (ed.) *Ancient Cultures of the Uralic Peoples* (Budapest, Hungary: Corvina Press, 1976)

Halperin, C. *Russia and the Golden Horde* (Bloomington, United States: Indiana University Bloomington, 1985)

Halperin, C. *The Tatar Yoke* (Columbus, United States: Slavica Publishers, 1986)

Halperin, C. *The Kipchak Connection: The Ilkhans, Mamluks and Ayn-Jalut* (Bulletin of the School of Oriental and African Studies, Vol. 63, Issue 2, 2000) pp. 229–245

Hambly, G. *Central Asia* (New York: Dell Publishing Co., 1969)

Hartag, L. de *Ghenghis Khan Conqueror of the World* (London: I. B. Tauris & Co Ltd., 1989)

Henthorn, W. E. *Korea: The Mongol Invasions* (Leiden, The Netherlands: Brill, 1963)

Henthorn, W. E. *A History of Korea* (New York: Free Press, 1971)

Hoang, M. *Ghenghis Khan* (London: Saqi Books, 1990)

Honeychurch, W. *Inner Asia and the Spatial Politics of Empire: Archaeology, Mobility, and Culture Contact* (New York: Springer, 2015)

Hookham, H. *Tamburlaine the Conqueror* (Kent, United Kingdom: The Camelot Press Ltd., 1962)

Hostler, C. W. *The Turks of Central Asia* (London: Praeger, 1993)

Howorth, H. *History of the Mongols from the 9th to the 19th Century* (London: Longmans, Green; New York: Burt Franklin, 1876)

The Independent. *Tankers Begin to Offload Oil Through China-Myanmar pipeline Bypassing Singapore Altogether* www.theindependent.sg/tankers-begin-to-offload-oil-through-china-myanmar-pipeline-bypassing-singapore-altogether/, 2017 (Accessed 9 June 2017)

Ipsiroglu, M. S. (Tr. by E. D. Phillips) *Paintings and Culture of the Mongols* (London: Thames and Hudson, 1967)

Ischboldin, B. *Essays on Tatar History* (2nd rev and enl ed.) (New Delhi, India: New Book Society of India, 1973)

Islamov, B. 'Post-Soviet Central Asia' in *Central Asia in Historical Perspective* (ed.) B. Manz (Boulder, United States: Westview Press, 1994) pp. 202–219

Ivanov, D. *Eurasian Union- A Trinket for Three Comerades* www.euinside.eu/en/analyses/Eurasia-Union-Putin-Kazakhstan-Belarus, 2011 (Accessed 9 June 2017)

Jackson, P. *Early Mission to the Mongols: Carpini and his Contemporaries* (London: Hakluyt Society, 1994)

Jackson, P. *The Mongols and the West 1221–1240* (Harlow, United Kingdom: Longman, 2005a)

Jackson, P. 'The Mongols and the Faith of the Conquered' in *Mongols Turks and Others* (eds) R. Amitai and M. Biran (Leiden, The Netherlands: Brill, 2005b) pp. 245–290

Jackson, P. *Studies on the Mongol Empire and Early Muslim India* (Farnham, United Kingdom: Ashgate, 2009)

Jackson, P. *Mongol Khans and Religious Allegiance: The Problems of Confronting a Minister-Historian in Ilkhanid Iran* (British Institute of Persian Studies, Iran, Vol. 47, 2009) pp. 109–122

Jackson, P. *The Mongols and the Islamic Lands from Conquest to Conversion* (London: Yale University Press, 2017)

Jackson, P. and Morgan, D. (eds) (Tr. Peter Jackson) *The Mission of Friar Rubruck: His Journey to the Court of the Great Khan Mongke 1253–1255* (London: Hakluyt Society, 1990)

Juwayni, A-M. *Kitab-i Tarikh-i Jahangushay, Sayyid Jalal al-Din Tehrani* (Tihran, Iran: Matba'ah-I Majlis, [1351–1352]1932–1933)

Kalra, P. and Varadzhakov, S. *The Customs Union between Russia, Kazakhstan and Belarus: First Steps Towards the Revival of the Silk Road SSRN* www.euinside.eu/en/analyses/Eurasia-Union-Putin-Kazakhstan-Belarus, 2011 (Accessed 9 June 2017)

Kaplan, E. H. and Whisenhunt, D. W. *Opuscula Altaica Essays Presented in Honour of Henry Schwarz* (Bellingham, United States: Centre for East Asian Studies, Western Washington University, 1994)

Kaplonski, C. 'The Mongolian Impact on Eurasia: A Reassessment' in *The Role of Migration in the History of the Eurasian Steppe, Sedentary Civilizations vs 'Barbarian' and Nomad* (ed.) A. Bell-Fialkoff (London: MacMillan, 2000) pp. 251–274

Kauz, R. 'The Maritime Trade of Kish during the Mongol Period' in *Beyond the Legacy of Ghenghis Khan* (ed.) L. Komaroff (Leiden, The Netherlands: Brill, 2006) pp. 51–67

Kauz, R. (ed.) *Aspects of Maritime Silk Road: From the Persian Gulf to the East China Sea* (Wiesbaden, Germany: Harrassowitz Verlag, 2010)

Khazanov, A. and Wink, A. (ed.) *Nomads in the Sedentary World* (London: Curzon Press, 2001)

Klimkeit, H. J. 'Manichaeism and Nestorian Christianity' in *History of Civilizations of Central Asia Vol IV* (eds) C. E. Bosworth and M. S. Asimov (Paris: UNESCO, 2000) pp. 69–81

Komaroff, L. (ed.) *Beyond the Legacy of Ghenghis Khan* (Leiden, The Netherlands: Brill, 2006)

Kotkin, S. *Defining Territories and Empires: From Mongol ulus to Russian Siberia 1200–1800* (Princeton, United States: Princeton University, Slavic Research Centre, 1996)

Kramarovsky, M. 'Jochid Luxury Metalwork: Issues of Genesis and Development' in *Beyond the Legacy of Ghenghis Khan* (ed.) L. Komaroff (Leiden, The Netherlands: Brill, 2006) pp. 43–50

Kwanten, L. *Imperial Nomads: A History of Central Asia 500–1500* (Leicester, United Kingdom: Leicester University Press, 1979)

Lamb, H. *March of the Barbarians* (London: R. Hale, 1941)

Lattimore, O. *Desert Road to Turkestan* (London: Methuen & Co Ltd., 1928)

Mann, J. *Kubilai Khan* (London: Bantam Press, 2006)

Manz, B. *The Rise and Rule of Tamerlane* (Cambridge, United Kingdom: Cambridge University Press, 1989)

Manz, B. *Central Asia in Historical Perspective* (Boulder, United States and Oxford, United Kingdom: Westview Press, 1994)

Marshall, R. *Storm from the East* (London: Penguin Books, 1994)

Martin, H. D. *The Rise of Chinggis Khan and His Conquest of North China* (Baltimore, United States: The John Hopkins Press, 1950)

Martin, J. *The Land of Darkness and the Golden Horde: The fur Trade under the Mongols, XIII–XIVth Centuries* (Cathiers du Monde russe et sovietique, Vol. 19, No. 4, 1978) pp. 401–421

Martinez, A. P. 'Institutional Development, Revenues and Trade' in *The Cambridge History of Inner Asia* (eds) N. Di Cosmo, A. J. Frank, P. Golden (Cambridge, United Kingdom: Cambridge University Press, 2009)

Masuya, T. 'Seasonal Capitals with Permanent Buildings in the Mongol Empire' in *Turko-Mongol Rulers, Cities and City Life* (ed.) D. Durand-Guedy (Leiden, The Netherlands: Brill, 2013) pp. 223–257

May, T. *The Mongol Art of War* (Barnsley, United Kingdom: Pen and Sword Military, 2007)

Morgan, D. *The Mongol Armies in Persia* (Der Islam, Vol. 56, 1979) pp. 81–96

Morgan, D. *The Mongols* (Oxford, United Kingdom: Basil Blackwell, 1986)

Morgan, D. 'The "Great Yasa of Chinggis Khan" Revisited' in *Mongols, Turks and Others* (eds) R. Amitai and M. Biran (Leiden, The Netherlands: Brill, 2005) pp. 291–308

Morgan, D. 'The Mongol Empire in World History' in *Beyond the Legacy of Ghenghis Khan* (ed.) L. Komaroff (Leiden, The Netherlands: Brill, 2006) pp. 425–437

Mostaert, A. and Cleaves, W. *Les letters de 1289 et 1305 des Ilkhan Arghun et Oljeitu a Phillipe le Bel* (Cambridge, United States: Harvard University Press, 1962)

Mott, C. E. *The Formless Empire* (Yardley, United States: Westholme Publishing, 2015)

Moule, A. C. *Christians in China before the Year 1550* (London: Society for Promoting Christian Knowledge, 1930)

Moule, A. C. *Quinsai with other notes on Marco Polo* (Cambridge, United Kingdom: Cambridge University Press, 1957)

Moule, A. C. (Tr.) and Pelliot, P. (ed.) *Marco Polo: The Description of the World* (London: Routledge, 1938)

Nazarbayev, N. *Nurly Zhol: The Path to the Future* www.kazakhembus.com/content/nurly-zhol-path-future, 2014 (Accessed 15 July 2017)

Novogorodova, E. 'Turkic and Mongol Art' in *History of Civilizations of Central Asia Vol IV* (eds) C. E. Bosworth and M. S. Asimov (Paris: UNESCO, 2000) pp. 449–455

Okada, H. 'China as a Successor State to the Mongol Empire' in *The Mongol Empire and its Legacy* (eds) R. Amitai and D. Morgan (Leiden, The Netherlands: Brill, 1999)

Olschki, L. *Guillaume Boucher: A French Artist at the Court of the Khans* (Baltimore, United States: The John Hopkins Press, 1946)

Olschki, L. *Marco Polo's Asia* (Oaklands, United States: University of California Press, 1960)

Parker, E. H. *A Thousand Years of the Tatars* (London: K. Paul, Trench, Trubner & Co. Ltd., 1924)

Pelliot, P. *Notes on Marco Polo (3 Volumes)* (Paris: Impremerie nationale, 1959)

Petkov, K. *The Voices of Medieval Bulgaria Seventh-Fifteenth Century* (Leiden, The Netherlands: Brill, 2008)

Pfeiffer, J. *History and Historiography of Post-Mongol Central Asia and the Middle East: Studies in Honour of John. E. Woods* (eds) J. Pfieffer and S. Quinn (Wiesbaden, Germany: Harrassowitz, 2006a)

Pfeiffer, J. 'Reflections on a "Double Rapproachment": Conversion to Islam along the Mongol Elite during the Early Ilkhanate' in *Beyond the Legacy of Ghenghis Khan* (ed.) L. Komaroff (Leiden, The Netherlands: Brill, 2006b) pp. 369–389

Pfeiffer, J. *Politics, Patronage and the Transmission of Knowledge in the 13–15th Centuries Tabriz* (Leiden, The Netherlands: Brill, 2014)

Phillips, E. D. *The Royal Horses* (London: Thames & Hudson, 1965)

Prawdin, M. *The Mongol Empire* (New York: Collier MacMillan, 1967)

Praznik, R. *Sienna on the Silk Road* (Journal of World History, Vol. 21, No. 2, June 2010) pp. 177–217

PwC's Growth Market Centre. *China's New Silk Route: The Long and Winding Road* www.pwc.com/gx/en/growth-markets-center/assets/pdf/china-new-silk-route.pdf, 2016 (Accessed 9 June 2017)

Raby, J. and Fitzherbert, T. *The Court of the Ilkhans 1290–1340* (Oxford, United Kingdom: Oxford University Press, 1996)

Rachewiltz, I. de *Personnel and Personalities in Northern China in the Early Mongolian Period* (Journal of Economic and Social History of the Orient, Vol. 9, 1966) pp. 88–144

Rachewiltz, I. de *Papal Envoys to the Great Khans* (London: Faber and Faber, 1971)

Rachewiltz, I. de *The Secret History of the Mongols: A Mongolian Epic Chronicle of the Thirteenth Century (Volume 1 and 2)* (Leiden, The Netherlands: Brill, 2004)

Rachewiltz, I. de, Chan, H-L., Ch'i-ch'ing, H., Geir, P. W. (eds) *With the Assistance of May Wang, In the Service of the Khan: Eminent Personalities of the Early Mongol-Yuan Period* (Wiesbaden, Germany: Harrassowitz Verlag, 1993)

Rashid al-Din, F. a-H., Khashshab, Y., Nashat, S., Sayyad Fuad A. a-M., Handawi, M. M. *Jami al-Tawarikh* ('al-Qahirah, Egypt: Wizarat 'al-Thaqafah wa-al'Irshad 'al-Qawmi 'al Idarah'al Ammah lil-Thaqafah, 1960)

Ratchnevsky, P. *Ghenghis Khan and His Life and Legacy* (Hoboken, United States: Blackwell Publishers, 1991)

Riasanovsky, V. A. *Fundamental Principles of Mongol Law* (Bloomington, United States: Indiana University and The Hague, Belgium: Mouton, 1965)

Rockhill, W. (ed.) and Rubruck, W. (author) *The Journey of William Rubruck to the Eastern Part of the World as Narrated by Himself, with Two Accounts of the Earlier Journey of John of Pian de Carpine* (Hakluyt Society Second Series, No. 4, London, 1900)

Ronay, G. *The Tatar Khan's Englishman* (London: Cassell, 1978)

Ross, D. *The Tarikh-i-Rashidi: A History of the Moghuls of Central Asia* (London: S. Low, Marston and Co., 1895)

Rossabi, M. *Khubilai Khan and the Women in his Family* (Studia Sino-Mongolica; Festschrift fur Herbert Franke ed. Wolfgang Bauer) (Wiesbaden, Germany: Steiner, 1979) pp. 153–180

Rossabi, M. 'The Muslims in the early Yuan dynasty' in *China under Mongol Rule* (ed.) J. D. Langlois (Princeton, United States: Princeton University Press, 1981) pp. 257–295

Rossabi, M. *Chinese Myths about the National Minorities: Khubilai Khan, a Case Study* (Central and Inner Asian Studies, I, 1987) pp. 47–81

Rossabi, M. *Khubilai Khan* (Oakland, United States: University of California Press, 1988)

Rossabi, M. 'The Legacy of the Mongols' in *Central Asia in Historical Perspective* (ed.) B. Manz (Boulder, United States: Westview Press, 1994) pp. 27–44

Rossabi, M. 'Tabriz and Yuan China' in *Aspects of the Maritime Silk Road: From the Persian Gulf to the East China Sea* (ed.) R. Kauz (Wisbaden, Germany: Harrassowitz, 2010) pp. 97–107

Rossabi, M. *How Mongolia Matters: War, Law and society* (Leiden, The Netherlands and Boston, United States: Brill, 2017)

Saunders, J. J. *The Nomad as Empire Builder A Comparison of the Arab and Mongol Conquests* (Diogenes, Vol. 13, Issue 92, 1965) pp. 79–103

Saunders, J. J. *The History of the Mongol Conquest* (London: Routledge and K. Paul, 1971)

Saunders, J. J. *Muslims and Mongols: Essays on Medieval Asia* (ed.) G. W. Rice (Christchurch, New Zealand: Whitcoulls for the University of Canterbury, 1977)

Saxena, S. and Kalra, P. 'Asiatic Roots and the Rootedness of the Eurasian Project' in *The Eurasian Project and Europe: Regional Disparities and Continuities* (eds) D. Lane and V. Samokhvalov (London: Palgrave Macmillan, 2015)

Schurmann, H. F. *Mongol Tributary Practices of the Thirteenth Century* (Harvard Journal of Asiatic Studies, Vol. 19, No. 3/4, December 1956a) pp. 304–389

Schurmann, H. F. *Economic Structure of the Yuan Dynasty: Translation of Chapters 93 and 94 of the Yuan Shih* (Harvard-Yenching Institute Studies, Vol. 16, 1956b)

Shujie, Y. *China Pays Serious Attention to Davos for a More Stable World Order* www.telegraph.co.uk/news/world/china-watch/business/china-at-davos-2017/, 2017 (Accessed 15 July 2017)

Sinor, D. (ed.) *Aspects of Altaic Civilization* (Bloomington: Indiana University Press, 1963)

Sinor, D. and MacKellar, M. *Conqueror of the World* (Edinburgh, United Kingdom: Oliver & Boyd, 1967)

Smith, J. M. *Mongol and Nomadic Taxation* (Harvard Journal of Asiatic Studies, 9, 1956) pp. 304–389

Smith, J. M. *Mongol Manpower and Persian Population* (Journal of the Economic and Social History of the Orient, XVIII, 1975) pp. 271–299

Spuler, B. (Tr. Geoffrey Wheeler) *The Mongols in History* (London: Pall Mall Press, 1971)

Starr, F. *Lost Enlightenment: Central Asia's Golden Age from the Arab Conquest to Tamerlane* (Princeton, United States: Princeton University Press, 2013)

Stefanova, T. and Stepenov, T. *The Bulgars and the Steppe Empires in the Early Middle Ages* (Leiden, The Netherlands: Brill, 2010)

Thackston, W. *Mirza Haydar Dughlat's Tarikhi i Rashidi: A History of the Khans of Moghulistan* (Cambridge, United States: Harvard University, Department of Near Eastern Languages and Civilizations, 1996)

Thackston, W. *Classical Writings of the Medeival Islamic World Persian Histories of the Mongol Dynasties by Mirza Haydar Dughlat Vol I* (London: I. B. Tauris, 2012a)

Thackston, W. *Classical Writings of the Medieval Islamic World 'Persian Histories of the Mongol Dynasties' by Khwandmir Vol II* (London: I. B. Tauris, 2012b)

Thackston, W. *Classical Writings of the Medieval Islamic World Persian Histories of the Mongol Dynasties by Rashiduddin Fazlullah Vol. III* (London and New York: I. B. Tauris, 2012)

Togan, I. *Flexibility and Limitation in Steppe Formation* (London: Brill, 1998)

Twitchett, D. C., Frank, H. and Fairbank, J. K. (eds) *The Cambridge History of China: Volume 6, Alien Regimes and Border States 907–1368* (Cambridge, United Kingdom: Cambridge University Press, 1994; online edition, 1998)

Vasary, I. *Turks, Tatars and Russians in the 13–16th Centuries* (Oxford, United Kingdom: Variorum Collected Studies Series, Ashgate, 2007)

Vasary, I. 'The Jochid Realm: The Western Steppe and Eastern Europe' in *The Cambridge History of Inner Asia* (ed.) N. Di Cosmo, A. Frank, P. Golden (Cambridge, United Kingdom: Cambridge University Press, 2009)

Veit, V (ed.) *The Role of Women in the Altaic World* (Permanent International Altaic Conference 44th Meeting, Walderberg; Wisebaden, Germany: Harrassowitz Verlag, 2007)

Vernadsky, G. *The Mongols and Russia* (New Haven, United States: Yale University Press, 1953)

Vinokurov, E. and Libman, A. *Eurasian Integration Challenges of Transcontinental Regionalism* (London: Palgrave Macmillan, 2012)

Vladimirstov, B. *The Life of Chinggis Khan* (London: G. Routledge & Sons Ltd., 1930)

Waley, A. *Travels of an Alchemist: The Journey of the Taoist Monk, Ch'ang-ch'un from China to the Hindukush at the Summons of Chinggiz Khan Recorded by his Disciple, Li Chih Cha'ng* (London: G. Routledge & Sons Ltd., 1931)

Waley, A. *The Secret History of the Mongols and Other Pieces* (London: George Allen & Unwin Ltd., 1963)

Watson, O. 'Pottery under the Mongols' in *Beyond the Legacy of Ghenghis Khan* (ed.) L. Komaroff (Leiden, The Netherlands: Brill, 2006) pp. 325–345

Weissleder, W. (ed.) *The Nomadic Alternative Modes and Models of Interaction in the African-Asian Deserts and Steppes* (The Hague, The Netherlands: Mouton Publishers, 1978)

Wood, F. *The Silk Road 'Two Thousand Years in the Heart of Asia'* (London: The British Library, 2003)

Woods, J. E. *The Aqquyunlu Clan, Confederation, Empire* (Minneapolis and Chicago, United States: Bibliotheca Islamica Inc., 1976)

Woods, J. E. *The Timurid Dynasty* (Bloomington, Indiana: Indiana University, Research Institute for Inner Asian Studies, 1990)

Yingsheng, L. 'A Lingua Franca along the Silk Road: Persian Language in China between the 14th and the 16th Centuries' in *Aspects of the Maritime Silk Road: From the Persian Gulf to the East China Sea* (ed.) R. Kauz (Wisbaden, Germany: Harrassowitz, 2010) pp. 87–97

Yoshita, H. *Shang-tu: The Summer Capital of the Yuan Dynasty* (Tokyo: The Toa-koko-gaku-kwai or the Far Eastern Archaeological Society, 1941)

Yule, H. *Cathay and the Way Tither* (London: Hakluyt Society, 1913–1916)

Yule, H. *The Travels of Friar Odoric* (Grand Rapids, Michigan, United States: W. B. Eerdmans Pub. Co., 2002)

Zimonyi, I. and Karatay, O. (eds) *Central Eurasia in the Middle Ages Studies in Honour of Peter B. Golden* (Wiesbaden, Germany: Harrassowitz Verlag, 2016)

Index

Page numbers in *italics* denote figures.

For Product Safety Concerns and Information please contact our EU representative GPSR@taylorandfrancis.com
Taylor & Francis Verlag GmbH, Kaufingerstraße 24, 80331 München, Germany

www.ingramcontent.com/pod-product-compliance
Ingram Content Group UK Ltd.
Pitfield, Milton Keynes, MK11 3LW, UK
UKHW022124190926
475702UK00013B/1626

* 9 7 8 0 3 6 7 4 3 8 7 0 8 *